*Daylight Robbery*

# Daylight Robbery

### How Tax Shaped Our Past and
### Will Change Our Future

## DOMINIC FRISBY

## WITHDRAWN

**BUSINESS**

PENGUIN BUSINESS

UK | USA | Canada | Ireland | Australia
India | New Zealand | South Africa

Penguin Business is part of the Penguin Random House group of companies
whose addresses can be found at global.penguinrandomhouse.com.

First published 2019
001

Copyright © Dominic Frisby, 2019

The moral right of the author has been asserted

Typeset in 12/14.75 pt Dante MT Std
by Integra Software Services Pvt. Ltd, Pondicherry
Printed and bound in Great Britain by Clays Ltd, Elcograf S.p.A.

A CIP catalogue record for this book is available from the British Library

HARDBACK ISBN: 978-0-241-36086-6
TRADE PAPERBACK ISBN: 978-0-241-36083-5

www.greenpenguin.co.uk

For Samuel, Eliza, Lola & Ferdie
I love you all so dearly

# Contents

# Contents

# Contents

# Chapter 1

# *Daylight Robbery*

*The art of taxation consists of so plucking the goose as to obtain the most feathers with the least possible hissing.*[1]

Jean-Baptiste Colbert, finance minister to Louis XIV (1661–83)

It was the early 1690s and the king needed money.

King William and Parliament had brought this problem on themselves. To gain popularity they had just got rid of a hated tax. Now he was short of cash.

What to do?

Every home had a hearth, and the English had been paying hearth taxes one way or another, usually to the church, since before the Norman invasion of 1066, when they were known as 'smoke-farthings' or 'fumage'. But in 1662, hearth money became statute. Every home worth more than 20 shillings (about US$5,000 in today's money)[2] had to pay one shilling twice a year for every stove, hearth or fireplace. People who had been out of the range of direct taxes suddenly found themselves liable. Even paupers were listed. Tax collectors were operating on commission and 'enforced their rights to the last farthing'.[3] They demanded entry into people's homes every six months to count their fireplaces, and so infringed on the Englishman's sacred privacy. Worse yet, the idea had come from France. The English hated it, and it was a huge source of grievance when the Glorious Revolution came in 1688.

Here was a means to quickly ingratiate the new monarchs, William and Mary, with their people. They abolished hearth money 'to erect a lasting monument of their Majesties' goodness in every hearth in the kingdom'.[4]

But it left a major problem. The Dutch were owed money for equipping William's invasion to overthrow the previous king, James II. There was conflict in Ireland and war on the Continent, the Nine Years War, to be paid for. There were allies of James II in Scotland to expel. There was also the small matter of a currency crisis at home.

How to pay for it all?

In 1696, a solution was found. Surprise, surprise, it came in the form of another tax: the Duty on Houses, Light and Windows. Otherwise known as the window tax.

Now a collector could walk past somebody's house and count the number of windows from outside. He didn't have to venture in. No privacy was violated. No engagement with the taxpayer was required, nor any declaration on his part. You can't hide windows, so it was a hard tax to avoid. Thanks to hearth money, the infrastructure was already in place to collect the tax. It also seemed a fair tax: the more windows somebody had, the wealthier they were likely to be and so the greater their ability to pay.

Like so much permanent government legislation, window tax was introduced on a temporary basis. The amounts payable were low at first, starting with a flat rate of two shillings per house with up to ten windows. But over the years, they crept up.

Soon, rather than pay, people began blocking up their windows. By 1718, it was already noted that the tax wasn't raising as much revenue as hoped. The reaction was not to lower the tax, but to increase it. The result was even more extreme avoidance tactics. Homes were built with fewer windows. Some were built with windows already bricked up, thus giving the owner the option to knock through and glaze at a later stage, if desired. In some cases, apartment buildings were constructed with entire floors of windowless bedrooms. At a time when electric, gas and oil lighting had not yet been invented and light came from the smoky flames of tallow candles or rush lights (reeds dipped in fat), blocking out sunlight and fresh air was no small sacrifice.

A further 'absurd impost on light',[5] as the medical journal *The Lancet* later called it, came in 1746, when the government of King George II introduced a tax on glass. Between them the two taxes became 'a cause of deformity in building',[6] according to John Stuart Mill, yet they guided architecture for 150 years, determining how the villages, towns and cities of Britain and France (which would have its own 'impôt sur les portes et fenêtres') would look – and, in many places, still look today. The thresholds – or notches, as they were known – of the tax determined how many windows a building would have. Some aspirational villagers in Wiltshire even painted the exterior bricks of their homes in black and white to resemble the windows that were now missing. When the prime minister, William Pitt, tripled the tax in 1797, one carpenter reported to Parliament that a whole street had asked him to brick or board up their windows.[7]

The glass tax inhibited the growth of an entire industry. Between 1801 and 1851, the United Kingdom population grew from 11 million to 27 million.[8] London alone saw a 170% increase in its population, from 1 million to 2.7 million.[9] There was a building boom to accompany the extraordinary population growth. Yet thanks to the tax, glass production levels remained largely unchanged over the period.[10]

Windows became a symbol of wealth, even in fiction. 'Elizabeth saw much to be pleased with,' writes Jane Austen in *Pride and Prejudice*. 'Though she could not be in such raptures as Mr Collins expected the scene to inspire, and was but slightly affected by his enumeration of the windows in front of the house, and his relation of what the glazing altogether had originally cost.'[11]

Though the tax never made it to the USA, in 1798 fear of it sparked an entire rebellion – the Fries rebellion. When assessors in Pennsylvania rode about surveying property for the Direct House Tax, German and Dutch settlers thought they were about to try and levy a window tax. They rose up in an armed revolt that spread across the state and took the federal troops of President John Adams the best part of two years to quash.

Nor did the window tax prove progressive. 'A house of £10 rent in the country', wrote Adam Smith, 'may have more windows than a house of £500 rent in London',[12] yet the poorer country house owed more tax. Rural dwellers were hit hard. But it was the urban poor who suffered most. They lived in large tenement buildings, which, having many windows, proved heavily susceptible to the tax. Landlords – on whom the tax fell – simply boarded up the tenement windows to reduce costs. This led to the tax's most pernicious unintended consequence: it made people sick. The numerous epidemics of disease in cities during the Industrial Revolution – typhus, smallpox and cholera in particular – were made worse by the cramped, damp, windowless dwellings. *The Lancet* called the tax 'a direct encouragement to disease'.[13] An official scientific inquiry concluded that 'the blocking up of the numerous windows caused by the anxiety of their owners to escape the payment of the tax, has, in very many instances, greatly aggravated, and has even . . . been the primary cause of much sickness and mortality'.[14] Even so, the tax continued.

By the nineteenth century, opposition to it was everywhere. 'The adage "free as air" has become obsolete,' fumed Charles Dickens. 'Neither air nor light have been free since the imposition of the window-tax.'[15] Campaigning against it went on for decades. Pamphlets were handed out, songs were sung, speeches were made. In 1845, shortly after the reintroduction of income tax, Sir Robert Peel repealed glass taxes, but the window tax remained. Only in 1850 was a motion finally put before Parliament to repeal it. Legend has it that MPs cried 'Daylight robbery!' when the matter was debated. The idiom has lived on as an expression for outrageous charging.[16] The motion, however, failed to pass. Only after another national campaign was the tax finally repealed in 1851. France would not repeal its version for another 75 years.

The window tax was just one tax and, in the context of history, not a particularly long-lived one, but it is a great example of how a tax comes into being and the consequences that follow. In its evolution we see the typical life cycle of a tax.

It is enacted at a time of need, usually to fund some kind of war. It is presented as temporary, but becomes permanent. The amount payable is low at first, but increases over time. It violates basic freedoms, in this case the right to light and fresh air. Many go to great lengths to avoid paying it, and it thus distorts how people behave and the decisions they make. There are all sorts of unintended consequences, which get worse as the tax matures. Much of the money raised is wasted or spent in a way with which the taxpayer does not agree. Finally people have had enough, and there is some kind of movement – a campaign, a protest, even a revolution – to get rid of it, which government is slow and reluctant to do.

It is too simplistic to say the window tax was good or bad. It worked well for a while, then it didn't. The money raised helped pay, among other things, for the essential defence of the nation. At its heart is the moral dilemma of so many taxes. On the one hand, it was an invasion of private property rights, with grave unintended consequences; on the other, it was the most practical solution at the time to pay for what some would deem to be the vital workings of government. We can see why Winston Churchill, among many others, described taxes as 'a necessary evil'.[17] The big question is: how much evil is necessary?

## Chapter 2

# How an Extraordinary Situation Could Offer an Extraordinary Solution

*In this hard world we have to earn before we spend.*

John James Cowperthwaite, Hong Kong financial secretary (1961–71)

Now let me tell you a very different story.

Hong Kong never looked like a very promising place. Just some craggy islands and shearing sea stacks in the South China Sea at the mouth of the Pearl River. The land was of little use. There were no minerals to mine nor oil to drill. Most of it was too rocky to farm. But in the deep water between one of the larger islands and the mainland was its main redeeming feature: a large natural harbour.

Sixteenth-century Portuguese explorers established a post there from which to pursue trade with China, but that disappeared with the isolationism of the Ming dynasty. Eighteenth-century British traders rediscovered the archipelago; the Opium Wars of the nineteenth century saw Britain seize control, and it remained in British hands until the Second World War.

The name Hong Kong means 'fragrant harbour', perhaps because of the many incense factories that once lined the docks. To London, Hong Kong was a strategically important trading outpost of the Empire, but when the Second World War came, it was deemed too difficult to defend. 'We must avoid frittering away our resources on untenable positions,' wrote Churchill.[1] In 1941, the Japanese invaded (without declaring war) and Hong Kong quickly

6

fell. Almost four years of harrowing martial law followed, leaving the island starving and destitute.

Franklin Gimson took up the position of Hong Kong Colonial Secretary two days before the Japanese invasion. He spent the war in a Japanese prison camp. In 1945, as soon as he heard word of Japanese surrender, he left the camp and declared himself the territory's acting governor. He had offices up and running within a fortnight. This quick and decisive action, before China or the US had decided on any strategy, would have a profound effect on Hong Kong's destiny. It stayed British.

In the years that followed the war, Britain relinquished much of its empire, but, for fear it would be annexed by China, not Hong Kong. A team of civil servants was sent out to help get the colony back on its feet. One of them was a quiet, determined and deeply principled Scot by the name of John James Cowperthwaite.

Cowperthwaite had studied classics at both Edinburgh and Cambridge, but he had also studied economics at St Andrews, where he became deeply versed in the ideas of the Enlightenment, particularly Adam Smith. In 1951, he rose to the position of deputy financial secretary, and in 1961 he became financial secretary. 'For about 25 years,' says his biographer, Neil Monnery, 'he was absolutely central to Hong Kong economic policy.'[2] During that period, Hong Kong experienced one of the most extraordinary periods of economic expansion the world has ever seen.

What made it all possible was the colony's tax policy.

Cowperthwaite and his team arrived in late 1945. Their first task was to get industry up and running again. The governor announced that Hong Kong was a free port. There would be no tariffs on any goods bar a few commodities, no export subsidies and few import restrictions. Imports and exports resumed, and many who had fled the war were now returning. Trade grew quickly. It was patently apparent to Cowperthwaite that business was picking up by itself.

Cowperthwaite was an observant man. He would walk the streets, and visit the factories and ports to keep an eye on activity.

The more he watched, the more progress he observed – all without the civil service having to do anything. Hong Kong did not need an economic plan, he decided. As long as the framework was right, the colony was fine by itself. Its people and its businesses could do the heavy lifting. Steeped as he was in Adam Smith (it is said he slept with a copy of *The Wealth of Nations* by his bed), this was an observation Cowperthwaite, a classical liberal if ever there was one, was glad to make.

His second task was to manage the department responsible for getting essential supplies to the island – buying, selling and distributing food and fuel, and administering price controls. The department was beset with problems. 'That was a formative influence for him,' says Monnery, 'to see how difficult it was for a set of civil servants to run a trading business.'[3] Cowperthwaite developed a low opinion of bureaucrats. 'I trust the commercial judgment only of those who are themselves taking the risks,'[4] he said. 'When Government gets into a business it tends to make it uneconomic for anyone else.'[5]

He was beginning to formulate a theory he would later call 'positive non-intervention'. His idea was that government intervention in an open economy often does more harm than good. The default position should be not to intervene, unless careful consideration gives good reason to do so. 'Clumsy bureaucratic fingers' should be kept out of the 'sensitive mechanism' of the economy, he said.[6] It is better to rely on the 'hidden hand'. 'A multiplicity of individual decisions by businessmen and industrialists will . . . produce a better and wiser result than a single decision by a Government or by a board with its inevitably limited knowledge of the myriad factors involved, and its inflexibility.'[7]

Hong Kong's tax policies were the polar opposite of those pursued by Britain over the same period. Where Britain – and most of the West – had high levels of taxation, government spending, deficit financing, industrial planning and economic intervention, Hong Kong went the other way. Most people – 'all but the well-to-do'[8] – paid no income tax at all. Even higher earners only paid 15%. There were no tariffs or duties, no sales taxes or VAT, no taxes on capital gains, on interest or on overseas earnings. But there was a land value tax. The overall tax burden never exceeded 14% of GDP.

Meddling and change was kept to a minimum. The principle was that 'taxes should be constant over long periods (provided, that is, that they are neither burdensome nor inequitable)'.[9] At the same time, the collection of taxes should not be overly aggressive. Cowperthwaite spoke of 'the benefits to our economy, particularly in terms of investment and enterprise, both local and from overseas, of not having the inquisitorial type of tax system inevitably associated with a full income tax'.[10]

The Keynesian deficit financing that Western governments pursued to boost their economies was a no-no. 'It is wholly inappropriate to our economic situation . . . we don't, and can't, produce more than a small fraction of what we consume, and increased consumption would merely mean increased imports without matching exports; and a severe balance of payment crisis, which would destroy Hong Kong's credit and confidence in the Hong Kong dollar; and which we could not cure without coming close to ruining ourselves. Keynes was not writing with our situation in mind.'[11]

Government borrowing, meanwhile, was equally unacceptable – 'high national debt . . . is the surest precursor of high taxation',[12] Cowperthwaite said. 'I am sceptical of the theory that we have a right, if we could, to pass on our capital burden to future generations . . . Our predecessors had not passed any significant part of their burden on to us.'[13]

There was no industrial planning, no subsidies or economic intervention. 'I must confess my distaste for any proposal to use public funds for the support of selected, and thereby, privileged, industrialists, the more particularly if this is to be based on bureaucratic views of what is good and what is bad,'[14] he said in one of the many budget debates at the Legislative Council. 'I do not believe that any body of men can have enough knowledge of the past, the present and the future to establish "development priorities" . . . I should have thought that a desirable industry was, almost by definition, one which could establish itself and thrive without special assistance in ordinary market conditions.'[15]

Red tape was reduced to the point that a new company could be registered with just a one-page form. The tax code itself was kept short and simple. Even today, international tax lawyers regularly deem it the world's most efficient. At 300 pages and fewer than 150,000 words, it is 1.5% the size of the UK's.

Meanwhile, the currency was pegged to the pound, thus eliminating the possibility for taxation by inflation (at least by Hong Kong). In 1963, the economist Milton Friedman asked Cowperthwaite to explain the mechanism by which he pegged the currency, but he refused. Even HSBC, the bank that operated the peg, did not understand it, he said. 'Better they shouldn't. They would mess it up.'[16] He was right. Hong Kong abandoned the link after he stood down and HSBC was given a bigger say in monetary affairs. In 1983, the Hong Kong dollar met with a currency crisis, at one stage losing 13% in just two days. It had to be pegged to the dollar to stave off collapse.

Nor were there any capital controls. 'Money comes here and stays here because it can go if it wants to,' Cowperthwaite said. 'Try to hedge it around with prohibitions and it would go and we could not stop it and no more would come.'[17]

Hong Kong was no transparent democracy. It was a British colony. The governor, advised by the Legislative Council, had wide powers to make and enforce laws. In the wrong hands, the system could have been easily corrupted. But the civil servants (there were many others like-minded to Cowperthwaite) saw it as their duty to act in the best interests of the people of Hong Kong. Cowperthwaite had words to say about that too. 'If people want consultative government, the price is increased complexity and delay in arriving at decisions. If they want speed of government, then they must accept a greater degree of authoritarianism. I suspect that the real answer is that most people prefer the latter so long, that is, as government's decisions conform with their own views.'[18]

Cowperthwaite was only able to do what he did because of the unique circumstances in which Hong Kong found itself: in need of rebuilding, located far away from societies where Keynesian ideology had taken hold of government policy, not answerable to anyone. The British largely left it to its own devices. When they did get involved, they were often given short shrift. Denis Healey, the British Secretary of State for Defence, said, 'I always retired hurt from my encounters with the redoubtable financial secretary.'[19] As the transcripts of his speeches to the Hong Kong Legislative Council show, Cowperthwaite was a formidable arguer.

He was by no means a lone force. His successes built on the framework preceding financial secretaries had set. They were continued by his successor, Philip Haddon-Cave. They all strongly believed in laissez-faire, and had the support of their governors. But it was Cowperthwaite who would become the main architect.

The economic consequences to Britain and Hong Kong of their differing tax policies would be dramatic, though it is hard to put numbers on just how successful Hong Kong was, because another of Cowperthwaite's policies was to avoid compiling statistics. He believed such figures led officials to start fiddling in the economy, remedying perceived ills that didn't need remedying and thus hindering the work of the invisible hand in the market. (He constantly made such references to Adam Smith.) 'If I let them compute those statistics, they'll want to use them for planning,'[20] he explained to Friedman. He batted away request after request, both at home and from abroad.

When British officials came to find out why unemployment data was not being collected, he sent them back on the first available flight. When he met with pleas for GDP numbers from members of the Legislative Council, this was a typical response:

> Such figures are very inexact even in the most sophisticated countries. They do not have a great deal of meaning. That other countries

make use of them is not, I think, necessarily a good reason to suppose that we need them. I am not entirely clear what practical purpose they would serve in Hong Kong... The need arises in other countries because high taxation and detailed Government intervention in the economy have made it essential to be able to judge (or to hope to be able to judge) the effect of policies... We are in the happy position, where the leverage exercised by Government on the economy is so small that it is not necessary, nor even of any particular value, to have these figures available for the formulation of policy.[21]

Later in life he was asked what poor countries should do to turn their economies around. The first thing he said was 'abolish the office of national statistics'.[22]

In 1962, Cowperthwaite had come under such pressure to provide GDP numbers and other such statistics that he hired a professor to do the necessary research. He could then declare that he had set up a study to look at the feasibility of collecting the information. For seven years he sent back the poor professor's drafts: either something needed further clarification, or it needed investigation, or it needed development. In 1969, when no data was forthcoming, he explained that the professor was having difficulties coming to closure on how it should be collated.[23] The unfortunate academic had been set up to be a fall guy.

But we do know this much.

In 1945, after years of war and Japanese occupation, Hong Kong was destitute and broken. Many people were starving. Where its pre-war population was over a million, now it was 600,000.[24] Yet in the span of little more than a generation, this tiny territory with no significant natural resources to speak of would become the world's busiest port and an international manufacturing and financial powerhouse. Its population would grow by over ten times.

Even in the 1950s, the many refugees fleeing civil war in mainland China meant it was little more than a shanty town. Friedman described his visit there in 1955, saying that 'the temporary dwellings that the government had thrown up to house the refugees were one-room cells in a multistory building that was open in the front: one family, one room'.[25] Today Hong Kong is a futuristic city state.

Its wealth has grown at a similarly extraordinary rate. We do not have official GDP per capita for the 1940s, of course, but it's likely that it was below $300, on a par with much of Africa. In 1960, it was $429 (according to the OECD, not Cowperthwaite), compared to $1,380 for the UK and $3,007 for the US.[26] Within 33 years its GDP per capita exceeded that of the UK. Within 50 years it overtook the US.[27] Today it ranks among the ten richest nations in the world. Its per capita GDP is 40% higher than the UK's.

In all this time, taxes were kept low, and government spending to a minimum. The government ran a budget surplus every year after 1946 bar one,[28] usually keeping a year's worth of spending in reserve and never creating any national debt. 'Even I, who have always believed in the vigour of our economy under our present tax regime, have been surprised by the growth of revenue generated at our present tax rates,' Cowperthwaite said.[29] Today it has become an annual event that the financial secretary underestimates the surplus – 2015 was the eighth year in succession,[30] and in 2018 it happened again.

Every year, the Washington DC economic think tank the Heritage Foundation compiles a detailed index of economic freedom for 186 countries around the world. It defines economic freedom as the amount of control people have over their own labour and property, and it has '12 quantitative and qualitative factors' by which it measures it.[31] In every year since 1995, when the Heritage Foundation began compiling its index, Hong Kong has ranked first – the most economically free nation on earth.[32]

On the supply side, it is not as though Hong Kong's services lack in any way. The territory has the fourth best education system in the world, according to Pearson,[33] and it ranks top of Bloomberg's healthcare index.[34] Its public transport was ranked the world's best last year,[35] and it is consistently used as a model elsewhere, regularly achieving a 99.9% 'on-time success rate', with 94% of the population living within one kilometre of a railway station.[36] It is also one of the world's most profitable systems.

Laissez-faire economies tend to be painted as ruthless and heartless, but Cowperthwaite was adamant that his policies were for the good of all. Tax was an imposition, an obstacle to growth. Lower taxes meant greater profits. Greater profits meant more growth. More growth meant more jobs, better-paid jobs and greater wealth for all. 'I am more concerned with the creation of wealth than with its distribution,' he said. 'The rapid growth of the economy, and the pressure that comes with it on demand for labour, both produce a rapid and substantial redistribution of income directly of itself.'[37] In other words, leave the economy alone, and redistribution will take care of itself.

But here was a key point for Cowperthwaite: 'It also makes it possible to assist more generously those who are not, from misfortune temporary or permanent, sharing in the general advance.'[38] The interests of those at the very bottom were close to Cowperthwaite's heart, and a booming economy put the government in the best possible position to help them.[39] As he remarked, 'Due to our low tax policy . . . revenue has increased.' The evidence of Hong Kong's growth bears out his argument. Eventually, 'funds left in the hands of the public will come into the Exchequer', Cowperthwaite said, but 'with interest'.[40]

Hong Kong dealt with every challenge thrown at it, but with almost every crisis – public housing aside – the default position of the government was not intervention, but 'positive non-intervention'. In 1950, Hong Kong's main industries sprang from its role getting goods in and out of China – warehousing, shipping, shipbuilding, insurance and so on. When the Korean War began, and the US imposed sanctions, the colony's trade with China collapsed by around 90% over the next four years.[41] Hong Kong should have ground to a halt, but it didn't. Immigrants fleeing civil war in China brought their cotton spinning skills with them, and the colony would grow to dominate international textile markets instead, to the extent that the UK and the US both resorted to dramatic protectionist measures to support their domestic textile industries. Hong Kong businesses adapted to the strict import quotas on Hong Kong cotton by growing their synthetic textile output instead. They diversified into other forms of manufacturing – especially electronics and plastics. In 1967, the devaluation of the pound meant a loss of some £30 million to Hong Kong's foreign exchange reserves, but the colony took that in its stride too, as it did the destabilising impact of Mao's Cultural Revolution in China and the Asian crisis of 1997.

When Hong Kong was handed back to China in 1998, the expectation was that it and its policies would effectively be annexed. In fact, the opposite happened. The rest of Asia had noticed Hong Kong's success and they were copying it. Soon after Lee Kuan Yew became the first prime minister of Singapore, in 1959, he adopted the colony's low-tax, non-interventionist model, with similarly successful results. South Korea and Taiwan, even Japan to an extent, all had their own adaptations of low-tax, high-export models and all enjoyed huge periods of economic growth of their own. China itself would do something similar.

After Chairman Mao's death in 1976, reformers in China, who had observed the extraordinary growth of Hong Kong and Singapore, thought Cowperthwaite's model could work on the mainland too. In 1980, Shenzhen was chosen to be a 'special economic zone' – light on taxes and regulation. The population then was 30,000. It has grown to nearly 13 million, as more and more people have gone there seeking their fortune. At one stage its growth rate was an astonishing 40%.[42] Today it is another Hong Kong.

China wanted to 'appropriate capitalism for the good of socialism', as the National People's Congress put it in their legislation.[43] 'We didn't pay enough attention to developing the productive forces,' said Deng Xiaoping in his famous 1984 speech, 'Build Socialism with Chinese Characteristics'.[44] Given what these tiny islands had achieved, what was China capable of? Today China, with its own brand of authoritarian capitalism, is the second-largest economy in the world, in purchasing power parity terms perhaps the biggest.[45]

There is no doubt that Hong Kong was an extraordinary situation in an extraordinary time, but its low taxes and positive non-intervention are where the Asian economic miracle began. Cowperthwaite's achievement lay not so much in what he did do, but in what he didn't. 'I did very little,' he said with typical humility. 'All I did was to try to prevent some of the things that might undo it.'[46]

# Chapter 3

## *Why Tax?*

Taxation is as old as civilisation itself.

Even in early hunter-gatherer societies there existed a sense of duty to the greater collective, so when man first settled some 10,000 years ago, leaders were already requisitioning labour and produce. In all the years since, not a single civilisation has existed without taxation.

Yet how much do we actually think or talk about tax? During the Enlightenment, the ethics of taxes, as well as the practicalities, were intensely and extensively discussed, but today, somehow, the arguments have faded. Taxes are the dull domain of accountants and economists. While we resign ourselves to their payment, politicians rarely seem to think beyond adding a little here or taking away a little there. The moralities of many taxes, particularly income tax, are rarely, if ever, questioned. Major reform is left to another day.

My aim with this book is to get people thinking and talking about tax again. When you look at the world through the prism of taxation – at the world around us today, at the past and at the future – so much becomes clear: why things are as they are, why events happened in the way they did, how the future will pan out – and what must be done to change it. Civilisations are shaped by the way they are taxed. A large part of a nation's destiny – whether its people will be prosperous or poor, free or subordinated, happy or depressed – is determined by its system of tax.

Tax is power. Whether king, emperor or government, if they lose their tax revenue, they lose their power. This rule has always applied, from the first king of ancient Sumer[2] to the social democracies of today. Taxes are the fuel on which the state's operations run. Limit taxes, and you limit ruling power.

Every war, from ancient Mesopotamia to modern Iraq, was paid for by some kind of tax. Taxes make wars possible. If you want to end war, end taxes. The aim of every conqueror, from Alexander the Great to Napoleon and beyond, was to take control of the tax base: the land, the labour, the produce and the profits. Conquerors plunder and then they tax. 'Taxes are the chief business of a conqueror of the world,' said George Bernard Shaw's Caesar. When Genghis Khan took China, his plan was to kill everyone, as was his way. This was no small undertaking, as China then, as now, was the most populous nation on earth. One of his counsellors, however, a little-known man by the name of Yeliu Ch'uts'ai, pointed out that dead peasants pay considerably less tax than living. Genghis saw the light and millions of lives were saved.

The same goes for revolution and revolt. Inequitable taxation almost always lurks near their heart. 'No taxation without representation' was the cry of the American revolutionaries. Ruinous taxes levied by the tsar against peasant farmers led to the Russian Revolution. Perhaps most explicitly of all, the Philippine Revolution began with the Cry of Pugad Lawin, exhorting rebels to tear up their tax certificates. From Spartacus to Boudicca to Robin Hood to Mahatma Gandhi, the greatest rebels in history were usually tax rebels.

History looks different when viewed through this lens of taxation. There is a tax story – often an overlooked one – somewhere near the heart of almost all of humanity's defining events. Jesus was only born in Bethlehem because Mary and Joseph were there to pay tax. Taxes paid for man to take his first steps on the moon. Tax stories lurk within even apparently unconnected episodes. Take women's suffrage, for example: that women joined the workforce and paid income taxes during the First World War was a major factor in their being given the vote. Even natural disasters often incorporate tax stories. The Plague, for example, effectively ended the feudal system in Europe and created a new class of tax-paying workers. Usually the tax story occurs in the rebuilding effort that follows the disaster. After the Great Fire of London, the funds to rebuild the city came mostly from taxes on coal (indeed, it has even been suggested that the Great Fire was started by tax evasion – the not uncommon scam of knocking through to the chimney next door in order to avoid hearth money).

Many of our greatest buildings – from the Pyramids to the White House – were, one way or another, built on the back of taxes. Some were constructed for the purpose of collecting them. We presume the Great Wall of China was intended to protect against invasion – and it was – but, manned at its peak by as many as a million men, it was also built to collect duties on goods coming in and out of the nation, especially along the Silk Road; in other words, to protect government revenue. Hadrian's Wall served the same purpose for the Roman Empire.

Even the names we have, we have because of tax. Prior to the thirteenth century, ordinary people in the British Isles and (to a slightly lesser extent) Europe did not have surnames. By the end of the fourteenth century, they did, typically based around their occupation (for example, Smith); their paternity (Jackson, Matthews, MacDonald); some defining geographical feature where they lived (Hill or Ford); or, as in my case, the village they came from (Frisby). Sometimes, especially in Gaelic cultures, the name derived from a physical characteristic – Cameron, for example, means 'crooked nose', Kennedy 'shaggy head', Connolly 'valiant'. The reason surnames came about? To distinguish people for the purposes of levying poll taxes.

In China, surnames are rather older. They go back, legend has it, all the way to 2852 BC and Emperor Fuxi.[3] The reason for their existence, however, is the same: to facilitate taxation.

The word 'tax' only appeared in the English language in the 1300s, as coinage became more widespread. Prior to that, we used the word 'task', from Old French, and taxes were often paid in kind – rulers took a share of the harvest, and debts were paid with labour. But whether we call it tax, burden, duty, tribute, tithe, charge, corvée, toll, impost or tariff, the principle is the same. The close relationship between taxation and freedom is even apparent in the evolution of language. Censorship and tax assessment (as in census) both have their origins in the same Latin word. The censor was an ancient Roman magistrate who maintained the census, supervised public morality and oversaw certain aspects of the government's finances. Censorship and taxation both involve the restriction of freedoms – whether economic or otherwise.

Leaders will use taxation as a means of control – to influence behaviour and the decisions people make. Peter the Great wanted to modernise Russia and he felt beards were unfashionable, so he levied a tax against them. Russians had to shave, or pay the tax. To prove they had paid it, they had to hang a copper token from their beard on which was written, 'The beard is a superfluous burden.' Often such taxes do change behaviour, though not always in the way intended. If you tax cigarettes, some people choose not to smoke, but others take up smuggling. Tax fuel, and some will change the way they travel, others will not travel at all. Tax labour heavily, and some will work harder, others will relocate offshore and others will not bother working. Tax, as I'll show, even affects the number of children people decide to have. With all such taxes there is an underlying moral argument: what is the role of the state? What one might see as sensible planning, another will see as nanny-state meddling beyond the remit of government.

Today taxes are taken without choice, often by stealth, at source and by force. My agent hates me saying that – 'They are not taken by force,' she insists. She is right in that armed guards do not collect them. Where the force comes in is that if you do not pay them, you face jail. In many cases, the option to not pay and risk jail is not even there, because taxes are deducted at source. As comedian

Chris Rock thundered, 'You don't even pay taxes, they take taxes. You get the cheque – money gone. That ain't a payment, that's a jack.'

In ancient Greece, many taxes were voluntary. At the other extreme, in authoritarian or totalitarian societies such as Soviet Russia or North Korea, people have virtually no ownership of their labour, their produce or their profit. Government takes it all. The developed world today sits somewhere in the middle of those two extremes. Excluding inflation (itself a form of tax, as I'll show), if you are a typical American, roughly 38% of everything you ever earn is taken from you in taxes.[4] In the UK, 45%.[5] In France, the figure is an eye-watering 57%.[6] These high levels of taxation are a recent development. At the turn of the twentieth century, taxes played a much less prominent role in our lives. Government spending (which mostly derives from taxes) was much lower. In the US, it was around just 7% of GDP; in the UK, it was 9%; in France, 13%.[7] Of nations in the modern era, Sweden in 1870 had the lowest spending, at just 5.7% of GDP.[8] These low rates of tax ended with the First World War and have never been seen since.

Today taxes permeate everything we do. There is barely an activity that does not involve it in some way. Thinking and, to an extent, sex are among the few activities that have proved immune. In ancient Rome there was even a tax on urine,[9] though thankfully not today.

As a result, almost wherever you are in the twenty-first-century developed world, the most expensive purchase you ever make in your life is not your home, as many people think it to be, but your government. For a typical British middle-class professional over the course of his or her life, the bill totals £3.6 million ($5 million)[10] – considerably more than the typical house. You will spend a full 20 years of your life or more in obligatory service to the state.[11] On a time basis, the state owns as much of your labour as the feudal lord did that of the medieval serf, who gave half his working week to farm the land of his lord in exchange for his protection. In exchange, you receive the protection of the state and its services: defence, healthcare, education and so on, for yourself and others. Some people are content with today's arrangement, others are not, but whatever your political leanings, you have no choice. If you want to work to earn a living, you must work for the state as well as yourself. We are not as free as we may think we are.

What if you are opposed to the way in which the state spends your taxes – on a war in the Middle East, say, some wasteful infrastructure project, or enforcing a law you consider immoral? No matter. Beyond a vote of questionable impact every four or five years, you have little say in how your money is spent. 'Taxes are what we pay for a civilised society'[12] are the words inscribed on the outside of the IRS building in Washington DC, but is that civilised? A form of forced labour for something against which you are morally opposed?

The social democrat sees taxes as a way to equalise society: to redistribute wealth, to provide equal access to education and welfare and to balance out the distortions of the market economy. The socialist takes a more extreme position along the same line of thinking. The libertarian says tax is theft: an invasion of an individual's freedom and a violation of their property rights; that government spending is wasteful and immoral, that the individual would spend his own money better.

Without taxation, there can be no government: one leads to the other. Thus, though usually obscurely, tax is at the heart of just about every political argument: what should the government spend money on? How much should it spend? Who pays? And how?

So many of the problems we face today, not least the enormous wealth gaps between rich and poor, and between generations, can be traced back to our systems of tax. Tax reform is one of the few ways by which politicians really can change the world. If we are to think about the future, the kind of world we want for our children and grandchildren, then we must think about the way we tax people.

In this book we will stroll through history to consider some stories in the evolution of taxation. We will consider the bind in which so many governments find themselves today. And we will look at the future of tax.

Many governments' finances across the world are in trouble. The debt they owe is so extraordinarily large as to be unpayable, but in an increasingly globalised, digitalised world, in which borders are becoming blurred, taxes will become harder to collect. The pressure to raise money to meet spending needs is growing, but when a populace is already heavily taxed and is fast losing faith in its leaders, how keen will it be to accept higher taxes – especially as technology makes so many existing government services look redundant?

The large-state social democratic model by which we currently live, with government the main provider of welfare, education, healthcare and other essential services, is in jeopardy. It may even be that within a generation, many nation states, as we currently know them, will no longer exist. Tax will be at the heart of it all. Tax will determine what follows.

As well as what is likely to happen, I will also outline what 'should' happen. I'll offer some ideas as to how we should levy taxes in the twenty-first century. Whether they are practicable or not, and whether indeed that is the kind of society you would want, is something you can decide for yourself.

# Chapter 4

## *The Cradle of Taxation*

*You can have a God, you can have a king, but the man to fear is the tax collector.*[1]

Ancient Sumerian proverb

Civilisation 'began' some 7,000–10,000 years ago as nomadic tribes settled on the fertile plains between the Tigris and the Euphrates. It was the mud that persuaded them to stay. Crop yields were the like of which no one had ever known. They found the mud made good tools – pots, even sickles, axes, hammers and nails, for which we later used metal. If you mixed the mud with straw and baked it in the sun, it made bricks. These bricks built houses, which would eventually become man's first cities.

The Eridu were the first, but other tribes soon followed – the Ukuk, Kish, Ur, Umma and Lagash – to form their own cities. For perhaps the first time in history, man produced more than he actually needed. The Eridu began to trade their produce for whatever they were short of – metals, wood, stone and other types of food. Thus the mud found another use: money. Moulded into tokens – a cone for a small measure of barley, a disc for a sheep – accounts could be kept. Traders baked the tokens inside clay balls, and then stamped the balls with marks to represent their signatures. The balls were kept until debts were settled, then smashed open. Taxes were the most common debt that was owed, and an ancient form of tithing, known as *esretu*, in which a tenth of someone's labour or produce was taken, was probably the first formal tax system.[2]

In time, rather than bake these tokens in balls, the ancients began to inscribe the clay with pictures instead, and thus the first systems of writing developed. The earliest examples of human writing are tax records: tablets logging tithes and tributes. Those who mastered this new art of writing and record-keeping – the scribes – became the tax collectors. Early accounting, money, debt, taxes and writing – they all evolved together.

As the settlements of ancient Mesopotamia thrived and grew into cities, wars began to break out between them, especially over resources. Umma and Lagash seemed to be the most prone to fall out. How were those wars to be paid for? Taxes, of course.

One war over water resources continued for four generations. Lagash eventually won it and Umma then had to pay them a levy in order to use the disputed water reserves. But the king of Lagash carried on levying taxes on his people, even after the war had finished. From one end of Lagash to the other, wrote a scribe at the time, 'there was the tax collector'.[3] If a man separated from his wife, he had to pay five shekels of silver. If a shepherd sheared his sheep, he had to pay five shekels of silver. If a husband died, the widow had to pay silver from their inheritance. 'The head boatman appropriated boats, the livestock official appropriated asses and sheep, the fisheries inspector fish,' wrote a Sumerian scribe.[4] So followed one of the first recorded revolts, in which the king was deposed by one of history's first tax reformers, Urakagina, who 'replaced the conventions of former times'.[5] He fired the tax collectors, cut taxes, exempted widows from inheritance dues and legislated to protect citizens from unscrupulous taxation.

The birthplace of civilisation was the birthplace of taxation. In all the years since, there has never been a civilisation without taxation.

## The ancient origins of income tax

*He will take the tenth of your seed, and of your vineyards, and give
to his officers, and to his servants. And he will take your menservants,
and your maidservants, and your goodliest young men, and your
asses, and put them to his work. He will take the tenth of your
sheep: and ye shall be his servants. And ye shall cry out . . .*

1 Samuel 8:15–18

The practice of giving a tenth of what you earn or produce – or having it taken from you – was adopted not just in Mesopotamia, but across ancient cultures, whether Chinese, Egyptian, Indian, Greek, Roman, Carthaginian, Phoenician or Arabic. We tend to think of the tithe as a tax paid to the church, but the distinction between god, king, ruler, church and government was not always clear, and often they were one and the same. Some scholars argue that ancient cultures arrived at the figure of one tenth because we have ten fingers, and calculations were often made using one's fingers. It is a natural number.

Just like taxes today, tithing paid for wars and defence, for buildings and infrastructure, for the lavish lifestyles of leaders, but also for alms. Almsgiving is an essential feature of just about every religion – indeed, I would say it is a part of human nature – and one of the main roles of the church through history was to provide the contemporary equivalents of welfare, healthcare and education – responsibilities that have now largely passed to government. *Zakat* (almsgiving) is one of the Five Pillars of Islam, and the tithe is known as *ushur*. The Sikh tithe is *dawandh*. In Buddhism, almsgiving is where the journey to Nirvana begins, though the 10% figure is not specified. In Hinduism, almsgiving – or *dana* – is a duty (*niyama*). Another is observing sacred vows, or *vratas*, one of which is *dashama bhaga vrata*, which translates from the Sanskrit as the 'one tenth part vow'.

As for Judaeo-Christianity, from early in the Book of Genesis, tithing is repeatedly mentioned in the Old Testament. Abraham thanked God by giving him 'a tenth of everything', after God secured him a stunning victory in battle (Melchizedek, king of Salem, received the donation on behalf of God, which was most selfless of him).[6] 'Of all that you shall give me I will surely give the tenth unto you' was a pledge made by Jacob to God.[7] In return for their political and religious services, the landed tribes of Israel were required to give the Levites 'all the tenth . . . for ever throughout your generations'.[8] Christianity followed Jewish principles of tithing, and the practice was embedded in canon law at the Synod of Mâcon in 585.

Before money and coin were widespread, the tithe was often taken in kind. A farmer might give 10% of his produce – his grain, his wool, his meat or his milk; an artisan 10% of his output; a worker 10% of his labour. In many religions, the first fruits of the harvest were also given to the church. Paid with your labour or the products of your labour, the tithe was, effectively, an income tax. The revenue bestowed immense wealth and thus power on those who collected it, especially given the cumulative effects.

In France, the tithe died with the Revolution. In England, its expiry was more gradual. In the sixteenth and seventeenth centuries, after the Reformation, a great deal of land in England passed from the church to lay owners. With the land came the entitlement to receive tithes, but by the early nineteenth century, against a backdrop of industrialisation, religious dissent, agricultural depression, income tax, and more widespread money and coin, the tithe payment in kind had become both out of date and unpopular. Inability to pay was one of the many factors that drove peasants from the countryside to the cities during the Industrial Revolution. An Act of Parliament in 1836 required tithes in kind to be converted to more convenient monetary payments called 'tithe rentcharge'.[9] The tithe paid to landowners would, over time, effectively become rent.

Many still give a percentage of their earnings to the church. Germany still operates a church tax, but it is much lower than the

10% of total earnings that was the tithe. With the state now ultimately responsible for many of the services previously carried out by the church, the tithe has faded away.

Political ideology may have replaced religion, but the principle of almsgiving remains. Whether believer or non, a passionate insistence prevails that large amounts be paid to fund the modern equivalent of what tithes were once supposed to have covered – healthcare, education and welfare. Indeed, some have compared the devout worship of the National Health Service in Britain to a creed. 'The NHS is our religion,' says the *Guardian's* Polly Toynbee; its birth was 'the proudest social-democratic moment in our history'.[10] The NHS is 'the closest thing the English people have to a religion', according to former Chancellor Nigel Lawson.[11] I suggest that the passion many feel about its protection is because almsgiving, compassion, the need to know that people are cared for are all engrained in us. Taxation is the means to enforce that ideology.

## One of the most important archaeological discoveries of all time was a tax document

The Rosetta Stone is regarded as one of the most important archaeological discoveries of all time. It was found in 1799 by one of Napoleon's officers in the northern Egyptian town of Rosetta – today Rashid – as French soldiers plundered ancient Egyptian tombs for relics to send home to France. Today, much to the consternation of the Egyptian authorities, the stone sits in the British Museum, perhaps its most prized asset.

This celebrated slab of black granite has been dated to 196 BC, to the Hellenistic period, when Egypt was ruled by the Ptolemaic Greeks. Its importance lies in the fact that it was inscribed in three different ancient scripts – ancient Greek (the language of the rulers), demotic (the language of the people) and hieroglyphs (the language of the temples). The three scripts together meant that scholars were finally able to decipher these ancient languages, especially the hieroglyphs, which had hitherto baffled them – and so 4,000 years of ancient culture were unlocked.

We know that something important was being said because of the decision to inscribe the words in stone, rather than use papyrus. Set in stone, it would last. We also know it was important because of the trouble taken to inscribe it in three different languages. This way, as many people as possible would understand it. What exactly was being said that was so important?

The stone is a fragment of a larger stone inscribed with a decree made by the child king Ptolemy V after an uprising. It seems to have been an attempt to make peace following a victory against Egyptian secessionists – to restore 'the civilized life of men'.[12] The form of the peace seems to have been amnesty for the secessionists, in particular tax amnesty.

According to the decree, Ptolemy V has 'dedicated to the temples revenues in money and corn and has undertaken much outlay to bring Egypt into prosperity'.[13] 'Of the revenues and taxes levied in Egypt some he has wholly remitted and others he has lightened, in order that the people and all the others might be in prosperity during his reign.'[14] He forgives the debts 'which they in Egypt and in the rest of the kingdom owed'. He decrees that 'gods shall continue to enjoy the revenues of the temples' and that priests 'should pay no more as the tax for admission to the priesthood'[15] than they did in his father's time.

In short, he was outlining a reflation programme. The Rosetta Stone was a tax plan.

If a historian wants to learn about an era, tax documents are often the most fruitful port of call. They tend to be well kept – no surprise given the importance of their revenue to a ruler. And the way a society is taxed says a great deal about that society.

## *The ancient Greeks: How tax can be voluntary*

*We do not have, and never had, and could not have a 'voluntary'*
*tax system.*

Donald C. Alexander, US Commissioner of Internal
Revenue (1973–77)

Imagine a tax that fell only on those most able to pay; in which the
rich voluntarily paid *more* than obliged, voluntarily, rather than
trying to avoid, evade or minimise; where the money was spent
according to the wishes of the person paying the tax; and which
involved barely any bureaucracy. Impossible, you may say. History
would argue otherwise. Whether it's mathematics or science,
drama or philosophy, we have a great deal to admire the ancient
Greeks for. We should add their early system of tax to the list.

Like the philosophers of the Enlightenment, the Greeks put
taxation in the field of ethics: the liberty or despotism of a
society – how free or oppressive it is – could be measured by its
system of taxes. 'It is fair that he who has much should pay much,
while he who has little should pay little,' said Aristotle.[16] Where
we should admire them is not so much in the way that they taxed,
but in the way that they didn't. There was no tax on income, nor
were taxes the way by which the wealth of the rich was shared
with the people. Instead, this was achieved by a voluntary alternative: liturgy.

The word liturgy – from the ancient Greek *leitourgia* – means
'public service' or 'work of the people', and the idea of benefaction, public service and self-sacrifice, with its roots in Greek
mythology, was embedded in the ancient Greek psyche. The Titan
Prometheus created mankind, but when Zeus refused to give
humans the gift of fire, Prometheus stole a lightning bolt from the
god and gave that to them instead, so they would discover fire
anyway. Thus did he became mankind's greatest benefactor

– though the transgression saw him sentenced by Zeus to torment for all eternity. The goddess Athena gave the citizenry the olive tree, symbol of peace and prosperity, and so the city of Athens was named after her.

Aristotle developed the theme. His 'magnificent man' gave vast sums to the community. Poor men could never be 'magnificent', by Aristotle's definition, because they did not have the financial means. True wealth consists of doing good, he argued in *The Art of Rhetoric*, of handing out money, giving scarce and costly gifts, and helping others to maintain an existence.[17] The physician Hippocrates, the 'founder of medicine', was another who believed in this social responsibility, advising doctors to 'Sometimes give your services for nothing, calling to mind a previous benefaction or present satisfaction. And if there be an opportunity of serving one who is a stranger in financial straits, give full assistance to all such.'[18]

Perhaps the city needed some kind of improvement to its infrastructure – a new bridge, for example. Perhaps a war loomed and military spending was required. Perhaps some kind of festivity was deemed necessary. Then the rich stepped forward. The rationale was that they should shoulder the expenses of the city given the unequal share of its wealth they enjoyed. Not only did they pay for the undertaking, they carried it out as well: it was their responsibility to oversee the work in question. Thus did undertakings tend to be well executed: the liturgist's reputation was on the line.

At various times, depending on need (in times of war, the number went up), there were anywhere between 300 and 1,200 liturgists in Athens, some minor, some major. In most cases, they volunteered. Liturgy was not enforced by law or bureaucracy, but by tradition and public sentiment. The motivation for volunteering, as well as benevolence and a sense of public duty, was the reward of honour and prestige. If an assignment was carried out well, the patron's standing among their fellow elites, as well as ordinary people, would rise. While in early ancient Greece only warriors could become 'heroes', later, liturgists could earn heroic status by acting in the public interest for the welfare of others. The result was that many gave *more* than was expected, as much as three or four times – a far cry from today's culture of paying as little as is legally possible. The self-interest of the benefactor was exploited for the benefit of the city.

The most prestigious and important liturgy – and by far the most expensive – was the navy, known as 'trierarchy'. The trierarch had to build, maintain and operate a warship – a trireme. These kept the Athenian navy strong – at one time the strongest in the world – and shipping lanes free from pirates. Their role in protecting the trading centre that was Athens was essential. Many of the buildings of ancient Greece were constructed by benefactors competing for honour. The Panathenaic Games and the theatrical festival of Dionysia came about for the same reason. The 'choregy' involved selecting, financing and training teams to compete in athletic, dramatic or musical contests at Athens' many festivals.[19] If his contestants won, the prestige of the choragus rose. Some of the bronze tripods and monuments erected to commemorate the choregoi who had sponsored the best works can still be seen today.

No doubt the system was exploited for individual gain, in particular political gain. One of the ways the young Pericles made his mark on Athenian society, before he became a military commander, was by presenting Aeschylus's drama *The Persians* at the Great Dionysia festival to demonstrate his benefaction. His principal political opponent, Cimon, responded similarly, gaining public favour by lavishly handing out portions of his sizeable personal fortune.

Liturgists who, for whatever reason, did not want to participate risked public scorn, but there were exemptions, particularly for those who had previously rendered services to the city or had other ongoing liturgies. There was also 'antidosis'.[20] A liturgist could argue that another citizen – citizen B – was wealthier and therefore better able to bear the financial burden of the liturgy. Citizen B then had three choices: to accept the liturgy, to submit to a trial within a month in which a jury determined who was the wealthier, or to swap assets. It was a pretty effective system for determining how wealthy somebody actually was, as opposed to how rich he said he was.

But the mounting costs of the Peloponnesian War (431–404 BC) meant that Athenians found themselves having to pay war taxes, and *eisphora*, in which they were directly taxed on their wealth. Voluntary liturgy withered and died as ancient Athens followed the pattern of many great societies: the low taxes and freedoms that underpin them in their early days fade as the society evolves and its government obligations, especially in the form of war, increase.

# Chapter 5

# *Judaism, Christianity, Islam – and Tax*

*The economic and political story of the Jews has been one continuous struggle after another against outrageous taxation.*

Charles Adams, *For Good and Evil* (1993)[1]

If ancient Mesopotamia was one cradle of civilisation, ancient Egypt was the other.

By 1300 BC, the Hebrews had been settled in Egypt for around 450 years, but their growing wealth, and their growing numbers, meant that they were seen as a threat. The Egyptians became 'ill-affected' towards the Hebrews, said first-century Romano-Jewish scholar Titus Josephus, and 'touched with envy at their prosperity'.[2] 'Behold, the people of the children of Israel are more and mightier than we,' the Bible quotes Pharaoh (probably Ramses II) as saying. 'Let us deal wisely with them; lest they multiply.'[3]

To deal wisely with the Hebrews was to tax them. In his *History of the Jews*, Heinrich Graetz explains that at that time, somebody could only be enslaved if they were a prisoner of war or a criminal, or if they had failed to pay their debts or taxes.[4] The oppression began, as has so often been the case in history, with taxation. Taxes were increased to punitive levels as the Egyptians 'set over them [the Hebrews] taskmasters to afflict them with their burdens'.[5] This was then escalated. 'The Egyptians made the children of Israel to serve with rigour,' continues the Book of Exodus. 'They made their lives bitter with hard bondage, in mortar, and in brick, and in all manner of service in the field.'[6] By the time Moses led them out of Egypt, the once free Hebrews had become slaves. Slavery – in which you have no ownership of your labour, indeed your entire self – is, in many ways, the ultimate form of taxation.

Moses led the Hebrews into the Sinai to escape their bondage, thus making them some of history's first tax exiles. From there we have the Ten Commandments, the belief system on which Judaeo-Christianity is built. At the heart of Judaism is a tax story.

## Jesus and the tax collectors

Judaism is not the only religion to have a tax story at its heart.

'And it came to pass in those days,' says the gospel according to St Luke, 'that there went out a decree from Caesar Augustus, that all the world should be taxed, and all went to be taxed, every one into his own city. And Joseph also went up from Galilee, out of the city of Nazareth, into Judaea, unto the city of David, which is called Bethlehem . . . to be taxed with Mary his espoused wife, being great with child.'[7]

The reason Mary and Joseph were in Bethlehem when Jesus Christ was born was to pay taxes. Some versions of the story have it that they went to Bethlehem for a census (ordered by Augustus Caesar as part of his extensive tax reform), but given that the census was taken for the purposes of collecting taxes, the argument is the same. One way or the other, tax brought Mary and Joseph to Bethlehem. Without the levy, Christianity would never have evolved in the way that it did.

Tax is a recurring theme throughout Jesus's life. No wonder. He was a revolutionary. He had considerable grievance with the injustices, as he perceived them, of the Roman tax system, particularly the temple tax, which Rome levied against any temples in which Roman gods were not worshipped. He complained that the Roman 'kings of the earth' taxed some religions, but not their own. But he still advised paying up, 'lest we should offend them'.[8] However unjust the taxes, the consequences of not paying them – death or slavery – were not worth it.

There is also the famous story of Jesus and the Pharisees. Arriving at the temple of Jerusalem, Jesus, to his horror, found traders at work inside. He 'began to cast out them that sold therein, and them that bought'.⁹ Once he had cleansed the temple, he began preaching. This was, unsurprisingly, to the great annoyance of the Pharisees and their scribes. Their businesses had been disrupted, the revenues they collected for Pontius Pilate, the man responsible for collecting taxes in Judaea on behalf of Rome, jeopardised and thus the relationship they enjoyed with him prejudiced. They wanted rid of this Jesus. The problem was that Jesus was popular. So they hatched a plan to trick him into incriminating himself: they would 'trap him in his words'.¹⁰ First, they flattered him, praising his devotion to truth, his integrity and his impartiality. Then they asked him whether it was right for Jews to pay the taxes demanded by Caesar, hoping he would say that it wasn't – then they would have reason to hand him over to Pontius Pilate. 'They sent spies,' writes Luke, 'who pretended to be righteous, that they might seize on His words, in order to deliver Him to the power and the authority of the governor.'¹¹

Jesus, however, seems to have rumbled the ruse. 'Why do you test me, you hypocrites?' he said. 'Show me the tax money.' One of them showed him a denarius, to which Jesus responded, 'Whose image and inscription is this?' They replied, 'Caesar's,' to which he uttered the immortal retort: 'Render therefore to Caesar the things that are Caesar's, and to God the things that are God's.'¹² They had no answer.

Jesus got away with it on that occasion, but tax laws, eventually, would bring about his downfall.

Some religions were allowed by the Romans. Judaism was one such *religio licita*. It was not savagely suppressed or all but wiped out in the same way as, for example, the druidry of Celtic religions or the periodic outbreaks of Bacchanalian cults, which were deemed little more than a *superstitio*. Non-Roman kings, however, were not tolerated. They were a threat to both Rome's authority and its tax revenues. Roman law had long since decreed that anyone who claimed to be a king was guilty of sedition.

Moreover, Roman citizens could not be crucified, only non-Romans, and only for one of three crimes: attempting to escape from slavery, highway robbery, or piracy and sedition. 'We found this fellow perverting the nation,' cried the mob who brought Jesus before Pontius Pilate, 'and forbidding to give tribute [i.e. tax] to Caesar, saying that he himself is Christ a King.'[13] Sedition, which he encouraged by non-payment of taxes, was the charge for which he was crucified.

At the birth of Christ, at his death and throughout his life, there is a tax story.

## Tax and the rise of Islam

*The poverty of the people is the direct cause of the devastation and ruination of a country; the main cause of the poverty of the people is the desire of its ruler and officers to amass wealth and possessions.*[14]

Ali ibn Abi Talib, fourth caliph (656–661)

Islam began with the prophet Muhammad. By the time of his death in 632, thanks to victory in battle, astute occupation of trade routes and promises of equal treatment for all, he had unified the tribes of Arabia. Within barely three decades of his death, Islam had become one of the largest empires in the world. It continued to grow. Historians argue as to why and how it was that it spread so quickly and so successfully in the seventh and eighth centuries. Muslim tax policy explains all. It secured more converts than perhaps any proselytising tool the world has ever known.

Abu Bakr, Muhammad's close companion and father-in-law, was his successor – the first caliph. Like the fiercely loyal and highly organised armies of the early Roman Republic, Bakr's army consisted entirely of volunteers. To the north-east of him there was political, social, economic and military weakness in the Sasanian Empire of Persia. Once a major world power, the Sasanian Empire was exhausted after decades of warfare against the Byzantines, to the north-west, who were almost as spent. Whether Persian, Byzantine or Roman, they all suffered with heavy taxation. Bakr believed that his cause would find support if he lightened the load. He declared that those who 'accept Mohammed's religion and pray his prayers'[15] would be relieved of taxes.

Under Bakr's orders, his general Khalid ibn al-Walid took Persia. The conquered people, mostly Zoroastrians, were made to pay a poll tax, known as the *jizya*, but following Bakr's instructions, those who converted to Islam were exempted from the tax and given their freedom.[16] Even those who did not convert were not so badly treated – as long as they paid up. Those who failed to pay, however, were imprisoned, enslaved or killed. 'In the name of God, the Merciful and Compassionate,' exhorted the conquering general, 'become Muslim and be saved. If not, accept protection from us and pay the poll tax. If not, I shall come against you with men who love death as you love wine.'[17] Death, taxes or Islam – that was the choice. Many chose Islam.

Bakr's successors, Umar, Uthman and then Ali, had a similar approach. The armies of Muhammad swept across North Africa and eventually into Spain. All fell before them. 'Death to the infidel!' was the cry, but Islam's success had as much to do with judicious tax policy as it did the sword or the Koran. Conquered lands put up little resistance. Heavily burdened with taxes as they were under their previous regimes, they had neither the means nor the inclination. 'Burdens were so grievous', wrote one contemporary historian, that 'many of the rich and poor denied the faith of the Messiah'[18] – the largest body of converts were Christians.

Even those who did not convert were often glad of the relief the Islamic invaders brought. One story from Judaea tells of overextended Muslim forces retreating from a large body of Roman troops marching from Antioch. As they evacuated, the chief tax collector was ordered to reimburse the conquered people's poll tax, as the Muslims were not able to ensure their safety and the poll tax was 'nothing but the price of protection'.[19] Conquered Christians were brought to tears by the gesture, crying, 'May God bring you back to us', while conquered Jews pledged that 'the Roman emperor shall not take the city as long as the spark of life scintillates in our bodies'.[20]

Like the invaders of the early Roman Republic before them, the Muslims tended to leave existing local tax infrastructure in place in conquered territories, yet, to find favour with newly conquered peoples, they imposed lower rates of tax, and less aggressive means of collection. In Egypt, for example, Ali, the fourth caliph, wrote to his chief governor instructing him to exercise great care 'to ensure the prosperity of those who pay taxes'. 'The proper upkeep of the land in cultivation is of greater importance than the collection of revenue,' he advised, 'for revenue cannot be derived unless the land is productive.'[21]

'He who demands revenue without helping the cultivator to improve his land,' Ali added,

> inflicts unmerited hardship on the cultivator and ruins the state. The rule of such a person does not last long. If the cultivators ask for a reduction in their land tax for having suffered from epidemics, drought, excessive rainfall, soil infertility, floods impairing the fertility of the land or crop damage, then reduce the tax accordingly, so that their condition may improve. Do not mind the loss of revenue on that account, for that will return to you one day manifold in the hour of greater prosperity of the land and enable you to improve the condition of your towns and to raise the prestige of your state.[22]

Ali was also insistent that taxpayers should never be humiliated. 'If you disobey my commands God will punish you,' he said.[23]

Something similar was observed in the Islamic conquest of Spain. 'The Muslims were victorious over their enemies,' says twelfth-century Arabic-Andalusian philosopher Abu Bakr Muhammad at-Turtushi, 'as long as the tax-paying peasants were treated kindly . . . They cared for them as a merchant cares for his merchandise. The land flourished, there was plenty of money, and the armies were well supplied.'[24]

The first four caliphs (632–661) – the Rashidun – can be credited with the military expansion of Islam, but it was under the Umayyad dynasty (661–750) and then the Abbasid (750–1258) that the Islamic empire solidified. It would grow to become one of the greatest empires in history, making huge contributions to advances in mathematics, chemistry, optics, surgery, music, architecture and art. Its trade routes brought coffee (via Ethiopia) and gunpowder (via China) to Europe for the first time.

Over time, however, a shortage of infidels led to a shortage of revenue. Religious immunity to poll taxes would become a thing of the past. One ruler in Egypt begged the caliph to reinstate poll taxes on converts, and so he did. Revenue usually takes precedence over principle. Instead of the option to convert, there was a pact, known as the *dhimma*, in which non-believers were granted protection as long as they paid taxes, did not strike Muslim men and kept their hands off Muslim women. One or two dinars per year was the rate, though, like all taxes, it would eventually go up. Taxing non-believers eventually proved so lucrative that Christian Europe began to copy the practice, and Jews, especially, fell foul of it.

Islam was never a republic like early Rome, but an autocracy more like Rome in its imperial days. The distant caliph had little audit control and local sultans kept more and more of what they collected. With the passage of time, Islamic armies no longer brought liberation from oppressive taxation, they perpetrated it. The annual burden of one dinar became four. Crop taxes of 25% became commonplace. There are many reports of taxpayers being beaten or humiliated as they came before the tax collector to pay.

Some even had receipts tattooed on their necks to protect against double payment. One Muslim minister argued for a capital tax of two thirds of the value of assets owned by Christians or Jews.[25] Another in Egypt triggered a revolt when he tried to increase land taxes on the same day one of his wives wore a 30,000-dinar dress. A brave adviser pointed out the injudiciousness of the action, adding, 'and that is only one dress and one wife'.[26] In Spain, in the words of a contemporary, tax collectors 'devoured the subjects and misappropriated their money and exhausted them, so that the subjects fled and could not cultivate the land. The revenues brought to the Sultan diminished, the armies became weak, and the enemy grew strong against the lands of the Muslims and seized many of them. The Muslims were inferior and the enemy victorious.'[27] Perhaps it was not so much the Pyrenees, but excessive taxation that halted the Islamic advance into Europe.

The very first caliph, Abu Bakr, at the time of his death refunded to the state treasury the entire amount he had drawn during the period of his caliphate.[28] Such selflessness was a thing of the past. By the fifteenth century, and possibly before, Islam's golden age was behind it. Higher taxes had become the order of the day.

One the empire's greatest philosophers was the fourteenth-century Tunisian Ibn Khaldun. In his magnum opus, *The Muqaddimah*, he described a common cycle of taxation:

> In the early stages of an empire, taxes are light in their incidence, but fetch in large revenue. As time passes and kings succeed each other, they lose their tribal habits in favour of more civilised ones. Their needs and exigencies grow . . . owing to the luxury in which they have been brought up. Hence they impose fresh taxes on their subjects . . . and sharply raise the rate of old taxes to increase their yield . . . But the effects on business of this rise in taxation make themselves felt. For businessmen are soon discouraged by the comparison of their profits with the burden of their taxes . . . Consequently, production falls off, and with it the yield of taxation.

He might have been describing Rome or Greece before, Britain or the US after. Low taxation and small government accompanies the ascent of great civilisations, high taxation and big government their demise.

## High tax rates do not mean more revenue

It may be counter-intuitive, but it is an observation that goes back centuries. Low tax rates often bring in greater revenue, while higher tax rates bring in less.

Khaldun was not the first to take note. It was a guiding philosophy of the fourth caliph, Ali, who, as we have seen, wanted to protect the prosperity of taxpayers at all costs. Eighteenth-century Scottish philosophers David Hume and Adam Smith made the same observation, as did John Maynard Keynes, J. F. Kennedy and Ronald Reagan – and many more besides – in the twentieth century. In 1924, US Secretary of the Treasury Andrew Mellon wrote, 'It seems difficult for some to understand that high rates of taxation do not necessarily mean large revenue to the government, and that more revenue may often be obtained by lower rates.'[29] But perhaps the most famous proponent of this argument was the American economist Arthur Laffer.

In 1974, Laffer was having dinner in Washington DC with two of (recently impeached) President Richard Nixon's former advisers, Dick Cheney and Donald Rumsfeld, as well as a writer for the *Wall Street Journal* by the name of Jude Wanniski. Laffer was arguing that the incumbent president Gerald Ford's recent tax increases were flawed and would not lead to increased government revenue. To illustrate his argument, so the story goes, he drew a curve on a napkin showing the relationship between tax rates and revenue. At very low rates of tax, government revenue is low; but it is also low at high rates (because the economy is weaker, profits are down, earnings are down, evasion is higher and so on), so the curve is bell-shaped. The top of the bell is the point of maximum revenue – that is, the sweet spot at which to place tax rates if your goal is to maximise government revenue. Laffer's argument caught the imagination of those present; Wanniski would later dub it 'the Laffer Curve', even though Laffer later stressed, 'The Laffer Curve, by the way, was not invented by me',[30] and mentioned many others, from Keynes to Khaldun, who had observed the same phenomenon (perhaps we should call it the Fourth Caliph Curve).

As President J. F. Kennedy once said, 'It is a paradoxical truth that tax rates are too high today and tax revenues are too low, and the soundest way to raise the revenues in the long run is to cut the tax rates.'[31] It is a lesson that mankind – and the Islamic empire was no different – continually seems to forget, and one that continually needs reteaching.

# Chapter 6

# The Greatest Constitutional Document
# of All Time

*Taxes, hahaha! Taxes! Beautiful, lovely taxes! Aha! Aha!*

King John in Disney's *Robin Hood* (1973)[1]

Rulers have a long history of justifying taxes on moral grounds. Former Chancellor George Osborne's sugar taxes were introduced not for the good of government coffers, but for the good of your health. French president Emmanuel Macron imposed fuel taxes for the good of the climate. The spin is apparent even in the language of tax – a tax is your 'duty', your 'tribute', your 'due'.

Medieval England saw one such example. Knights who, perhaps not unreasonably, did not want to follow their king to war had to pay a tax instead – 'scutage'. It was also known as cowardice tax. Levying it proved lucrative for the medieval English king.

In 1187, when the great Kurdish leader Saladin annihilated the armies of the Crusaders and took Jerusalem, the Christian cause was shaken to its core. There must be a new crusade, said the kings of England and France, and to pay for it Henry II levied a special tithe, the Saladin tithe. It was a 10% tax on revenues and movable properties, with special exemptions for the 'arms, horses and garments of knights' and the 'horses, books, garments and vestments, and all appurtenances of whatever sort used by clerks in divine service'.[2] Everyone else paid – though if you joined the crusade you were exempted, which proved an extremely effective recruiting

44

tool. The Saladin tithe became the largest tax ever collected in England. Needless to say, it wasn't popular. As the church had been so involved in its collection, the Archbishop of Canterbury, Baldwin of Exeter, received much of the blame. Wisely, he disappeared to Wales for the year.

But Henry never even made the crusade. Instead, he fell into war with Philip of France, and then his own son, before a bleeding ulcer killed him a year later, in 1189. His son, Richard 'the Lionheart', who saw England as a place to tax, rather than rule (he spent less than six months of his ten-year reign there), succeeded him. On being crowned, Richard found the coffers full and immediately set off on the Third Crusade, in which he failed to take Jerusalem back from Saladin. On his way home, he was captured and handed over to the Holy Roman Emperor, who then demanded an extortionate ransom: 100,000 pounds of silver, roughly the amount the Saladin tithe had raised the previous year. So another tithe was levied to secure his release, this time at 25% rather than 10%, and the clergy were not exempted. In addition, scutage was also levied and a new land tax was implemented.[3]

Richard died five years later, in 1199, to be succeeded by his brother John, who had actually tried to bribe the Holy Roman Emperor to keep Richard for longer. John picked up where his brother left off to become one of the most infamous tax collectors in history. He raised scutage 11 times in his 17-year reign, often in the absence of actual military campaigns. He levied new land taxes based on Richard's system. Those who refused to pay had their lands confiscated. He levied yet another royal tithe. There were new import and export duties. He instigated a kind of inheritance tax, in which relief payments were demanded when estates and castles were inherited, often in excess of what barons were able to pay. He sold expensive sheriff appointments and the new incumbents would then endeavour to make back their investment through fines and penalties, particularly in the forests. Thus do we have the legend of Robin Hood and the Sheriff of Nottingham. John sold the rights to establish new towns – one such royal charter saw the foundation of Liverpool. He created a special tax for the Jews, who had already been targeted during the Saladin tithe, now known as the tallage of 1210, which left them 44,000 pounds of silver worse off. He even taxed widows who wished to remain single. This must have been especially hurtful to those women who had lost their husbands fighting John's wars.

As if things couldn't get worse, a succession of poor harvests led to a shortage of food and then rising prices. Despite John's attempts to steady the inflation with a re-coinage in 1204–5, there was social unrest. The English had had enough.

In the north and the east barons renounced their feudal ties to the Crown, proclaimed themselves the Army of God and marched on London, which they took. The Archbishop of Canterbury, Stephen Langton, attempted to broker peace talks with the king. On the banks of the River Thames in Runnymede, about 20 miles west of London, a charter was agreed with wide proposals for political reform. New taxes could only be levied with the consent of the barons. Limits were placed on scutage and other feudal payments. Barons were protected from illegal imprisonment and granted access to swift justice. The rights of the church were also protected, as, to an extent, were those of free men. The barons agreed to surrender London and demobilise their troops.

They did neither. They did not trust John to keep his word, which, as expected, he did not. He appealed to the pope, who duly declared the charter 'shameful, demeaning and unjust' and excommunicated the rebel barons.

The ensuing war was one John would not survive, but it was dysentery, not fighting, that took him. His nine-year-old son, Henry III, succeeded him, under the protection of William the Marshal, 'the best knight that ever lived', according to the archbishop.[4] Langton may have had a point.

Marshal had served under four kings. With John out of the way, and Marshal as protector, many rebel barons changed sides, so that the royalists, led by Marshal, who was still charging into battle at the age of 70, actually won the war. But at the ensuing Treaty of

Lambeth, Marshal needed to make sure of rebel allegiance. Old as he now was, he knew his time would soon be up and he wanted peace and stability for his nine-year-old liege. He was deeply loyal to the Crown, but he had also seen the consequences of the previous three kings' pernicious taxes. The failed charter made beside the Thames two years previously was his best chance. Ignoring criticisms that he was being too generous to the losing side, he reissued it. He himself would be one of the witnessing barons and it would be used as a basis for future government. It was called 'the great charter', or, to give it its Latin name, Magna Carta.

Henry III reissued the charter again in 1225, in exchange for permission to levy taxes, and his son, Edward I, did the same in 1297; thus did it became statutory law in England.

## When myth is more powerful than fact

*To the meadow came the king and the barons. Their parlays culminated in the greatest constitutional document of all time.*[5]

Lord Thomas Denning, English judge (1957)

The celebrated British judge Lord Denning was just one of Magna Carta's many admirers, but perhaps the myth of Magna Carta and the protection of ancient freedoms it is supposed to have enshrined is greater than the document itself. Denning called it 'the foundation of the freedom of the individual against the arbitrary authority of the despot',[6] but in fact it was less concerned with the rights of ordinary people than with the relationship between the barons and the king. Of its many clauses, only three remain law today. The rest have been repealed, most two or three hundred years ago.

The myth, however, has remained powerful and iconic, a great symbol of freedom. It persisted through the English Civil War, when it was argued that Magna Carta made the king as much subject to the common law of the land as ordinary citizens. It was believed to have formed the origin of the trial-by-jury system. It heavily influenced political thinking during the Glorious Revolution of 1688. Perhaps most significantly of all, when English colonists set off for the New World, they took with them royal charters emphasising that they would have the same 'liberties, franchises and immunities'[7] as people born in England. The colonists believed Magna Carta to be a fundamental law. When they fought back against their English overlords in the American War of Independence, they believed they were fighting not so much for new freedoms as to preserve those Magna Carta had already enshrined.[8]

'During the American Revolution,' the US National Archives tell us, 'Magna Carta served to inspire and justify action in liberty's defense. The colonists believed they were entitled to the same rights as Englishmen, rights guaranteed in Magna Carta. They embedded those rights into the laws of their states and later into the Constitution and Bill of Rights.'[9]

The Fifth Amendment of the US Constitution contains the phrase 'no person shall be deprived of life, liberty, or property, without due process of law'. This derives from one of the three clauses in Magna Carta that still remain part of English common law: 'No Freeman shall be taken or imprisoned, or be disseised of his Freehold, or Liberties, or free Customs, or be outlawed, or exiled, or any other wise destroyed; nor will We not pass upon him, nor condemn him, but by lawful judgment of his Peers, or by the Law of the land.'

'The democratic aspiration is no mere recent phase in human history,' said President Franklin Delano Roosevelt in his 1941 inaugural address to the people of America. 'It was written in Magna Carta.'

Magna Carta, conceived some 700 years earlier in reaction to King John and his predecessors' pernicious taxation, shaped the national mentality of the United States of America. Even today it is still an integral part of that great nation's character.

# Chapter 7

## How the Black Death Changed the Tax Structure of Europe

*We will ourself in person to this war:*
*And for our coffers, with too great a court*
*And liberal largess, are grown somewhat light,*
*We are inforc'd to farm our royal realm,*
*The revenue whereof shall furnish us*
*For our affairs in hand.*

William Shakespeare, *Richard II* (Act I, Scene IV)

The medieval system of rule known today as feudalism was, essentially, a tax structure. At the top was the king. As he had acquired his right to rule from God, he owned all the land, the primary source of wealth. He kept some for himself, perhaps around a quarter, gave some to the church and the rest to the barons. In exchange, the barons gave the king a share of their produce, their revenues, their service, their knights and soldiers, when required, and their loyalty.

The same dynamic – land and protection in exchange for produce, profit and labour – applied all the way down the food chain to villeins and serfs at the bottom. The latter were probably the descendants of Roman slaves and their status was little better. They had to provide their lord, be it knight, baron, church or king, with their labour. Roughly half their week was spent working their lord's land; the other half they kept for themselves to work the strips of land of which they were given possession. At harvest time they gave a share of their crop. They were obliged to grind their grain at the noble granary, and the noble would take his share. If an animal was slaughtered, some of the meat was given. Serfs were attached to the land. If the land changed ownership, so did they. They were not allowed to leave without their lord's permission – and if they did, they would find themselves outlaws. Like the knights and barons above them, their position was heritable, trapping them for generations in this slave-like status.

It was, essentially, a tax structure: a system of control and rule, enforced by military strength.

Then, in the mid 1300s, came the Black Death.

The Black Death killed some 50 million people, 60% of Europe's entire population. It was especially devastating in rural areas, where some 90% of people lived.[1] Estimates vary, but it's thought England's population shrank by around two thirds, from roughly six million to two million people.

Across Europe, the effect on feudalism was dramatic. 'There was such a shortage of servants for all sorts of labour as it was believed had never been before,' said one contemporary chronicler.[2] Villeins were in short supply. Land, however, now unmanaged or abandoned, was not. Wages went up; landowners' profits went down. Between 1340 and 1380, the purchasing power of rural labourers rose by 40%.[3]

Many serfs found themselves lordless and, as a result, free – without having had to buy their freedom. To encourage survivors to stay, lords gave peasants their freedom and even paid them to work on their land. Peasants handled money for the first time.

The reaction of the ruling classes was to legislate against this unwanted upwardly mobile dynamic. In 1349, little more than a year after the Black Death arrived in Britain, legislation was passed to cap wages and prices. It didn't work. Two years later, the Statute of Labourers Act set out maximum daily rates of pay for just about every job you can think of – farmers, saddlers, tailors, fishmongers, butchers, brewers, bakers. People were barred from charging more than pre-Plague prices for their goods or labour, with the penalty of branding or imprisonment if they broke this law. Laws were enforced by justices, who, typically, also happened to be local landowners. In 1359, legislation was brought in to punish migrants, and in 1361, further legislation to strengthen the Statute of Labourers Act. Never had the government allied itself with local landowners in such an unpopular way.[4] But the legislation could not halt the tide. The lower classes began wearing better clothes, often similar clothes to their superiors, and their diet improved. In reaction, in 1363 a sumptuary law was passed to limit the diet and detail the quality and colour of cloth that lay people at different levels of society could wear.

Meanwhile, Britain and France were in the midst of what would become known as the Hundred Years War. In 1377, with Richard II still a minor, his uncle, the military commander John of Gaunt, Duke of Lancaster, the richest man in Britain, was the effective head of government. He imposed a poll tax to cover the spiralling costs of the war. This was to be paid by peasants as well as landowners. The barons supported the tax. They would be collecting it and could take a cut. What was new about the tax, as far as the lower orders were concerned, was that it was to be paid in money, not in kind – four pence per person. It reflected the huge change in the economy that had taken place as a result of the labour shortage – the lower orders were now handling cash.

It was meant to be a one-off, but the tax was repeated two years later. That didn't raise as much as was hoped, so a third tax was imposed: a flat rate of 12 pence – a full shilling – per person over the age of 15. This was almost a week's wages, and the poor paid as much as the rich. It was seen as a tax on the labouring classes.

People began looking for ways to avoid the tax. Many refused to register. When the returns were examined, John of Gaunt was furious to discover that so little had been collected. He appointed commissioners to interrogate local communities in an attempt to find those who had refused to comply. One such commissioner was a justice of the peace named Thomas Bampton.

Bampton arrived at the village of Fobbing in Essex on 30 May 1381 and summoned the villagers to appear before him. They arrived armed with bows and sticks. Not only would they have to pay the tax a second time, Bampton explained, they would have to pay for those who had failed to turn up. Thomas the Baker represented the people of Fobbing. He said his village had already paid its taxes and no more would be forthcoming. Bampton ordered him arrested. Thomas the Baker resisted. In the fighting that followed, three of Bampton's clerks were killed, though he managed to escape.

The following day, Chief Justice Sir Robert Belknap arrived at the village with several soldiers and the simple plan to execute the ringleaders, thereby scaring everyone else into paying their taxes. To his surprise, he was attacked and his men beaten. The villagers then 'made him swear on the Bible that never again would he hold such sessions nor act as Justice in such inquests'. Once released, 'Sir Robert travelled home as quickly as possible.'[5]

So began the Peasants' Revolt.

## The tiler who spat at the king

*Now the time is come in which ye may cast off the yoke of bondage and recover liberty.*[6]

John Ball, preacher (1338–1381)

History has been rather mocking of the Peasants' Revolt, depicting it as a ramshackle, even comic affair. The truth is otherwise. Even the word peasant, itself derogatory, is inaccurate. As much as they were peasants, the rebels were ordinary workers, artisans and small businessmen. Today we might call many of them middle class. Moreover, this was not some spontaneous uprising, but a well-orchestrated operation, with a clear and, in many ways, quite brilliant strategy – to take out the tax system. It came close to overthrowing the power structure of England.

The movement's ideological champion was a priest by the name of John Ball, whose brushes with authority, particularly the Archbishop of Canterbury, saw him both excommunicated and landed in prison several times. He had been preaching about economic injustice for at least 20 years. When the bishops banned him 'from preaching in parishes and churches', he began 'to speak in streets and squares and in the open fields'[7] instead, where he would pour forth fiery words. Ball's sermons drew large crowds. He was 'popular with the ignorant people', according to one of the many deprecatory contemporary chroniclers,[8] and had many listeners, 'whom he always strove to entice to his sermons by pleasing words, and slander of the prelates'.[9] Like a medieval Marxist, Ball declared that 'things would not go well with England until everything was held in common'. 'They are dressed in velvet and furs, while we wear only cloth,' he cried. 'They have wine, and spices and good bread, while we have rye bread and water. They have fine houses and manors, and we have to brave the wind and rain as we toil in the fields. It is by the sweat of our brows that they maintain their high state. We are called serfs, and we are beaten if we do not perform our task.'[10]

Ball had become such a thorn in the Archbishop of Canterbury's side that the archbishop, who was loathed for his taxes, ordered all people listening to the priest's sermons to be punished. When that failed, he locked Ball up in Maidstone Castle. Ball predicted that he would be freed by 20,000 men.

Word had quickly spread of the riot in Fobbing. All over Essex, Kent, Hertfordshire and Suffolk, as tax collectors arrived, people banded together in resistance. Tax collectors who lost their lives had their heads put on poles, to be paraded around neighbouring villages. Within a week of that first riot in Essex, rebels in Kent had mobilised to take Maidstone Castle and free Ball, whose prediction came true. It seems the revolt had been planned. More than that, it was Ball who had been urging his followers not to pay their taxes in the first place. Now that he was freed, the uprising was blessed with a man of God: it had been legitimised too.

Little is known about the man the Kentish rebels elected to be their leader, except that his name was Walter, he had served in the army in France and he was a 'tiler of roofs and a low person'.[11] For tax purposes, he was identified as Walter the Tiler. Wat Tyler is how we know him today.

From Maidstone, the Kentish rebels marched to Rochester, then on to Canterbury. They targeted any buildings that housed tax documents and burned them down, so that all records were destroyed, including people's names, the rent they paid and the services they carried out. Lawyers and legal records were specifically targeted. The instruction was to kill 'all lawyers, and the men of the Chancery and the Exchequer'.[12] The Archbishop of Canterbury's complicity in the poll tax was clear to them, and they marched on the cathedral to depose him. Luckily for the archbishop, he was in London, but the rebels declared him deposed nonetheless. The city gaol was opened and the prisoners set free. This was an attempt to destroy the system itself.

The following day, they marched on London. The march had been timed to coincide with that of rebels north of the Thames estuary. Those from Essex, Hertfordshire, Suffolk and Norfolk camped at Mile End, those from Kent on Blackheath. Not even a fortnight had passed since Thomas Bampton had been chased out of Fobbing, yet here was a coordinated army of many thousands. The chronicler Thomas Walsingham said that 'two hundred thousand had gathered together'. Even if the number was more likely between 30,000 and 50,000, this was no spontaneous uprising. It was arranged for when the royal armies were absent. The closest force was up north fighting off the Scots, otherwise the armies were overseas.

The rebels' beef was not so much with the king as with those who advised him. The king was in Windsor when word of the rebellion reached him. He set off for London on the royal barge. A meeting was set for 13 June at Rotherhithe, close to the rebels' Blackheath camp. As the barge approached, Richard's advisers saw the huge crowds and would not let him land. Angry and frustrated, the peasants closed in on London.

Londoners were sympathetic to the cause. Though the king ordered the gates of the city to be shut, they left London Bridge open for the Kent rebels coming from the south, and Aldgate open so that the Essex rebels could enter from the east. The rebels ran riot. As at Canterbury, prisons were broken open and the inmates freed. All the legal paperwork at the Temple was brought out and burned in the street, the buildings systematically demolished and the lawyers murdered. Anyone with a link to tax collection was targeted for attack.

Looking for John of Gaunt, the peasants marched on his Savoy Palace and broke in, but he was up north defending against Scottish invasion. Rebels burned the duke's furnishings, smashed his precious metalwork, ground up his jewellery and gems, set fire to his records and threw everything they could not break into the sewers or the Thames. But they stole nothing, so the story goes. Here were self-declared 'zealots for truth and justice, not thieves and robbers'.[13]

At the end of that first day in London, the rebel forces congregated outside the Tower, where the king, in horror no doubt, watched the city burn. There was only the castle's garrison and his immediate bodyguard – several hundred soldiers at most – against a rabble of many thousands. The king could not rely on military force. But he had to get the mob out of the city. To do so, he agreed to meet them the following day at 8 a.m. outside the city, at Mile End.

As with so many medieval negotiations, skulduggery was the order of the day. Tyler laid out the peasants' demands. They wanted an end to the poll tax. They wanted the abolition of serfdom and unfree tenure – men should be employed to work, not compelled. They wanted free trade – to be able to buy and sell goods as they wished. They wanted a rent limit of four pence per acre and an end to feudal fines through the manor courts. And they wanted charters that guaranteed them the rights and privileges of free men, as well as pardons for all those involved in the rebellion. What was more, they had drawn up a list of 'traitors' – the hated officials of the law who had so persecuted them for taxes. They wanted these officials surrendered for execution. Among those on the list were the Archbishop of Canterbury and John of Gaunt.

With his hands tied by lack of military force, the king quickly agreed to most of the demands on condition the rebels disperse back to the countryside. He declined to hand over the officials, instead promising that he would personally implement any justice that was required. Thirty clerks began writing out charters. Once they had them, many of the rebels from Hertfordshire, East Anglia and Essex began the journey home, believing their demands had been met.

The Kentish rebels did not get their charters that day, however, and it seems they were suspicious. The gates of the Tower of London had been left open to receive Richard on his return, but some 400 rebels got there first. Inside, they found many 'traitors' – Simon Sudbury, the Archbishop of Canterbury; Sir Robert Hales, the king's treasurer; and John Legge, the tax commissioner. They dragged them all out onto Tower Hill, and beheaded them. That night the rebels continued their scourge of London, seeking out and killing John of Gaunt's men, and anyone associated with the legal system.

The following day, Tyler and the king met again, this time at Smithfields, inside the city walls. Again the peasants had the critical mass of numbers, though not by as much as the previous day. Tyler's success so far, it seems, had rather gone to his head. 'He came to the King with great confidence, mounted on a little horse, that the commons might see him,' says one chronicle, and when he dismounted, he only 'half bent his knee', nor did he remove his hood (a sign of disrespect before the king). He then 'took the King by the hand, and shook his arm forcibly' and called him 'Brother'.[14]

'Be of good comfort and joyful,' he told Richard, 'for you shall have, in the fortnight that is to come, praise from the commons even more than you have yet had, and we shall be good companions.'[15]

The chronicle continues: 'And the King said to Walter, "Why will you not go back to your own country?" But the other answered, with a great oath, that neither he nor his fellows would depart until they had got their charter such as they wished to have it.'[16]

'And he demanded that there should be only one bishop in England . . . and all the lands and possessions (of the church) should be taken from them and divided among the commons . . . And he demanded that there should be no more villeins in England, and no serfdom . . . that all men should be free.'[17]

The king acceded to Tyler's demands, though judging by the way Tyler then acted, it seems he did not believe him. He 'sent for a flagon of water to rinse his mouth, because of the great heat that he was in, and when it was brought he rinsed his mouth in a very rude and disgusting fashion before the King's face. And then he made them bring him a jug of beer, and drank a great draught, and then, in the presence of the King, climbed on his horse again.'[18]

It was around about now that the king's – or his advisers' – plot came into action. 'A certain valet from Kent, who was among the King's retinue, asked that the said Walter, the chief of the commons, might be pointed out to him. And when he saw him, he said aloud that he knew him for the greatest thief and robber in all Kent.' 'For these words Wat wanted to strike the valet with his dagger,' says the *Anonimalle Chronicle*, but acting in such an improper manner before the king gave the Mayor of London, who was wearing armour, grounds to forcibly arrest him. When Tyler tried to fight him off, the mayor gave him 'a deep cut on the neck, and then a great cut on the head'. Then 'one of the King's household drew his sword, and ran Wat two or three times through the body, mortally wounding him'.[19]

Tyler attempted to ride back to his men, 'crying to the commons to avenge him', but he made it only a few paces before he fell. His men bent their bows to shoot – this was their last chance – but they hesitated because they were not quite sure what was going on. The young king, showing great presence of mind, rode out to them, shouting out that all their demands would be met, and told them to follow him to Clerkenwell Fields, outside the city walls, where they would be given their charters. This was their mistake: trusting the king.

With Tyler's demise, the bubble of rebellion had been popped. His head was placed on the end of a pole and processed through the city, before being left for all to see on London Bridge. The Peasants' Revolt had been quashed.

Then began the process of rounding up the troublemakers. Royal forces swept through Hertfordshire, Essex and Kent. As troops approached, rebels held up the pardons and charters they had been given, but were brutally cut down. The charter became a virtual death sentence. The king then granted pardons to those who executed rebels without due process. Villagers were promised that no harm would come to them as long as they named those who had encouraged them to join the rebellion. Those named were then executed. 'Serfs you are and serfs you will remain,' said the king. The promises he had made were long forgotten.

Ball was found in Coventry and sent to trial. He stood proud, made no apology for his 'unacceptable' beliefs and was sentenced to death. The Bishop of London delayed the execution in the hope that he would repent of his treason and so save his soul, but Ball would do no such thing. On 15 July, little more than six weeks after the first uprising in Fobbing, John Ball was hanged, drawn and quartered.

For its perpetrators, the Peasants' Revolt was a failure, but its impact was considerable. Parliament gave up trying to cap wages. Lords increasingly sold serfs their freedom; tenures gradually became leasehold arrangements. England did not see another poll tax for 300 years. Rather than raise taxes to pay for the Hundred Years War, Parliament decided that the military effort should be reduced – and as a result, this was a war England would eventually lose. Reluctance to raise taxes for overseas military spending persisted for over 100 years into the reign of Henry VII.

The English aversion to poll taxes never went away. Six hundred years later, tax rebels would again exploit it to bring down Britain's best-known post-war prime minister, Margaret Thatcher.

## How the Peasants' Revolt brought down Thatcher

Margaret Thatcher had been wanting to reform local taxes in Britain – known as rates – for some 16 years. She felt they were outdated and she wanted to bring some accountability to local councils, especially in cities, who were spending too much on needless schemes. In this, she had a point. This was the era of the 'Loony Left'. In London, Hackney ended its twinning arrangements with France, West Germany and Israel for new twinnings with the Soviet Union, East Germany and Nicaragua. Lambeth banned the word 'family' from council literature because it was discriminatory. An Inner London Education Authority school in Kennington made pupils write protest letters as part of the time-table, while one of its teaching packs, entitled 'Auschwitz: Yesterday's Racism', equated Thatcher's trade union legislation with that of Adolf Hitler.

Early in 1990, Thatcher introduced the community charge, which was a flat-rate per capita charge – everyone paid the same, in other words (with students and the unemployed given an 80% discount) – levied to pay for local services. As services differed from council to council, so would the charge. Thatcher's idea was that it would bring greater transparency and accountability to local government spending. It backfired horribly.

The tax brought too much accountability. Where council spending was out of control, residents found themselves with huge bills. Outrage at the perceived injustice of a flat rate was everywhere. 'The Duke of Westminster,' thundered the *Guardian*, 'who used to pay £10,255 in rates on his estate has just learned his new poll tax: £417. His house-keeper and resident chauffeur face precisely the same.'[20]

After 10 years in office, Thatcher's popularity was waning even amongst her supporters, but, here, finally, for her many ideological enemies, was a means to take her down. They were quick to rename her charge the poll tax, after the tax of 1381 that triggered the Peasants' Revolt. Thatcher tried to shake the name off, but it stuck. As in 1381, a huge non-payment campaign – Can't Pay, Won't Pay – sprung up encouraging people to resist. There were riots and protests. People found all sorts of ways to avoid payment. They abstained from the electoral register, so the council had no idea who was living in a given residence. Renters, especially students, simply moved on at the end of their tenancies, leaving an unpaid tax bill. Councils proved inept at collection, and as the number of defaulters grew, they were unable to cope with the burden of pursuing them. Opponents would clog up court processes by contesting liability orders, and then not attend court hearings arising from non-compliance, so that legal costs escalated. The sums demanded began to rise. As they did, and the inability of councils to enforce payment became more apparent, so more and more people refused to pay. At least one in five avoided payment. Within six months, Thatcher had resigned.

A flat-rate per capita tax seems simple enough, but, collected neither centrally nor at source, it was impossible to enforce. Residents felt directly the pain of out-of-control local government spending, yet rather than hold the perpetrators of the spending accountable, the blame was directed at the architect of the tax herself. Thatcher paid for it with her career.

### The business brain of Henry VII and the end of feudalism

The Peasants' Revolt did not end the feudal system in England. Such embedded systems of rule do not stop overnight. Its final disintegration did not come until the financial reforms of Henry VII, a hundred years later.

If ever there was a lesson in the value to a nation of a ruler who avoids war, it came from Henry VII. Henry ruled for 24 years, from 1485 to 1509, and his reign saw just one overseas conflict. Instead of war, he pursued overseas marriages and alliances. His tactical taxation and legislation of the nobility effectively ended the power of the barons and thus feudalism itself. It also established the supremacy of the Crown and the freedom of the mercantile classes, laying the foundations for the extraordinary period of expansion that occurred in Tudor England. He became the first English king for centuries to run a surplus.

His reign began with his victory at the Battle of Bosworth in 1485, which brought the Wars of the Roses to an end. He moved quickly to pardon his enemies, and to marry Elizabeth of his opposing house, so as to bring the houses of York and Lancaster together under one Tudor rose. He then took control of all the land owned by both houses, and much more besides.

He was determined to break the power of the barons and assert the supremacy of the Crown, and did so by acquiring wealth. Taxes, fines and pardons became a major source of revenue for Henry. He instituted a sort of inheritance tax, whereby if men died without an heir, their land passed to the Crown. He exploited an Act that meant anyone in prison for treason could be punished without trial. The penalty was execution – or they could forfeit their land to the Crown. Population decline meant that much manorial land had fallen into disrepair, but Henry enacted a kind of efficiency tax whereby he fined landowners who had let this happen. Meanwhile, he took great care to increase efficiency and maximise returns on all royal land and any more that he acquired.

After the Hundred Years War and the Wars of the Roses, the barons were weak and they put up little resistance. As well as taxing them, Henry further weakened them by banning private armies. Without armies, the barons could not enforce the collection of their tithes. Meanwhile, the exploding wool trade meant that enclosures to graze sheep replaced the open-field system of feudal England, in which a serf was responsible for a strip. The role of serfdom was falling away, and there were fewer serfs from whom barons could collect tithes. Britain was changing to a money- rather than land-based economy. For his allies Henry turned to the increasingly powerful mercantile classes.

He signed a trade deal with Philip IV of Burgundy known as the Intercursus Magnus, to boost trade. He then levied customs duties against wool, leather, cloth and wine. To encourage the development of the domestic cloth manufacturing industry, he placed a heavy export duty – often as high as 70% – on undressed wool. He developed a navy and a merchant marine – the latter would supplement the small royal navy, as well as allow England to control its own trade.

Having seen the devastating effect of French cannon on the English in the Hundred Years War, he took steps to manufacture cannon balls with which to defend England against Scottish invasion. England had its first blast furnace in 1496, and so began its iron industry.

Henry's financial reform saw the expenses of the royal household separated from the revenues of the state. He had new coins issued to ensure a standard currency. Weights were also standardised. His judicial reforms saw statutes passed to protect the poor from injustice, and to penalise dishonest juries, and a system of law began to replace noble whims.

Henry's many achievements lay in his business brain. Rather than resist economic change and new technology, he encouraged it. Rather than wage war, he avoided it. He built up an extraordinary wealth. And thus did feudalism fade away.

Even so, one of the first acts of his son, Henry VIII, two days after his coronation, was to arrest the two men responsible for collecting his father's taxes. Sir Richard Empson and Edmund Dudley were charged with high treason and duly executed.

## Chapter 8

# *How Taxes Gave Us the Modern Nation States We Know Today*

Though Tudor England was relatively stable, the country would soon be at war with itself again. Taxation, as always, was at the heart of it all.

At the turn of the seventeenth century, the Crown depended largely on Parliament for its revenue. Parliament was, mostly, made up of the gentry, and only they had the ability and authority to collect the most meaningful forms of taxation at local level.

A healthy relationship between Crown and Parliament was essential to any monarch, but after James I became king in 1603 – the first king from the House of Stuart – tension grew between the two. The Crown was in debt. There was inflation. The king had extravagant habits. Most significantly of all, with the Thirty Years War imminent in Europe, there would soon be overseas conflict to pay for. James needed money. In particular, he had his eye on the revenue from customs and excise. Parliament, for various reasons, would not give it to him.

The same tension between Crown and Parliament over tax revenue spilled into the reign of James's son, Charles I, who became king in 1626. That Charles had married a Catholic further exacerbated the enmity. Parliament refused to assign him the right to collect customs duties. Desperate for funds, he dissolved Parliament, assembled a new one, then dissolved that and avoided calling a new one for another 11 years. This period would become known as the Eleven Years Tyranny. The beauty of it all was that the king's lack of funds forced him to make peace in Europe, when he might have preferred war.

Charles resorted to other means to raise revenue. He used fines. He sold titles – and if you refused one, you were fined. There was a tax that didn't need parliamentary approval – ship money – and he tried to levy that. But ship money was only supposed to be levied during times of war. One politician, John Hampden, refused to pay and in 1637 stood trial. He lost, but the trial made him famous and it got the country thinking about the relationship between taxes and parliamentary representation. 'What an English King has no right to demand, an English subject has a right to refuse,' Hampden said.

When the Scots invaded England in 1639, Charles had to recall Parliament to raise money to fight them off. Parliament granted him funds, but only on condition that he execute his top advisers. The king believed his authority came from God. How dare Parliament hold him to account? He attempted to arrest his five biggest critics, one of whom was the same John Hampden who had refused him ship money. Civil war soon followed.

The English Civil War was actually a series of armed conflicts fought over many years, usually broken down into three wars. After the second, the Scots handed Charles I over to the English – in exchange for £100,000 and the promise of future payments.[1] That the king was then subjected to a trial set a precedent in itself.

Charles insisted that the trial was illegal, that his authority was God-given and that no court had jurisdiction over a monarch. The prosecuting barrister, one John Cooke, the Solicitor General, defied numerous threats against his life to make his case. Charles had used his power to pursue his personal interest rather than the good of the country, he argued. He was therefore guilty of treason. The king was 'trusted with a limited power to govern by and according to the laws of the land and not otherwise'.[2]

Charles I was found guilty and sentenced to death. At 2 p.m. on 30 January 1649, he was executed. With that one clean strike that took off his head, the divine right of kings was dead. Now they were subject to the law like everyone else. Parliament's control over tax revenue had made it possible.

He was briefly succeeded by his son, Charles II, who fled the country in 1651 after the Parliamentarian victory at the Battle of Worcester. The English Civil War was over. Some 300,000 people – 6% of the population – died in the conflict.

England became a protectorate under the puritanical military leader Oliver Cromwell, who took an extraordinary annual salary of £100,000[3] – the same figure paid to the Scots for Charles I. The protectorate did not last. When Cromwell died in 1658, his son, Richard, was unable to maintain the confidence of the army, and he soon renounced power. The ensuing vacuum meant the monarchy was actually restored, with Charles II – known as the Merry Monarch – as king. It seems he was just what the country needed after so many years of Puritan repression. Among other things, Cromwell had shut down the theatres and banned Christmas. Charles restored both, and allowed women to appear on the stage for the first time.

He certainly lived up to his nickname. He had at least a dozen children by seven mistresses. None of them were legitimate, however, so when he died in 1685 with the words 'I am sorry, Gentlemen, for being such a time a-dying', the rightful heir was his rather less vivacious brother James, who had converted to Roman Catholicism. Parliament, which was mostly Protestant, did not trust its new king. It suspected he was pro-French and pro-Catholic, and that he had designs on restoring absolute monarchy to Britain. When he then produced an heir, it moved quickly to eliminate the danger, allying with the Dutch king, William of Orange, to depose the troublesome new king.

James was easily defeated. Parliament then invited William and his wife, Mary, who was also James's daughter and rightful heir to the throne, to be joint monarchs – on condition they agreed to a Declaration of Rights, which stipulated they had to obtain Parliament's consent if they wanted to levy taxes. Parliament was enforcing what it had fought for; and it was limiting the power of the Crown by curtailing its ability to tax. The declaration also stipulated regular parliaments, free elections, and freedom of speech in Parliament. It set out basic civil rights, which granted greater legal protection for individuals' life, liberty and property. This was the Glorious Revolution.

The power structure of Britain had changed. Now it was set in law: an English monarch could not rule or raise taxes without Parliament's consent. It remains so to this day. Taxes are the property of the Crown, but only Parliament may deem where and how they are collected and spent. This has left the United Kingdom with a bizarre anachronism. As taxes belong to the Crown, the body in charge of collecting them, HMRC – Her Majesty's Revenue and Customs – is not directly accountable to Parliament.

A statue of John Hampden, the politician who refused to pay Charles I's ship money, now stands in the lobby of the Palace of Westminster, where the House of Lords and the House of Commons meet, the symbolic defender of the rights of Parliament. The five MPs whom Charles I tried to arrest – John Hampden, Arthur Haselrig, Denzil Holles, John Pym and William Strode – are commemorated each year at the State Opening of Parliament. The doors of the Commons chamber are slammed in the face of the monarch's messenger to symbolise the rights of Parliament and its independence from the Crown. The English Civil War, fought over tax, defined the system of rule that Britain knows today.

## America: Taxation without representation is tyranny

The rationale for John Hampden's stand against Charles I would become the slogan of the American revolutionaries. Their rallying cry still echoes today: 'No taxation without representation.' The 13 states stood up against the taxes of their British overlords. Their victory led to the formation of the United States of America, the most powerful nation on earth.

Yet the irony is that Americans did not have such a bad deal. The taxes Britain raised were mostly spent in America. The military victories on which those taxes had been spent had removed the threat of French armies and opened up the western frontier. The colonists had British military protection. The land was rich. Business was good. Americans were free of the restrictive social class structures of Europe that had held many back. Their sons could not be conscripted to fight in faraway places of little relevance to their own lives. The uprising was triggered not so much by the amounts levied, but by the way they were levied. The tax lesson of the American Revolution surely lies in the dangers of misjudged legislation.

It all began, as so often seems to be the way, with overseas conflict. The Seven Years War of 1756–1763, fought between the European nations but across five continents, had left Britain in debt. The British thought, not unreasonably, that their American cousins should shoulder some of the cost of pushing the French out of America. So in 1764, Britain introduced a tax on sugar (the majority of taxes came through customs and excise duties, often designed to protect British merchants).

Future US president John Adams said the Sugar Act imposed 'enormous taxes, burdensome taxes, oppressive, ruinous, intolerable taxes',[4] but it was the six states of New England, whose merchants were hit hardest, that were most upset. The other states were largely indifferent. What riled all 13 states as one, uniting them in a way that nobody had previously been able to do, was the tax that came the following year.

Britain had its own domestic problems. Riots in 1765 saw excise collectors mobbed. There was great pressure to look overseas for revenue, and when the prime minister, George Grenville, asked Parliament if the Crown had the right to collect taxes from the colonists, he met with approval. A new stamp tax was introduced to raise funds to station troops in the colonies.

Stamp taxes meant that stamps had to be bought from public officials and fixed on newspapers, playing cards, legal documents, land titles, business licences, diplomas and other such documents for them to be legitimate. Though stamp taxes were common in Europe, they were not in the colonies, and they aroused anger. Such direct taxes were unconstitutional, the colonists decided, a betrayal of the rights enshrined by Magna Carta. If they were to be implemented, the bare minimum was that the colonists should have representation in Parliament. A delegation that counted among its number one Benjamin Franklin went to Britain to petition for repeal of the Stamp Act. Despite Franklin's warning that the temper of America towards Great Britain was 'very much altered', when just two years earlier it had been 'the best in the world', the delegation was unsuccessful.

In America, there were town meetings, speeches, even riots. A political movement known as the Sons of Liberty sprang up, often using intimidating and violent tactics to hamper the distribution of stamps. Tax collectors were harassed. Their effigies were burned. Across the country there was a boycott of British-manufactured goods, and imports reduced to a trickle. British merchants came to oppose stamp taxes, and their influence was such that, with the Declaratory Act of 1766, the taxes were abolished. Jubilation followed, but only briefly.

The Declaratory Act came with an addendum, granted to appease those in Parliament who wanted to punish colonial impudence. It affirmed that Parliament had 'full power and authority to make laws and statutes of sufficient force and vitality to bind the colonies and people of America . . . in all cases whatsoever'.[5] This meant that Parliament had the power to tax, if it wanted, and the colonies could not take exception to any parliamentary law. Parliament wanted the right of absolute power. It's not hard to see why the now united colonists were unhappy, nor why taxation without consent should be against their disposition.

The Chancellor of the Exchequer, Charles Townshend, in order to be able to reduce land taxes at home, then introduced new duties on items from Britain – paper, glass, paint, lead and tea. The colonists quickly realised that this Act was not about regulating trade, but raising revenue. In essence, it was as bad as the direct stamp taxes. The worst aspect of the duties was their collection. Officials 'treated every trader as a cheat'.[6] Any breaches of the law meant the entire vessel, as well as its cargo – even the personal chests of ordinary seamen – could be seized. The rewards paid to informers – one third of confiscated property – created a culture of paranoia, mistrust and, occasionally, misinformation. It did not help that the army, for which the taxes were mostly being levied, aided and protected the officials who collected them.

Franklin wrote a telling piece of satire to show how misjudged British taxation was. He called it *Rules by Which a Great Empire May Be Reduced to a Small One*. Rule XI ran: 'To make your taxes more odious, and more likely to procure resistance, send from the capital a board of officers to superintend the collection, composed of the most indiscreet, ill-bred and insolent you can find . . . If any revenue officers are accused of the least tenderness for the people, discard them. If others are justly complained of, promote them . . .' Rule XV said: 'Convert the brave, honest soldiers of your navy into pimping tide-waiters and colony officers of the customs . . . scour with armed boats every bay harbour river creek cove and nook throughout the coast of your colonies; stop and detain every coaster, every wooden boat, every fisherman; tumble their cargoes and even ballast inside out and upside down; and if a penny worth of pins is found unentered, let the whole boat be seized and confiscated.'[7]

The Quartering Act, which required colonists to provide British troops with food and shelter, further exacerbated tensions. In Britain the army was not allowed to quarter troops in private homes if the owner objected. Why should the rules be different in America? Colonists felt their rights and freedoms were being violated. They were equal in status, not subordinate to the British.

Once again there was a boycott of British goods and trade slumped. The Sons of Liberty continued with their tactics of intimidation. Boston was where tensions were felt most, and one riot led to the infamous Boston massacre, in which British soldiers, while under attack, fired into a mob, killing five people. The ensuing investigation and trial saw widely different reports of events and became a major propaganda war between the two sides. John Adams wrote that the 'foundation of American independence was laid' that day.

Economic hardship and merchant petitioning meant that in 1770, Britain repealed Townshend's duties. As a symbolic gesture, however, a small duty on tea was retained. Though the compromise eased tensions, tea, that most British of drinks, would be the eventual trigger for revolution.

By 1773, American merchants had been boycotting English tea for five years. Ninety per cent of the tea drunk in the colonies was Dutch, and it was smuggled. Dutch tea was cheaper, and by drinking it, loathsome British duties were avoided. But Britain's East India Company was in trouble. To prop it up, Parliament passed the Tea Act and granted the company a monopoly over the British tea market. More significantly, it allowed direct sales into the colony with no taxes due. It meant British tea became cheaper than Dutch, and colonial merchants were cut out of the loop entirely. The implications for the American merchants' business revenues were so ghastly that, disguised as Indians, American merchants boarded British vessels and threw their tea into the harbour. This did not meet with wholesale American approval. It was a serious violation of private property rights. Many, Benjamin Franklin among them, felt full restitution should be paid to the owners of the tea. The British reacted by passing a series of coercive acts to re-establish dominion. Town assemblies were banned. The power of the House of Representatives was restricted. Boston harbour was closed until the East India Company was compensated (which it never was). This only made matters worse.

By 1775, full-scale war had broken out, the Patriots against the British, with the French, Spanish and Dutch all involved on the Patriots' side. Fighting went on for six years. The logistics of supporting troops 3,000 miles away eventually became too much for the British, and the Patriots emerged victorious. The British kept Canada. Spain took Florida. The United States took all the territory in between, as far west as the Mississippi.

The painful irony was that British taxes were a pittance compared to the obligations the US now faced. Tens of thousands of men had lost their lives. Many of those who survived returned home to bankrupt farms. The 20% of colonists who had remained loyal to Britain lost their properties and fled the country, either north to Canada or south to the Bahamas. War debts now had to be paid. The Continental Congress, which governed the United States during the revolution, could not afford its soldiers' back pay, nor the interest on its war debt, let alone the capital. Its currency, printed with abandon to cover war costs, met with hyperinflation (from where we derive the phrase 'not worth a continental').

The British, it seems, learned their lesson. 'Taxation by the Parliament of Great Britain,' as Parliament put it with considerable understatement, 'occasioned great uneasiness and disorder.'[8] So in 1778, King George III approved a new Act, which declared that Britain would 'not impose any duty, tax or assessment for the purposes of raising revenue in any of the colonies'.[9] From then on, local authorities had to give their consent before new taxes could be levied. The Patriots did not just win the war for themselves, but in a way for all colonies of the British Empire, until its eventual demise after the Second World War.

Poorly thought-through tax legislation was the cause. A nation built on low taxes was the result.

The United States was born.

## France: Liberté, egalité, fraternité

Louis XIV ruled France for 72 years, the longest-serving monarch in European history. In 1715, as he lay on his deathbed, he said to his heir, 'Do not follow the bad example which I have set you. I have often undertaken war too lightly and have sustained it for vanity. Do not imitate me, but be a peaceful prince, and may you apply yourself principally to the alleviation of the burdens of your subjects.'[10] He had left his country's finances in a parlous position.

For a short time his advice seems to have been heeded. Then came war after war. The 1740s saw the War of the Austrian Succession, followed by the Seven Years War, which saw France lose its North American colonies to the British, and the destruction of its navy. Then Louis XVI decided to support the colonial rebels in the American War of Independence, which cost millions, as well as the lives of at least 10,000 French troops. France seemed eternally plagued by profligate, warmongering kings, who imposed unpayable national debts on their nation. Decades of fight-now-pay-later policies and an out-of-touch decadence among the ruling classes meant there was little chance of those debts ever being paid back. Rising national debt inevitably leads to higher taxes, by one means or another.

Historians will discuss the causes of the French Revolution into eternity, but if you had to boil those causes down to one word, that word would surely be 'taxes'. There were too many. They were too high. They were inconsistent. They were unjust. And they could not cover the spending habits of France's elite. How ironic that France should support the American Revolution, founded as it was on unjust taxation, when its own system – riddled with corruption, incompetence and inconsistency – brought revolution on itself. If ever there was a tax story with a moral, it is the story of the French Revolution.

France was one of the highest-taxing regimes in Europe – and it did not have Britain's trading empire, or the productivity gains of the early Industrial Revolution, to compensate.

There was the *taille*, levied against each family based on the amount of land they owned. There was a poll tax, and the *vingt-ième*, a one-off tax to 'ease' the state deficit. Peasants also had to pay a tithe to their church, as well as seigneurial duties. They could not grow their holdings, as feudalism still existed, and they did not have the full rights of landowners. There were excises, and there were also customs duties, the *octroi*. As smuggling on the French coast was hard to prevent, these were mostly levied instead at the entrances to cities, further impacting ordinary people. A second wall was built inside the city of Paris to collect the *octroi* and prevent evasion. When revolution came, that wall was one of the first things to come tumbling down.

The salt tax, or *gabelle*, was the most hated of all. Some people were exempt. Others found themselves paying ten times the real price of salt.[11] Households had to purchase minimum quantities, usually at artificially inflated rates. Though these minimum quantities were supposed to be a household's average needs, they were in fact much larger amounts. Yet regulations stated that salt could not be given away, nor held over from one year to another, so the following year everyone would have to buy more. If someone then wanted to use salt to preserve fish or meat, they had to obtain written permission from the *grenier* – the official salt warehouse – and pay an additional tax. To avoid paying it, many went without.

At different stages in the seventeenth and eighteenth centuries, there were taxes on just about anything that moved, including food, alcohol and tobacco. You can imagine how popular these were in France. At one point there were five taxes on wine: on the vine, on the harvest, on the manufacture, on the transportation and on the sale. In France! Peasants drank cider instead.

Much tax collection in France was contracted out to tax farmers – *fermiers généraux*, as they were known. In their enthusiasm for their work, they frequently resorted to intimidation. With great efficiency, they divided the country into districts and formed large national corporations with their own system of bonds, which the government later used to settle debts. Tax farming was extremely lucrative. One tax farmer, Antoine Crozat, grew so rich he would count French Louisiana – all of it! – among his assets.

Local officials, who collected taxes, transferred the money to financial receivers, who transferred it to general receivers, who transferred it to the royal treasury. You can guess what happened along the way. Accounting was so backward that the royal treasury had very little means of knowing whether the amounts being paid to it were actually correct, nor how much had been siphoned off. One story tells of the king asking his advisers why so little revenue seemed to reach the treasury. In answer, a nobleman took a piece of ice and had it pass through the hands of all those at the table until it reached the king, by which time it had melted and there was nothing left.

To enforce the rules, and to counter smuggling, which was rife, there was extensive and rigorous surveillance. Investigators could conduct household searches unannounced. They frequently resorted to intimidation. Voltaire describes a scene on his estate that followed a dispute over salt taxes: 'The gendarmes of the tax farmers . . . marched about in groups of fifty, stopped all the vehicles, searched all the pockets, forced their way into all the houses and made every kind of damage there in the name of the king, and made the peasants buy them off with money.'[12]

Despite paying so many taxes, there was no seat for ordinary folk in government. The only means available to make themselves heard was uprising, which they resorted to frequently. But if the winemakers of Bordeaux revolted and forced down taxation, only they would see the benefit. The winemakers of Burgundy would have to stage their own revolt. There was no single fiscal policy, and it seems it was the inconsistencies, and the injustices they created, that made the populace angry as much as the taxes themselves.

Two classes of people avoided many taxes almost completely – the church and the nobility. The church had the option to make a voluntary contribution every five years called the *don gratuité*, but it was neither regulated nor compulsory. The nobility, as the military elite, apparently paid their dues in service and in blood. As a result of such exemption, a new business emerged of buying noble status, government office and other such tax-exempt positions of influence. This only added to the inconsistency. Selling government offices became such a notorious racket, the US Founding Fathers would insert two clauses in their constitution to make sure it could not happen there.

Every attempt to reform the system ran up against the brick wall of the nobility. The 1750 *taille* reform plan, for example, removed tax exemptions for church lands, noble lands and certain provinces. But then the king, under pressure from the nobility, not only scuttled the plan, but removed the minister who had proposed it. The *taille* would eventually become known as 'the peasants' tax', because everyone else had found a means to avoid it.

However, the lower and middle classes were becoming increasingly aware of their situation. Thanks to the philosophers of the Enlightenment, such anarchic notions as *liberté*, *fraternité* and *egalité* were becoming more and more widespread. There was also the heretic thought that the monarchy was, in fact, not divinely ordained, but incompetent.

Word had got out of a revolution in America in which representation was demanded in exchange for taxation. The *Encyclopédie*, 27 volumes of revolutionary scientific and philosophical thought, had been widely distributed, with the stated aim 'to change the way people think'.[13] Contributions from contemporary leading thinkers included: 'in the matter of taxation, every privilege is an injustice' (Voltaire); 'He who only has the bare necessities of life should pay nothing' (Rousseau); and 'Of the poor man it [France's tax system] makes a beggar, of the workman an idler, of an unfortunate a rogue' (Raynal). France's heavily taxed bourgeoisie grew to resent its exclusion from political power and from positions of honour and privilege. It was increasingly frustrated with its decadent, promiscuous king, its frivolous and aloof ruling classes, its antiquated system of government, so incapable of reform, and its 'inconsistent, arbitrary, byzantine' tax system 'plagued with incompetence and abuse'.[14]

In February 1787, the state of the nation's finances had become so bad that the Controller-General of Finances, Charles Alexandre de Calonne, called an assembly of 'notables' to propose reforms designed to eliminate the budget deficit by increasing the taxation of the privileged classes. Still the exempted classes would not give way, and the problem was deferred again. Existing restlessness was compounded when 1788 saw a poor harvest, crop failure and rising food prices.

Finally, the three classes of society – the clergy (First Estate), the nobility (Second Estate) and the rest (Third Estate) – were called to an Estates General to resolve the issue. In anticipation of the meeting France was flooded with pamphlets discussing how the state should be reconstructed. Chief among the complaints in the *cahiers de doléances* – the lists of grievances prepared by the Third Estate – was taxes.

On 5 May 1789, the Estates General met at Versailles. They couldn't agree on how to vote. Frustrated at the failure to progress, the deputies of the Third Estate declared themselves the National Assembly and swore not to disperse until France had a new constitution. The king gave in and a National Constituent Assembly was formed.

Almost straight away, however, the king began mustering troops to dissolve this new assembly. Rumours of an aristocratic conspiracy to overthrow the Third Estate spread through the provinces. It was enough to provoke insurrection. On 14 July 1789, the Parisian crowd seized the Bastille, the fortress in the centre of Paris that symbolised royal tyranny. Across the country, hungry and angry, peasants rose up against their lords.

The Third Estate's National Constituent Assembly declared that the feudal regime and the tithe were abolished. Then it introduced the Declaration of the Rights of Man and of the Citizen, which proclaimed liberty, equality, the inviolability of property, and the right to resist oppression. The declaration said that taxes should be distributed equally among all citizens, according to their ability to pay; that all citizens had the right to have demonstrated to them the need for taxation, to consent to it freely, to watch over its use, and to determine its proportion, basis, collection and duration; and that society had the right to hold accountable every public agent of the administration.

The king refused to sanction it. The Parisians rose again and on 5 October marched on Versailles. The rest, as they say, is history.

Among the first steps taken by the victorious revolutionaries was to abolish tax farming. It was not just the king who would be so famously executed. Numerous tax farmers got the chop as well. The monarch lost the right to levy taxes. This now fell to the parliament, on behalf of the people. All the statutes and tax privileges of the nobility, the clergy, the provinces, cities and corporations were abolished. The former system of tax was history.

But the new government desperately needed tax money. It had condemned the salt tax, but then asked everyone to pay it until it could come up with something better. It was ignored. It tried asking everyone to donate 25% of their income – effectively an income tax – and was again ignored. Desperate for funds to pay off public debts, it confiscated the land of the Catholic Church – almost one third of France. It then used the land as backing for bonds, known as *assignats*, with which it paid off creditors. The holder could swap the *assignat* for confiscated land, or sell it on. In a country short of money, these bonds became a form of legal tender in themselves. But the government issued more and more of them, while existing ones were not destroyed even if they had already been used to redeem land. Faith in them was quickly lost; there was inflation, followed by hyperinflation and the eventual collapse of the currency by 1797.

The country badly needed a leader to give them direction. That man was the military general Napoleon. As he rode through Paris, the crowds cried, '*Plus d'impôts, à bas des riches, à bas la république, vive l'empéreur*' – 'No more taxes, down with the rich, down with the republic, long live the emperor!'[15]

Napoleon couldn't end taxation. But with the help of three men, Martin-Michel-Charles Gaudin, François Barbé-Marbois and Nicolas François-Mollien, he did bring tax reform to France. He created several new public bodies: the ministry of finance, the treasury and, in 1800, the Bank of France.

To address the problem of tax farmers, he established a department of professionals whose only job was tax collection, and whose income was fixed. To incentivise payment, he promised to name the most beautiful square in Paris after the first region to pay its taxes in full, and thus did Place des Vosges get its name.

He tried many new taxes, some with success, others without. In the end, there were land taxes, commercial taxes at 10% of annual rent, and various licence taxes. From workers and peasants he took three days' wages a year. There were taxes on wine, playing cards, carriages, salt, tobacco, windows and doors.

Spending by each ministry was closely monitored so as to ensure the budget remained balanced. The administration never devalued its currency. The cost of living stabilised. New debt was avoided – Napoleon disliked the high rates of interest – while the national debt was eliminated. The government balanced its books for the first time in over 70 years. All in all, taxes were lower, fairer and more efficient.

But they did not raise enough to pay for Napoleon's military adventures. Here he relied on conquest: he plundered and then taxed. He was especially convinced of the wealth of northern Italy, and he increased existing burdens there, as well as imposing new ones, based around his efficient new collection systems. Consumption and licence taxes, as well as the *octroi*, were all introduced. It did not inspire good feeling in the conquered territories, and meant his grip on them would be short-lived. His dependence on military success also made him vulnerable – he could not sustain defeat. Sooner or later, a Waterloo was inevitable.

French revulsion for taxes lasted for over a hundred years, despite the many changes in political regime. Income tax took hold in Britain and elsewhere, but not in France. It was proposed and debated several times, but the inquisition and the inequality of progressive rates were deemed unacceptable. Any tax the French settled for had to follow certain principles.[16] A tax must be on a thing not a person. Taxes on incomes from land or business must be estimated, not exact, based on the typical income of a given estate or operation over a span of years. Failure to declare income would not meet with punitive provisions; presumed income would be used instead. It was a system of tax for a nation of small proprietors, manufacturers and traders, with minimum contact between taxman and taxpayer. Tax was subordinate to liberty. The tax burden never exceeded 12%. France thrived.

Shortly after the American Civil War, France gave America its great statue – a robed woman representing the Roman goddess of freedom Libertas. She holds a torch above her head – a beacon of light, clarity and truth – and in her left hand carries a tablet inscribed with the date of the US Declaration of Independence. A broken chain lies at her feet. The Statue of Liberty has become an icon of freedom and of the United States. Inquisitional income tax was regarded by both the French and the Americans as an enemy, an affront to liberty.

It all changed with the Great War. By the end of it, the Frenchman's income tax form was as complicated and intrusive as the Englishman's many schedules. France, where government spending today amounts to 56% of GDP,[17] is one of the most heavily taxed nations on earth. The French, wearing their yellow gilets, are rioting again.

## When the British government stole 11 days

In the UK, the tax year begins on 6 April and ends on the 5th. Ever wondered why?

Until 1752, the new year in England did not begin in the middle of winter on 1 January. Instead the year was aligned with the seasons and began around the spring equinox (when the length of day and night is the same), on 25 March – Lady Day.

England operated on the Julian calendar, so named because it came into law under Julius Caesar. Lady Day was one of the four quarter days, the other three being Midsummer Day (24 June), Michaelmas (29 September) and Christmas Day. Quarter days were important days, when rents were paid, accounts were due, servants were hired and school terms began. The tradition went all the way back to medieval times.

As Lady Day fell between ploughing and harvesting, it became the date on which long-term contracts between farmer and landowner would begin. Farmers could often be seen travelling from old farm to new on Lady Day. It also came to be the first day of the fiscal and contractual year.

In 1582, Pope Gregory XIII introduced the more accurate Gregorian calendar, and Europe, led by France, began to adopt it. Scotland, both independent and Catholic at the time, switched in 1600. Protestant England, however, did not embrace this Catholic innovation and stayed with what it knew.

Eventually, in 1751, to address the growing problem of 'dual dating' (people using different calendars), and to fall in line with both Scotland and the rest of Europe, Parliament passed the Calendar Act, and so Britain switched from the Julian to the Gregorian calendar, with 1 January becoming the first day of the new year.

Although 1751 had become a short year, running only from March to December, England still had to correct by 11 days in order to align the two calendars. Wednesday 2 September 1752, it was decided, would be followed by Thursday 14 September. And thus did England 'lose' 11 days.

Taxes and other dues still had to be paid on Lady Day, 25 March, however. Collectors wanted the full amount. People wanted something for the 11 days they had lost. 'Give us our eleven days!' they cried. There are even stories of riots breaking out.

The problem was solved by moving the start of the fiscal year back 11 days, to 6 April. It remains to this day the beginning of the tax year.

## Chapter 9

# War, Debt, Inflation, Famine – and Income Tax

Income tax – 'this colossal engine of finance', as William Gladstone described it[1] – has had a greater impact on modern history than perhaps any piece of legislation ever enacted.

Not only was it the 'tax to beat Napoleon', income tax made the difference in the First World War, it funded the American contribution to the Second, thus winning the war for the Allies, and today it is the key funding component of welfare states in all their forms around the world.

Without income tax we could not have the public education, welfare, healthcare and pension systems that we do.

In the US, 65% of government revenue now derives from taxes on income.[2] In Germany, it is the same.[3] In the UK, it is 47%.[4] Income taxes have made possible the large-state social democratic model by which most of the developed world lives today. Society is designed the way it is because of income taxes.

English prime minister William Pitt the Younger is widely believed to be the man who introduced income tax to the world, when he brought it in in Britain in 1799. But there are many examples that precede him. The old republic of Holland tried it in 1674 and 1715. The French attempted to introduce it in 1793 after the revolution, and the Dutch brought it in again in 1796.[5]

And there was another example, which pre-dated Pitt by about 400 years. In the parliament of January 1404, a one-off income tax was granted to Henry IV, on condition that it should not be made a precedent in the future.[6] To keep it concealed from posterity, no evidence was preserved in the treasury or the exchequer, and every record was burned.[7] A contemporary chronicler, Thomas Walsingham, in his *Historia Anglicana*, described the tax as 'vexatious and burdensome', but said little more than that. He did not mention the amount that was raised, nor how it was assessed, though he knew the details. 'I would have inserted these into this work,' he said, but Parliament wanted it to remain secret forever. We will never know why, though we can imagine all sorts of reasons.

But really, not even this little-known tax of 1404 was the first income tax. As we have seen, its origins go all the way back to ancient Mesopotamia and the tithe.

## The tax to beat Napoleon

*More taxes were raised [by England] per capita in the war against Napoleon than in the war against Hitler.*

Andrew Lambert, historian (2005)[8]

When William Pitt came to power in 1783, annual tax revenues were about £13 million. The national debt was £234 million and the interest on the debt was £8 million.[9]

War with France broke out 10 years later and things began to balloon. Pitt was ideologically opposed to France's new revolutionary movement. He feared the insurgency might spread to Britain and he was determined not to let that happen. To support other European monarchs against revolutionary fervour, he poured money into the Continent. The 'Golden Cavalry of St George' it was called, because of the image of St George on the gold guineas he sent.

Almost all of Pitt's national expenditure in the five years between 1793 and 1798 came from loans.[10] By 1798, the debt was £413 million, and the annual interest payable had more than doubled.[11] Amongst those who lent the British money was the banker Nathan Mayer Rothschild, who would become the richest man on earth.

The situation was critical.

The Bank of England initially paid the interest quarterly in gold and silver, but as the payments increased, it started using notes instead, and then issuing more and more notes in smaller denominations. 'If put to the test,' said Thomas Paine, the bank 'had not money to pay half a crown in the pound . . . And on this slender twig hangs the whole funding system.'[12] Precious metal became worth more as bullion than its face value as money, and many began melting down coins and exporting the bullion to the Continent. The bank, realising it was running out of gold and silver, approached Pitt and asked him to pass an Act to free it from having to redeem its notes in gold and silver. Pitt obliged. The currency of the Crown became unconvertible and Britain effectively abandoned the gold standard.

As a result, through the course of the war, inflation would manifest itself at a rate 'unprecedented in the lives of the British citizen'.[13] The cost of bread, meat and beer rose by over 50%, dairy by 75%, salt by 270%. Rents rose by 76%. Wages, however, remained largely unchanged.[14] Thus did ordinary people pay the price of the debasement of money. With bad harvests in 1801–2, the inflation led to riots.

Pitt introduced his income tax in 1799 against this strained financial backdrop of debt and money-printing. The navy had mutinied, and the army was starving. He needed 'aid and contribution for the prosecution of the war'.[15]

It was said of the government at that time, 'Wherever you see an object, tax it!'[16] There was a tax on carriages, wagons, wains and carts. A tax on male servants. A tax on bricks, glass, windows and wallpaper, on carriage horses, riding horses, racehorses and game hunting. In 1795, Pitt introduced a tax on hair powder. In 1796, a tax on dog owners. In 1797, a tax on clocks and watches. In 1798, a tax on coats of arms, whether on carriages, seals, signet rings or on one's person.

He then introduced the triple assessment, which meant you had to pay from three to five times the amount you had been assessed for. Thus if you owed £20, you must pay £60. Alternatively, you could declare your annual income and pay 10% of that instead.[17] It was hoped the tax would raise £10 million a year. It fell short by 40%. Pitt complained about 'shameful evasion' and 'scandalous frauds', but really the fault was in the design.

## Making tax work: Collection at source

Peace in 1802 saw the tax abolished by Pitt's successor, Henry Addington. But when hostilities with France resumed a year later, income tax soon returned. However, Addington made some fundamental changes.

The main objection to Pitt's income tax was the intrusion it brought into people's private lives. Addington recast the whole scheme with two main objectives: to avoid intrusion and to avoid fraud. He introduced five schedules,[18] which, to an extent, still exist to this day.

His great innovation was to tax at source. Under Pitt's system, the taxpayer had been responsible for payment. With Addington, the tax was payable at the point at which the income arose. The bank paid the tax on the interest and deducted it before paying the bond holder. It deducted the tax on the company dividend before remitting to the shareholder. Salaries and pensions paid from public revenue were also taxed at source – something that would eventually spread into wider employment in the second half of the twentieth century, and is now the case in most countries today.

Addington's tax, though it was resented, succeeded where Pitt's had failed. Even though the maximum rate was 5% (at first), compared to Pitt's 10%, overall it raised 50% more money.[19] Given how much better Addington's system worked, in many ways he, not Pitt, should be seen as the author of modern income tax, though perhaps Pitt's failure was needed to show the way.

In 1816, one year after the Battle of Waterloo, with the war against France now over, there were some 379 petitions against the tax.[20] Though the Chancellor wanted to retain it, the House of Commons voted the other way and it was abolished again – to 'a thundering peal of applause'[21] that 'continued for several minutes'.[22] So loathed were the violations of privacy the tax brought that all records were cut into pieces and pulped. Some were burned by the Chancellor in public.

Yet duplicates had been sent to the King's Remembrancer, and, for reasons we will probably never know, these were never destroyed. More significantly, what also went unforgotten was that the tax had proved a practical means of raising revenue. Governments do not forget such experiences.

## The real cost of war: Perpetual debt

*Nothing is so well calculated to produce a death-like torpor in the country as an extended system of taxation and a great national debt.*[23]

William Cobbett, pamphleteer (1763–1835)

The Napoleonic Wars added over £600 million to the national debt. It cost three times as much as the previous four wars together.[24] The introduction of income taxes did reduce the government's dependence on loans, but still well over half of government expenditure was funded by debt.[25]

In 1853, Prime Minister William Gladstone tried to argue that 'our debt need not at this moment have existed if there had been resolution enough to submit to the Income Tax at an earlier period'.[26] The 'enormous weight and enormous mischief that have been entailed upon this country by the accumulation of debt' could have been avoided, he declared,[27] providing solid figures to back up his argument.

But such a war would not have been possible if its cost had been directly and immediately felt by the taxpayer. Taxes alone could not cover the enormous cost. The moneyed and propertied classes would not have stood for it. The middle classes and poor could not have paid for it. Indeed, Gladstone himself saw taxes as a check on war. 'The necessity of meeting from year to year the expenditure which it entails is a salutary and wholesome check, making them feel what they are about and making them measure the cost of the benefit which they may calculate.'[28] Government debt and abandoning the gold standard got through the exigencies and cloaked the real cost. They, as well as income tax, won the war for the British.

The irony was that France over this period remained on an orthodox, bi-metallic standard. As a result of its pre-revolutionary profligacy, France had no credibility. Britain had a better record of financial probity and an open budgetary process in Parliament, which meant it could borrow at much lower rates, as well as pursuing the inflation tax. William Cobbett, who would find himself in prison for his criticisms of the government, wrote an entire book, *Paper Against Gold*, railing against this sleight of hand and emphasising the need for sound gold currency. Easy debt made war too easy. Adam Smith had made a similar point, as did Gladstone half a century later: 'The system of raising funds necessary for war by loans practices wholesale systematic and continual deception on the people. The consequences are adjourned into a far future. The people do not know what they are doing.'[29]

But, to silence Cobbett and other critics, the government introduced higher taxes on publications, pamphlets, their advertising content and the paper they were printed on, effectively pricing them out of the reach of the working people they were aimed at, especially in the provinces. These became known as 'taxes on knowledge'.

The debt of the Napoleonic War and the interest payable effectively burdened the British people with a huge perpetual charge, which brought great hardship for the next 50 years. The conditions for the working class in the first half of the nineteenth century were as bad as they had ever been. Disraeli declared there was more serfdom in England then than at any time since the Norman Conquest. In their study of the impact of the Industrial Revolution on the working classes,[30] the social historians John and Barbara Hammond calculated that a labourer earning £22 paid £11 in indirect taxes imposed on the necessities of life. No wonder so many people fled to America in search of better opportunity. The great economic advances of the manufacturing towns in the nineteenth century eased the burden, but how much less poverty would there have been in the early part of the century without Pitt's debt?

When William Pitt died in 1806, it was discovered that he himself had debts over £40,000. His servants had been robbing him for years. He had been as careless with his own finances as he was with the nation's.

In 1842, barely 26 years after it had been abolished, income tax made its return in the first budget of Sir Robert Peel.

Peel had two pressing problems: Britain was in recession, and a £7.5 million budget deficit had been run up by the previous administration. Britain needed fewer taxes that generated greater revenue, Peel believed, and his solution was to bring back income tax, payable at 3%. It was a temporary measure, to be repealed as soon as government revenues were in balance. Over 175 years later, we are still waiting.

Income tax's effectiveness is what doomed its chances of ever being repealed. Even for Peel, the tax produced 50% more revenue than anticipated. William Gladstone became Chancellor in 1853 and he too was determined to abolish income tax, but the national debt tied his hands.

Gladstone did not like income tax. 'The inquisition it entails is a most serious disadvantage and the frauds to which it leads are an evil such as it is not possible to characterize,' he said. But he was stuck with it. War in Crimea in 1854 made things worse, and by 1860, government was even more reliant on the tax. 'If only our expenditure had continued to be stationary,' he said, 'or to rise only at the gentle and hardly perceptible rate of its growth during a quarter of a century before 1853, we should at this moment have been able to dispense with the Income Tax.'[31]

In the general election of 1871, both Gladstone and Disraeli opposed income tax. Disraeli won, but the tax stayed. 'Public expenditure' and 'the abandonment of the spirit of thrift' in government were to blame, said Gladstone.

By 1875, income tax was permanent.

## Sir Robert Peel – one of Britain's great tax heroes

Sir Robert Peel should be regarded as one of Britain's greatest tax reformers, even if some of his achievements were perhaps accidental. 'We must make this country a cheap country for living,' he declared,[32] and his reintroduction of income tax in 1842 – at a rate of seven pence in the pound on incomes over £150 per annum – meant he was able to remove over 600 duties and reduce rates on more than 500 further items. Thanks to his tax, trade and financial reforms, Britain actually ran a surplus.

Among the repeals were duties on sugar, livestock, cotton, meat and potatoes, as well as glass excise taxes. 'We hail with joy the abolition of the duty on glass,' said *The Lancet*, describing it as 'one of the most cruel [taxes] which a Government could possibly inflict on the nation; and only to be equaled in cruelty by the duties on corn'.[33] Peel would eventually repeal the duties on corn as well – in a move that ended his career.

The notorious Corn Laws were introduced in the aftermath of the Napoleonic Wars. To protect British crop producers against the falling cost of bread, the Tory government of Lord Liverpool introduced tariffs on imported grain. In protecting British landowners from foreign competition, there was less pressure for them to improve their own productivity. The cost of grain was kept high. The unnecessarily excessive cost of food increased the hardship on the already indebted British working classes, but it also created some of the richest British aristocratic dynasties in history. The wealth of the huge estates of Cadogan, Westminster and Bedford, which even today still occupy much of prime central London, were built on the back of these protectionist tariffs. The Duke of Westminster remains one of the richest people in the world. In his book *Wealth Secrets of the One Percent*, economist Sam Wilkin argues that many of the richest people in history, from Marcus Crassus in ancient Rome to John D. Rockefeller, J. P. Morgan and Andrew Carnegie in America's Gilded Age to Bill Gates today, owe vast amounts of their great fortunes not so much to brilliant risk-taking as to using legislation to defeat the forces of market competition. The Corn Laws are one such example.

Worse yet was the effect of the tariffs on Ireland. In the 1840s, the country was hit by the Great Famine. Blight struck the potato plant on which Ireland depended almost entirely as its staple crop. It was desperately in need of food supplies from abroad, and there was plenty of cheap grain waiting to be exported, especially from the US, but the tariffs made the cost too high. Over a million people lost their lives to starvation. A million more fled to the US to escape it. When you consider the impact of the Irish on the destiny of the United States – over 20 presidents, for example, claim to have been of Irish descent – and how much of that emigration was caused by the unintended consequences of the Corn Laws, you can see just what an impact even apparently minor taxes can have on human history.

Petitions to repeal the laws began as early as 1820, but there were so many landowners in Parliament that any attempt at reform met with opposition. Even Britain's tax commissioners came from the landed gentry (they would eventually form the Board of Inland Revenue in 1849). Some blame the Tories for the failure to get the Corn Laws repealed, but the Whigs held power from 1830 to 1841 and the laws remained. In 1838, free-trade campaigner Richard Cobden set up the Anti-Corn Law League, and in 1841, he was elected as an MP. He would eventually win Peel's ear. Peel had voted against repealing the laws each year from 1837 to 1845, but with food supplies growing scarce in mainland Britain and famine in Ireland, he changed tack. British farmers did not produce enough grain to meet the needs of its rapidly growing population at any time, let alone in a food crisis caused by potato blight.

Peel's proposed reforms were strongly opposed from within his own Conservative Party. It was felt by some that Ireland was exaggerating its problems. 'Apathy and unwillingness to attend to the business' was the diagnosis of one research report made on behalf of Parliament.[34] But Peel found Whig support and the laws were finally repealed in 1846. Going against his party would mark the end of his term as prime minister, and he resigned the same day. He never held office again.

But as Cobden foresaw, Peel's many repeals ushered in an era of free trade in Britain in the second half of the nineteenth century that in terms of innovation, invention and rising prosperity was perhaps the greatest in British history.

British agriculture was not so badly hit by the repeal at first. But within a couple of decades, advances in railways and steamships led to cheaper transport from Russian and US farms, while improved machinery in the US (Russia relied on cheap labour rather than machines) led to increased production. British farms were unable to compete with the vast amounts of imported grain. By 1880, agriculture was no longer the country's biggest employer. Trade and industry usurped it to become the powerhouses of the economy. By 1914, Britain imported four fifths of its grain. Rich on rent, landowners had been the wealthiest class. When that economic leadership was lost, so was their political leadership. Peel's tax reforms helped changed the power structure of Britain.

# Chapter 10

## *The Real Reason for the US Civil War*

*The people of the Southern States are not only taxed for the benefit of the Northern States, but after the taxes are collected, three-fourths of them are expended at the North. This . . . has made the cities of the South provincial. Their growth is paralyzed; they are mere suburbs of Northern cities.*[1]

*The Address of the People of South Carolina Assembled in Convention, to the People of the Slaveholding States of the United States*

No other episode in American history has been as studied and written about as the US Civil War.

The widely held view, and the one that is taught in schools, is that it broke out as a result of the long-standing controversy over slavery.

But slavery was not why Lincoln went to war.

Let me show you what the American Civil War was really all about.

In the first half of the nineteenth century, the US, broadly speaking, divided into three main economic regions: the north, the west and the south.

The north was moving from trade and shipping towards industrial production. The mighty wealth of the south was built on its agriculture, producing tobacco, sugar and as much as two thirds of the world's cotton. Out west, the US had effectively doubled its size with the infamous Louisiana Purchase of 1803, when it bought 800,000 square miles of land from France for $15 million,[2] or three cents an acre, in what must be considered the worst real-estate deal in history, at least from a French point of view. Expansion would continue until eventually the US reached the Pacific. The west needed better transport systems – canals and railroads – to get its raw materials to market.

While slavery had been illegal in the north since 1804 (in principle if not in practice), southern agricultural economies relied on it. Its status in the expanding west was still undetermined. It would go on to be one of the biggest, if not the biggest, social issues of the time.

In 1802 Thomas Jefferson said, 'It may be the pleasure and pride of an American to ask, what farmer, what mechanic, what laborer, ever sees a tax-gatherer of the United States?'[3] He was right. There were no income taxes, there was no window tax, there was not the plethora of petty taxes that existed in Europe. Government was small and local. Each state was a sovereign entity and could levy taxes as its people wished, but there was no nationwide tax system. Except for the years between 1812 and 1816, when the US was at war, the federal government collected no internal revenue.[4] Revenue came instead from the occasional sale of public land, but mostly from tariffs on imported goods. The system proved inequitable. It did not end well.

Our story starts with a little-known tariff, the Dallas Tariff of 1816. Ordinary Americans encountered very few taxes in their everyday lives. The War of 1812, between Britain and the US, actually lasted until 1815. Britain had already been blocking US trade with France, and between 1807 and 1815, US imports fell by over 90%.[5] British merchants had built up large stockpiles of goods during the war, and when hostilities ended, they flooded US markets. Usually their goods were cheaper and better than their American rivals', so the effect was to undermine US industry. In reaction to this, and with war debts to pay off, a new tariff was proposed with high import duties.

This tariff hit the south hardest. The south bought goods from Europe, including its farming equipment, and sold its cotton directly in return. Tariffs meant southerners had to pay more for what they bought. Their money would not stay in the south, however, but go north. Effectively, they were subsidising the rest of the nation.

Yet the south not only agreed to the tariff, in many cases it agitated for it. Why?

Southerners put national interests first. Further conflict looked possible. If the US was to survive, it needed its own manufacturing industry. There was enough economic prosperity in the south to shoulder the burden of the tariff. The cotton price was high. The tariff would only be temporary.

On 27 April 1816, the Dallas Tariff was approved – authorised for three years – and the price of British goods rose to more or less par with American.

## North v south: 30 years of tariff war

How often does a tax pitched as temporary become permanent? And how often does a subsidy, which effectively this was, create special-interest groups?

When the tariff expiry date came in 1820, the northern manufacturers, who had benefited from it, wanted more. A bill for a permanent tariff with higher duties and a long list of new items added was put forward. It was passed by the House, but failed in the Senate by a single vote.

This time it did not have the support of the south. The reasons they had supported the previous tariff no longer applied. The price of cotton had fallen in 1819, so they did not feel as wealthy. The threat of imminent war was gone. The war debts of 1812 had been paid down. Trade wars had all but vanished. Protecting northern manufacturing was no longer a national emergency.[6]

However, the protectionist desire remained strong in the north and west, and in 1824, another tariff was proposed. This one did pass. The tax on imported goods rose to 33%. Before 1816, the rate had been just 5%.[7]

Things only got worse. The next tariff – dubbed the Tariff of Abominations – passed in 1828. It saw 92% of imported goods taxed at 38%. Again the northern and western states allied to get it passed. Southerners were effectively paying as much as 75% of federal taxes.[8] The alternative to buying foreign goods and paying high taxes was to buy inferior northern goods and pay high prices. Either way, their money ended up in the north. The economic heart of the nation was shifting northwards, and much of the population was moving with it. No wonder southerners felt they were being legislated against. Their situation was made worse by the fact that cotton prices had declined by around 50% since 1819 – a decline the southerners blamed on tariffs.[9]

At this point South Carolina began making noises about disunion. They got strong support from Kentucky, North Carolina and Virginia. By 1832, representatives from Alabama, Georgia and Maryland had joined them. A convention was called in South Carolina. Tariffs were declared unconstitutional and therefore unenforceable.

So began the Nullification Crisis, during which President Jackson threatened to collect duties by force. The country was close to civil war. Had Jackson called in the armies, it is likely other southern states might have allied with South Carolina.[10] But South Carolina's former vice president, John C. Calhoun, agreed a compromise with Senator Henry Clay, one of the tariff's main proponents. Import taxes would drop by 10% every two years until they reached 20% by 1842. The Nullification Crisis was averted. For almost a decade, tariffs disappeared as an issue.

As 1842 approached, however, northern industrial interests began agitating for protection yet again. With Henry Clay as their champion, they revived the argument that they were vulnerable to British competition. In 1842, the Black Tariff passed in the House and the Senate by just one vote. The south had been waiting nine years for tariffs to fall to the agreed 20%. Instead they rose close to the levels of the Tariff of Abominations. Not surprisingly, the south protested vehemently.

'Revolution would be the effect,' said South Carolinian Robert Rhett.[11] Alabamians would 'prefer a bloody grave' to being slaves of the north, according to William Payne of Alabama. Protectionism would bring the country to civil war and 'peril the perpetuity of the union', said Lewis Steenrod of Virginia. Import rates rose to almost 40%, with specific duties for specific items. The most heavily taxed item was iron. Nails, for example, were taxed at over 100%. International trade declined almost immediately. Imports almost halved. Moses Leonard of New York called it 'one of the grossest acts of injustice ever perpetrated by an American Congress upon a free and intelligent people'.

But crisis was again averted when James K. Polk defeated Henry Clay in the US presidential race of 1844 and declared that reducing the Black Tariff would be the first of four great measures to define his administration. He instructed his Treasury Secretary, Robert Walker, to get to work.

Walker proposed reducing rates to 25% and standardising them (as opposed to having different rates for different items). He argued that low rates would stimulate trade, and as a result, government revenue would actually increase. North-westerners, now seeking world markets for their goods, allied with the southerners, and the tariff passed in 1846. Walker was proved right. Despite the low rates, by 1850 customs revenue had increased by 50% from $30 million to $45 million annually.[12]

Of course the antagonism between the north and south wasn't just over tariffs. Slavery was also an issue. And South Carolina actually threatened secession for a second time in 1850, over the status of slaves in the new states acquired after the Mexican–American War. If slavery was illegal in the new territories, southerners feared that they would have fewer allies in the nation's capital and would thus carry less political force. What was more, the more free states there were, and the more agitation there was for slaves to be freed, the greater the risk of insurrection at home. Secession would ensure that slavery remained in South Carolina, protecting the prosperity of the cotton producers. Elections in October of 1851 effectively became a referendum on the matter. The secessionists lost badly. Cooperationists won 58.5% of the vote.[13] The issue of slavery alone was not enough to drive even South Carolina, let alone the other southern states, to secession, especially when business was good.

In the 1850s, the US economy was booming. The south had few complaints. The tariff of 1857 saw rates reduced even further – back to around 15%, where they had been in that first, 'temporary' tariff of 1816.

Then came the Panic of 1857.

## When panic leads to protectionism

In Europe, the Crimean War saw European farming grind to a halt. American imports filled the gap. When the war ended, however, European farming resumed. Harvests were good. American imports declined. English purchase of American wheat fell by 90%.[14] The price of commodities generally fell too, by as much as 35%.[15] The Ohio Life Insurance and Trust Company, which had made numerous investments in agricultural businesses, went bust, causing financial panic. With fewer goods to transport, the railroad sector was hit. Thousands of workers lost their jobs. Investors lost their capital. The SS *Central America*, destined for New York, known as the 'Ship of Gold' for its cargo of 30,000 pounds of gold mined in the California gold rush, then sank in a great hurricane. The loss of that extraordinary amount of gold further shook public confidence in the economy, especially in banks.

This was the Panic of 1857.

The south was hit, but not as hard as the north or west. Though the price of cotton fell, it recovered quickly. There were fewer bank failures. If anything, the panic restored southern self-belief. It reinforced the conviction that their cotton was essential to world trade. The prodigious strides forward made by the economies of the north and west had met with a crash to which the south had been more immune.

But how often does panic lead to unwise legislation?

The Pennsylvanian Henry Carey was perhaps the best-known and most influential economist of his day. He saw protectionism as the way to foster industrial growth in America. He laid the blame for the financial crisis specifically at the feet of that 1857 tariff. His fervent views were widely circulated, and they gained traction. Efforts to bring back higher tariffs began in earnest once again. The newly formed Republican Party embraced Carey's views, and one of the party's founders, Justin Smith Morrill, sought his advice in designing a new tariff. He claimed the aim was only to go back to 1846 levels, but in reality, the rates were higher.[16]

The Morrill Tariff became a major area of contention for some two years, before it eventually passed the House in May 1860. It won just one vote in the southern states.

The Republican leader, Abraham Lincoln, supported tariffs and had always done so. 'I am in favour of the internal improvement system and a high protective tariff. These are my sentiments and political principles,' he had said in his first political announcement, in 1832.[17] These principles remained. 'My views have undergone no material change on that subject,' he said in 1860.[18] 'The tariff is to the government what a meal is to the family.'[19]

## Lincoln becomes president

In the battle to be the Republican nominee, William H. Seward was Lincoln's main opponent and, at first, the favoured Republican candidate. Seward was an outspoken enemy of slavery, famous for his 1850 declaration that 'there is a higher law than the Constitution'.[20] However, there were plenty who didn't see slavery this way. Lincoln, ever the wily politician, avoided the issue, so as not to alienate potential voters. He might have abhorred slavery privately, but publicly his strategy was 'to bite my lip and keep quiet'.[21] It was his vocal support of protectionist tariffs, especially in Pennsylvania, that won him the nomination.

When the election came, Lincoln's main rival was his old foe the Democrat Stephen A. Douglas. But the Democrats were divided, with northerners voting for Douglas, and southerners for John Breckenridge. To win, Lincoln needed only to make sure he beat Douglas in the north, where Douglas and the Democrats were locked into an unpopular anti-tariff position. Lincoln's simple strategy was to tone down the slavery and tone up the protectionism. It worked. No part of the Republican platform, says historian David M. Potter, was 'greeted with louder cheers than the tariff plank'. Pennsylvania went into 'spasms of joy . . . her whole delegation rising and swinging hats and canes'.[22]

On 6 November 1860, Abraham Lincoln was elected president of the United States. He only won around 40% of the vote and his victory came entirely from support in the north and west. In the states that eventually seceded, he won nothing. The Morrill Tariff was the twelfth of seventeen planks in the Republican platform. Republican control of Congress meant the return of protectionist tariffs with dramatic consequences. One by one, led by South Carolina, the southern states began withdrawing from the Union.

Southerners are 'taxed by the people of the North for their benefit, exactly as the people of Great Britain taxed our ancestors in the British parliament for their benefit', said the South Carolina Address.[23] The South Carolinians felt they were doing just as their ancestors had done when they cried 'No taxation without representation!' to their British rulers. They were in 'exactly the same position'.[24]

By 1 February 1861, Mississippi, Florida, Alabama, Georgia, Louisiana and Texas had followed South Carolina out of the Union. The seven states formed their own government, the Confederate States of America.

Meanwhile, the economist Henry Carey urged the president-elect to push through the new tariff. 'The success of your administration is wholly dependent upon the passage of the Morrill bill at the present session . . . There is but one way to make the Party a permanent one,' he said.[25] Without the opposition of the seceded states, the bill passed easily through Congress. Two days later, on 4 March, Lincoln gave his inaugural address.

'I have no purpose, directly or indirectly, to interfere with the institution of slavery in the states where it exists,' he said. 'I believe I have no lawful right to do so, and I have no inclination to do so.'[26] Congress, too, had offered the south constitutional amendments that protected it from federal government interference in slavery. The Supreme Court had also given its endorsement three years earlier, when in 1857 it ruled against Dred Scott, a former slave who had unsuccessfully tried to sue for his and his family's freedom. The president, Congress and the Supreme Court – the three branches of US federal government – had all effectively offered the south guarantees over slavery, yet still the Confederate states wanted no part of the Union. Tariffs and autonomy were the bigger issue and there, Lincoln would not compromise. The revenue tariffs generated and the protection they gave were too valuable.

'The power confided to me will be used to hold, occupy, and possess the property and places belonging to the Government and to collect the duties and imposts,' he said. 'Beyond what may be necessary for these objects, there will be no invasion, no using of force against or among the people anywhere.'[27] Lincoln would use force to collect taxes. It was clear. This was a stark choice for southerners: pay up or face the consequences.

While Republicans were pushing through the Morrill Bill, the seceded states drafted their own constitution. It was remarkably similar to the US Constitution. The most telling differences were in the sovereignty granted to each state and the limitations placed on federal power to collect taxes. Congress could only 'lay and collect Taxes, Duties, Imposts and Excises' to pay debts, provide defence and carry on government. No longer could it do so for the 'general Welfare of the United States'.[28]

'Nor shall any duties or taxes on importations from foreign nations be laid to promote or foster any branch of industry,' it specified. Leaving no room for doubt, it continued, 'Neither this, nor any other clause contained in the constitution, shall ever be construed to delegate the power to Congress to appropriate money for any internal improvement intended to facilitate commerce.'[29]

The issue of slavery was also addressed. The original US Constitution did not use the word 'slavery', instead referring to 'Person[s] held to Service or Labor' (which included whites in indentured servitude). The Confederate Constitution used the word directly. It banned any slave trade with Africa. It prevented states from abolishing slavery within their own borders (interestingly, this was the one area were individual states' rights were not sovereign) and it protected the rights of slave owners travelling with their slaves.

The south did not want a war. It could not defeat the north. It wanted peaceful secession. As 'an agricultural people, whose chief interest is the export of a commodity required in every manufacturing country', said Jefferson Davis, President of the Confederate States, in his inaugural address, 'our true policy is peace, and the freest trade which our necessities will permit . . . There should be the fewest practicable restrictions upon the interchange of commodities.'

One of Davis's first acts as president of the Confederacy was to write to Abraham Lincoln expressing a desire for peaceful relations.[30] He sent a peace delegation to Washington. Lincoln would not even meet with them.

## Lincoln's ruse to start a war

Fort Sumter controlled access to Charleston Harbor in South Carolina. One of many forts along America's coastline, it was the point at which tariffs were collected.[31] It was occupied by Union troops. The Confederacy had been trying for weeks to get them to leave peacefully. It had offered to pay compensation not only for Fort Sumter, but for all federal property in southern territory. Lincoln's Secretary of State, William Seward, had promised the Confederacy that the fort would be evacuated, but the commander holding the garrison, Major Anderson, refused to leave.

It was April 1861. No shots in the civil war had yet been fired. Unionist Colonel John Baldwin had been called before Lincoln to update him on events at the secession convention in Virginia. 'We have a clear and controlling majority of nearly three to one,' said Baldwin. He was confident of winning the convention 'with perfect certainty'.[32]

'Withdraw the troops at Sumter,' Baldwin begged the president, adding that he should do it 'for the sake of peace . . . If you take that position there is national feeling enough in the seceded States themselves and all over the country to rally to your support, and you would gather more friends than any man in the country has ever had . . . For every one of your friends whom you would lose by such a policy you would gain ten who would rally to you and to the national standard of peace and Union.'[33]

But Sumter was a tariff collection point.[34] 'What about the revenue?' said Lincoln. 'What would I do about the collection of duties?'[35]

'Sir, how much do you expect to collect in a year?' Colonel Baldwin asked.

'Fifty or sixty millions,' Lincoln replied.

'Why, sir,' replied the Colonel, 'say $250 million would be the revenue of your term of the presidency; what is that but a drop in the bucket compared with the cost of such a war as we are threatened with? Let it all go, if necessary; but I do not believe that it will be necessary, because I believe that you can settle it . . . If there is a gun fired at Sumter – I do not care on which side it is fired – the thing is gone . . . As sure as there is a God in heaven the thing is gone. Virginia herself, strong as the Union majority in the Convention is now, will be out in forty-eight hours.'

'Oh,' said Lincoln, 'sir, that is impossible.'

'You have the choice to make, and you have got to make it very soon. You have, I believe, the power to place yourself up by the side of Washington himself as the saviour of your country, or, by taking a different course of policy, to send down your name on the page of history notorious forever.'[36]

Lincoln chose war.

Baldwin was right. When the first shells of the American Civil War were fired at Fort Sumter one week later, none of Virginia, Arkansas, North Carolina and Tennessee had seceded. The initial votes, whether in convention or by popular vote, had all gone against secession.[37] They wanted to remain in the Union and they wanted the Union to remain. But when it was clear Lincoln was going to use force against the Confederacy, new votes were held. Then they voted in favour of secession – and heavily so, just as Baldwin had said.

Lincoln knew that shots in Fort Sumter could spark a war. He also knew that 'the power to make war against a State [which wishes to withdraw from the Union] is at variance with the whole spirit and intent of the Constitution'.[38] His ruse to justify unconstitutional action was to have the south perceived as the aggressor. He sent three unarmed ships with supplies. 'You know perfectly well,' said Baldwin, 'that the people of Charleston have been feeding them already.'[39]

'The attempt at reinforcement was a feint,' said the *New York Times* at the time. 'Its object was to put upon the rebels the full and clear responsibility of commencing the war.'[40] Lincoln had even told his cabinet that if South Carolina's artillery opened fire on the fort or the resupply ship, 'he could blame the Confederacy for starting a war'.[41]

As the supply ships neared Sumter, the Confederates again demanded Major Anderson surrender the fort, and again he refused. On 12 April, they began shelling. It was the reaction Lincoln wanted. He had enough to deem this a rebellion. Now bloodshed was 'forced upon the national authority',[42] even if no Union troops were killed in the bombardment and Anderson ceded the fort the following day. Confederate President Jefferson Davis 'ran blindly into the trap'.[43]

The south had no ambition to conquer the north, nor did it make any attempt. Almost every battle in the war took place in the south, with the majority of fighting in Virginia and Tennessee. Southern Pennsylvania was as far north as the fighting went. The south was defensive. It could not defeat the north. Its population was 9 million to the north's 22 million. Union soldiers outnumbered Confederates by almost two to one.[44] The north had the factories, the industry, the manufacturing. Davis said repeatedly that the south only wanted peaceful secession, and that the Confederacy did not want conflict with the Union. Shelling Sumter proved a terrible mistake. What little chance there ever was of Lincoln granting peaceful secession had evaporated. Now the south could only hope to hold on long enough that the north would grow tired of casualties and eventually allow the Confederacy to exist.

'The plan succeeded,' said Lincoln. 'They attacked Sumter – it fell, and thus, did more service than it otherwise could.'[45]

## Why the north could not allow peaceful secession, and the south was smeared

Federal coffers were already in bad shape when Lincoln was elected. Following secession, customs receipts quickly fell. No wonder, when looking at Sumter, Lincoln was asking, 'What about the revenue?' The government's largest source was disappearing.

Lincoln's oft-stated reason for going to war was to preserve the Union. But the Union depended on southern tariff revenue for its very existence. 'They know that the bulk of duties is paid by the Southern people,' said the *New Orleans Daily Crescent*, 'and that, by the iniquitous operation of the Federal Government, these duties are mainly expended among the Northern people. They know that they can plunder and pillage the South, as long as they are in the same Union with us . . . They are enraged at the prospect of being despoiled of the rich feast upon which they have so long fed and fattened, and which they were just getting ready to enjoy with still greater gout and gusto.'[46] The north needed the south. The south did not need the north.

With a civil war to pay for, Lincoln had to introduce a swathe of new taxes. The US saw property taxes for the first time. Income tax also made its debut. Unconstitutional or not, it was introduced in 1861 – on a temporary basis: 3% on incomes over $800. As barely 3% of the population had an income of over $800, the tax found widespread support. The following year the threshold fell to $600 and rates rose.

To make sure that taxes were collected, Lincoln also gave America the Internal Revenue Service, the IRS. His 1862 Revenue Act introduced another law that has remained to this day: American citizens living and working outside America still have to pay tax in the US, unless they work for the government.

But the war was about more than lost tariff revenue. Seceded states going into free trade with Europe was too big a threat to tolerate, because northern businesses – manufacturing, shipping and, perhaps most influentially, banking – would be cut out of the trade loop. The *Boston Herald* said this would 'cripple the North'.[47] The Union could not allow any such thing to happen. The entire economic model of the north would have been jeopardised. Peaceful secession was never even an option for Lincoln.

In the House of Commons, when Liberal statesman William Forster declared that slavery was the cause of the civil war, he was met with cries of 'No, No. The tariff!'[48] Lincoln did not go to war to end slavery. 'My paramount objective in this struggle is to save the Union,' he said, even as late as August 1862. 'It is not either to save or destroy slavery. If I could save the Union without freeing any slave, I would do it; and if I could save it by freeing all the slaves, I would do it; and if I could save it by freeing some and leaving others alone, I would also do that.'[49] The Emancipation Proclamation, which freed slaves in the south, was not issued until January 1863 – and only then because Lincoln felt 'we had about played our last card, and must change our tactics, or lose the game'.[50]

In 1862, Confederate diplomats in England indicated to British authorities that the Confederacy would be willing to abolish slavery in exchange for diplomatic recognition.[51] For sure, the south would have preferred to preserve slavery, at least for the time being.

Slave labour was essential to its economy. But they were willing to abolish it in order to save their Confederacy. In 1864, Confederate diplomats in Europe made an offer to this effect.[52] Independence was more important to them, but the north would not let them have it. It wanted the tax revenue. A free-trading rival on its doorstep could not be countenanced.

Slavery was one area of disagreement among many – tariffs, federal spending, border security, equal access to the territories, and the sale of public land, for example. But it was inequitable taxation that caused the division. The southern states wanted to keep what they had earned. Lincoln and the northern states wanted their wealth for the Union. In popular understanding of history, the Confederate cause has since been smeared, while the Union effort has been framed as some great and noble cause. In reality, both sides were fighting over their economic interests.

In 1861, Charles Dickens published a lengthy article in his magazine *All Year Round*, which declared, 'The quarrel between the North and South is, as it stands, solely a fiscal quarrel . . . The last grievance of the south was the Morrill tariff . . . it has severed the last threads which have bound the north and south together.'[53]

The American Civil War was no different to any other civil war, or any other great revolt. Somewhere near its heart, there is always a tax story, usually an overlooked one.

# Chapter 11

# The Birth of Big Government

*Tax is theft. War is mass murder funded by theft. Conscription is the moral equivalent of kidnapping.*

Roger Ver, entrepreneur (2018)[1]

At the turn of the twentieth century, England was the world's richest country. Yet 19 in 20 people still had no property.[2] Contracts offered working men little protection, and many were haunted by the constant insecurity of potential dismissal and unemployment. Working conditions were often bad. The ideas of Karl Marx and others were gaining traction, and a socialist tide was spreading across Europe. A new narrative was emerging that government should do more to redistribute wealth.

In Britain, the Chancellor of the Exchequer, David Lloyd George, and his young ally Winston Churchill were the political champions of this new narrative. They wanted to replicate the success of the friendly societies – voluntary organisations that had sprung up in communities across the country in the nineteenth century and into which people paid small amounts of their earnings each year. In exchange, the societies provided pensions, welfare, healthcare and other such services for their members and their families in times of need. Lloyd George and Churchill wanted this success at a national, rather than local level.

Lloyd George's reforms began with the People's Budget of 1909, then the most redistributive budget in British history. He framed his argument as a war on poverty. 'This is a war Budget,' he said.

'It is for raising money to wage implacable warfare against poverty and squalidness . . . All should be called upon to bear their share.'[3] There were land taxes, death duties and increases to income tax. The House of Lords, full as it was of landowners, blocked it – though they made it clear they would pass it if the government obtained an electoral mandate. An election was held in January 1910. It produced a hung parliament. The budget was eventually passed in April – though, no surprise, without the land value taxes.

Lloyd George would not have the Lords in the way of his spending plans, and so came the Parliament Act of 1911, which effectively broke their power to veto finance bills. The Lords passed the Act because Herbert Asquith, the prime minister, had said it was the King's intention to fill the upper house with enough new peers to get it passed, and the Lords feared an enormous liberal influx. Their power was broken and now the path was open to higher taxes, whether for wars or social reform. Society's imperfections, as tax historian James Coffield says, could now be 'remedied by state intervention. Income was redistributed by taxation, employees were protected against the worst kind of employers and decisions affecting life, health and liberty were made by an ever-growing army of civil servants.'[4] The traditional laissez-faire liberalism of the latter half of the nineteenth century began to wither.

Then came the 1911 National Insurance Act, which created compulsory state health insurance for industrial workers funded by contributions from employers, the government and the workers themselves. Its unintended consequence was to put the friendly societies, which it was supposed to be copying, out of business. Most people did not want to – and could not afford to – buy insurance twice. One was compulsory, the other voluntary. Which would survive was inevitable. National Insurance still exists in the UK today, although in a manner most upsetting to accountants (and with good reason), the government now spends the money it receives rather than putting it aside as was originally intended.

## The Great War – the great rise in taxes

Lloyd George's People's Budget did not see income taxes rocket. The rate stayed at 3.75% on earnings below £2,000, rising to 5% in the £2,000–5,000 bracket, with an additional 2.5% super tax levied on earnings above £5,000 (about half a million in today's money). Tax rates subsequently crept up, but in times of peace it is hard to significantly raise taxes *and* keep the public happy. Lloyd George had to resort to other means to fund his welfare. Like Pitt before him, he borrowed rather than confront the population with taxes. 'He has no thought for the final bill,' said the financier J. P. Morgan.[5]

Then, in the autumn of 1914, Britain stumbled into the Great War. If ever there was a turning point in the nature of Western government, the Great War was it. Now higher tax rates could be justified. The standard rate of income tax rose from 6% in 1914 to 30% by 1918. Higher rates went over 50%. The number of people paying income tax went from 1.1 million to almost 3 million.[6] An excess profits tax was levied on companies that benefited from war production. The total tax take went from £163 million in 1913–14 to £784 million in 1918–19. This was 17 times higher than it had been in 1905,[7] yet it only accounted for somewhere between 19% and 25% of spending on the war.[8] The rest was paid through debt and inflation – the unofficial taxes.

The national debt increased from £650 million in 1914 to £7.4 billion by the war's end. Only a century later, in 2015, was this debt finally settled.[9] Like Pitt's Napoleonic War debts, several future generations of British people would be saddled with the cost.

As for inflation, shortly after hostilities broke out, Britain came off the gold standard and debased its money to help pay for the war. By 1921, the cost of living was at least two and a half times higher than it was in 1914.[10]

As the number of people paying taxes increased, so the principles of democratic consent and the right to vote extended, culminating with the two Representation of the People Acts, in 1918 and then 1928. Taxation led to universal adult suffrage.

Like the Napoleonic Wars a century before, it could be argued that income tax made the difference between the two sides in the First World War. Germany had been preparing for war for decades and it had a war chest of six million pounds of gold. It thought the war would be over sooner than it was, and that the costs would be recouped in plunder and booty from a defeated enemy. As its gold ran out, Germany turned to debt to fund its war effort. It thought income taxes would be too big a burden on its people, and might potentially disturb the public peace, so they were not imposed at the federal level. Later in the war, taxes on war profits, coal and turnover were introduced, but taxes overall accounted for just 8% of the 170 billion marks Germany spent during the war.[11] The rest was borrowed from German banks and private citizens. It proved too difficult to borrow from abroad. German national debt rose astronomically, from just 5 billion marks in 1914 to 156 billion in 1918.

Germany encouraged its citizens to hand over their gold and take paper currency in return. The paper currency, however, was not redeemable in gold bullion and money became fiat (issued and controlled by government). Despite price controls, inflation crept up during the war. By the early 1920s, in one of the most notorious financial collapses in history, that inflation turned hyper. It destroyed the value of Germany's war bonds altogether, as well as the currency itself.

## Income tax comes to America

Income tax was first proposed in America as far back as 1814, when Treasury Secretary Andrew Dallas was looking to fund the War of 1812 against the British. An end to hostilities in 1815 meant his proposal was shelved. The idea was all but forgotten until war brought it back again, and Abraham Lincoln introduced it in 1861. The tax was abandoned in 1872, once the civil war was over, but then, towards the end of the nineteenth century, it was introduced again, with the declared purpose to replace tariffs. However, in what became an infamous case – *Pollock v the Farmers' Loan & Trust Co.*, 1895 – the Supreme Court ruled that income tax was unconstitutional, and so levying it became all but impossible.

The constitutionality of income tax is an argument that has ever dogged the US. The Constitution was drafted before income tax in its modern form was widespread, and there is a lack of clarity. The resulting grey area has meant that the argument never dies. Even today it goes on. It is quite easy to suppose that the Founding Fathers, born as they were in the Enlightenment, great believers in liberty, limited government and taxation with representation, would not have approved of income tax. But nor would they have approved of the inequitable consequences of the tariff system.

The Constitution does specify that taxes should be proportional: a state with one tenth of the total population should bear one tenth of the total liability. Such a clause makes levying income tax impractical: if one state has a low population with lots of high earners and another a large population with lots of low earners, how is that reconciled?

The Constitution also specified that 'The Congress shall have Power To lay and collect Taxes, Duties, Imposts and Excises, to pay the Debts and provide for the common Defence and general Welfare of the United States; but all Duties, Imposts and Excises shall be uniform throughout the United States . . .' Uniformity and income taxes don't go together because incomes are so variable. However, it did not specify that taxes must be uniform – only duties, imposts and excises.

But all such arguments, legally at least, were put to bed in 1913. Congress got round the Supreme Court's ruling with the Sixteenth Amendment to the Constitution, which reads: 'The Congress shall have power to lay and collect taxes on incomes, from whatever source derived, without apportionment among the several States, and without regard to any census or enumeration.' The path to a much more heavily taxed nation, and thus much larger government, was now open.

## How income tax gave America Prohibition

One of the unintended consequences of the Sixteenth Amendment was Prohibition, and Prohibition could never have happened without the generalship of a little-known but extraordinarily determined Ohio attorney by the name of Wayne B. Wheeler. As a young boy on his family farm, Wheeler was accidentally stabbed in the leg with a pitchfork by a farmhand who was drunk. The incident gave him a lifelong loathing of alcohol, and he dedicated his life to its opposition.

In 1893, after listening to a sermon on temperance, Wheeler, now a student, joined the newly formed Anti-Saloon League (ASL). He would turn it into perhaps the most effective political pressure group the United States has ever known. Indeed, he actually coined the term 'pressure group',[12] and pressure politics is sometimes known as Wheelerism.

The temperance movement had hundreds of thousands of adherents, but their message was diffused and there was no leadership to unite them. The Woman's Christian Temperance Union, for example, was also campaigning for vegetarianism. The Prohibition Party was also trying to influence forest conservation and Post Office policy. Wheeler made sure the ASL stood for one issue alone: to remove alcohol from American life. His early years saw him cycling from town to town speaking to churches and recruiting supporters. This evolved into telegram campaigns, demonstrations and even legal cases. Anyone who supported Wheeler's cause was a friend, no matter what else they stood for; anyone who opposed his cause was an enemy. It was that simple and he was utterly ruthless about it.

On this basis, in the early 1900s the ASL opposed 70 Ohio legislators – around half the legislature – some Republican, some

Democrat, some Populist. All that mattered was their stance on alcohol. It defeated all of them. Now it could get a law through so that local voters could determine whether they wanted their area to be wet or dry. But the governor, Republican Myron T. Herrick, amended Wheeler's bill to make it more workable (as he saw it). The uncompromising Wheeler was outraged.

The state of Ohio usually voted Republican, and Herrick had been elected with the largest plurality in the state's history. He was well funded, successful and popular. He had the support of the church for his vetoing of racetrack betting. No matter. Wheeler took him on.

As the next gubernatorial election approached, the ASL sponsored more than 300 rallies against Herrick. It said he was a pawn of the liquor interests, 'the champion of the murder mills'. When the Brewers' Association sent out a letter urging its members to lend quiet support to Herrick, Wheeler photographed the letter and sent it out to thousands of churches just in time for the vote. The election saw the largest turnout in Ohio history. Every Republican on the ticket was nominated except Herrick. 'Never again,' said Wheeler, 'will any political party ignore the protests of the church and the moral forces of the state.' The incident showed him just what was possible with his campaigning tactics. He would replicate what had happened locally at a national level.

With his friend-or-foe mentality, he forged alliances that bonded the most unlikely groups to this one cause – from the evangelical clergy to the Industrial Workers of the World, who felt alcohol was a capitalist weapon to keep workers in a stupor; from the women's suffrage movement (on whom Wheeler was particularly keen, as he felt women mostly voted for dry candidates) to urban progressives concerned about the effect of drunkenness on the urban poor; from the Ku Klux Klan, which despised drinking by blacks, Jews and Catholic immigrants, to actual Jewish and Catholic Irish and Italian organisations.

If there had been a referendum on Prohibition, the ASL would have lost. The Prohibition Party would never win the presidential election. But this issue alone, in a sea of others, was usually enough to tip the scales in favour of the dry candidate, especially in close-run elections. Wheeler could deliver his voters to one candidate or another and change the outcome. 'I do it the way the bosses do it, with minorities,' he said.[13] This critical minority of voters enabled him to exert disproportionate influence.

Wheeler championed those who stood for Prohibition. Those who opposed it were attacked, smeared and taken down. When the First World War came, he exploited anti-German sentiment to attack any German business or group that opposed Prohibition, particularly the brewers Pabst, Schlitz, Blatz and Miller. It reached the point where candidates almost had to support his cause if they were to be elected.

Eventually, according to a biography written by a former colleague, Wheeler 'controlled six Congresses, dictated to two Presidents . . . directed legislation . . . held the balance of power in both Republican and Democratic parties, distributed more patronage than any dozen other men, supervised a federal bureau from outside without official authority, and was recognized by friend and foe alike as the most masterful and powerful single individual in the United States'.[14]

None of it could have happened without income tax.

Even after Wheeler's initial breakthrough with the state legislature in Ohio in 1905, the goal of getting alcohol banned nationally was verging on the delusional. With so many settlers from Germany, Britain and Ireland, alcohol was as much a part of American culture as it was northern European. Drinking was a private right exercised by millions. More significantly, perhaps, alcohol was the fifth-largest industry in the nation and taxes on alcohol accounted for something like 40% of government revenue. If Wheeler was to have any chance of achieving his goal, he would first have to make it fiscally possible: he would have to find some alternate means of government funding to make up for the loss of revenue from alcohol taxes. Without a replacement, Prohibition was unthinkable. 'The chief cry against national Prohibition,' said a policy statement from the ASL, 'has been that the government must have the revenue.' The Sixteenth Amendment to the Constitution gave him the solution he was looking for.

In 1912, Democrat Woodrow Wilson became the first southerner to win a presidential election since the civil war. The stated goal of the New Freedom platform on which he ran was lower tariffs, and on winning the presidency, reducing tariffs became his first priority. His means to replace the lost revenue was income tax (and later, estate taxes). But given that income tax had only recently been deemed unconstitutional by the Supreme Court, bringing it in would be no easy task.

Wilson had already whipped up discontent with constant warnings that Washington DC was being overrun by lobbyists. His appeals to the public through the press meant that furious constituents were contacting their representative to demand tariff reform. Even though Democrats had control of the House and the Senate, Wilson still sensed that southern and western Democrats might not be on side, particularly those who favoured protection of local industries, and their support was essential. He met with them extensively before doing something no president had done in over 100 years. He appeared in Congress to make an appeal. The joint session became a sensational event, with extraordinary newspaper coverage. There was a huge crowd, and every seat in the House was taken. Wilson only spoke for a short time. He made the case for tariff reform. A repeat of the embarrassment of the failed reform of 1894 would be unacceptable, he said, leaving the burden of responsibility on his party to approve his reforms or face the blame. He got his way.

The Revenue Act of 1913 saw tariffs reduced from 40% to 26%. The Sixteenth Amendment to the Constitution passed. Income tax would replace the lost revenue. But now the government's dependence on alcohol taxes was also removed. The main argument against Prohibition had disappeared. The First World War would soon show just how much revenue it was possible to raise through income tax. While in 1913 it only impacted higher earners and rates ranged from 1% to 7%, by 1918 they had risen to an eye-watering 77% for top-rate earners.[15]

Once income tax had been made law, there came what the ASL called 'the Next and Final Step': 'National Prohibition, [to] be secured through the adoption of a Constitutional Amendment'. After another five years of ruthless campaigning, in the aftermath of the First World War Wheeler achieved his dream, and the National Prohibition Act – the Volstead Act – which he mostly drafted, though it would be named after the congressman who sponsored it, was enacted in 1919.

Wheeler might have succeeded in making alcohol illegal, but he could not stop Americans drinking. Numerous legal loopholes were exploited, and anybody who wanted a drink in a city was easily able to find one (there were 32,000 illegal liquor establishments in New York alone, according to one police commissioner).[16] Meanwhile, there was unintended consequence after unintended consequence. Prohibition gave rise to the previously unknown phenomenon of organised crime. Bribery and corruption within the police, the courts and politics became common, as did disrespect for the law. The penal system became overburdened. Hundreds of thousands of people lost their jobs, with all sorts of terrible consequences, both economic and personal. A culture of binge drinking was created, with considerable health consequences, made worse by the fact that so much of the alcohol was poor quality – bad alcohol killed as many as 50,000 people,[17] not to mention those who died as a result of the new crime wave. People with alcohol problems were prevented from being treated properly – instead, they were viewed as criminals. Thousands of legitimate businesses went bust, to be replaced by illegitimate operations that paid no tax. This further increased the government's dependence on income tax – and thus did the burden of income tax on the American people increase.

None of these reasons was enough, however, to get Prohibition repealed, even though by the late 1920s the country was sick of it. The establishment was still scared of the Prohibition lobby. What forced its hand was the loss of tax revenue in the face of the Great Depression. Alcohol's taxability was what moved politicians to overturn Prohibition. Roosevelt needed money for his New Deal, and thus, in his 1932 election campaign, did he promise that the federal treasury would be enriched by hundreds of millions of dollars from beer revenue alone. Wheeler was no longer there to oppose him. He had died in 1927. By 1933, Prohibition was over. Tax revenue on alcoholic beverages reached $613 million by 1940.[18]

In 1932, the Hoover campaign, which stood against Roosevelt, conducted a poll, which has only recently been uncovered.[19] It shows that Americans did not blame the government for the Depression. Across the board, the biggest issue of the day was Prohibition. Hoover was a staunch defender, but the American people overwhelmingly favoured repeal. That was what the Democrats offered. Perhaps the repeal of Prohibition, rather than the prospect of his New Deal, was what won Franklin D. Roosevelt the presidency.

# Chapter 12

# *The Second World War, the US and the Nazis*

*The biggest piece of machinery ever designed to separate dollars from citizens.*[1]

Time magazine (October 1942)

The greater the war, the greater the tax burden. The Second World War gave the world even higher taxes. As US President Franklin D. Roosevelt said, 'War costs money.'[2]

In the US, taxes in total paid around 22% of the cost of its First World War effort.[3] Debt and money-printing paid for the rest. But ordinary Americans were still largely out of the range of income tax. That changed with the Revenue Act of 1942. The number of Americans paying income tax rose from 13 million to over 50 million. Suddenly 75% of working Americans found themselves paying. It 'will demand and get more money from more people than at any time in the history of the republic', lamented *Time* magazine.[4] Its prediction was correct.

The act was dubbed 'the Victory Tax' and a huge propaganda effort was instigated to make it palatable. Seeking both to educate people about how to pay their taxes and to reduce public resentment, Secretary of the Treasury Henry Morgenthau Jr commissioned Walt Disney to make a film. It was called *The New Spirit* and Donald Duck was cast as the star. The US turned to other entertainers in its mission to promote the payment of tax not just as a patriotic duty but also as a joy. Irving Berlin wrote a song, which Gene Autry sang: 'I Paid My Income Tax Today'. It proudly celebrates how an ordinary working man's taxes helped pay for a thousand planes to bomb Berlin. Was ever there a lyric that so casually depicts the link between taxes and war?

By 1944, the top rate of income tax was 94%.[5] Asked in February 1944 whether they considered the amount of tax they paid to be fair, 90% of people said yes.[6] Those who paid the top rate might have been less enthusiastic.

Over the course of the war, America bought roughly 13 million guns, 40 billion rounds of ammunition, 100,000 tanks, 300,000 air-craft, 10 battleships, 27 aircraft carriers and 200 submarines. The financial burden was enormous. The total cost of the war to the US federal government was ten times more than The First World War – some $321 billion.[7] This time taxes covered 48% of the cost.[8] The remainder was financed by borrowing and inflation. US national debt sextupled, reaching 110% of GDP by the end of the war.[9] Infla-tion is rarely included in calculations, though it should be. It is estimated that currency debasement may have accounted for 21% of the cost of the war.[10] In Europe, inflation was higher.

The arrival of the USA is said to have swung the war in favour of the Allies. The major part of that involvement was funded by this new income tax.

Debt aside, income tax was now America's main source of rev-enue. The era of large government had well and truly begun.

## Works, welfare and war: The funding of Nazi Germany

The Nazis came to power in Germany in 1933 in the face of the Great Depression. Unemployment was at 30% and the unemploy-ment insurance system had broken down.

The historical consensus is that the economic causes of the Nazis' rise lay in the effects of the Great Depression and the Treaty of Versailles, made after the First World War, and the enormous financial burdens it placed on Germany. However, voting data between 1930 and 1933 indicates that other factors contributed, in particular the government's tax increases and spending cuts. Had the previous Chancellor, Heinrich Brüning, pursued a more expansionary fiscal policy, it is argued, the Nazis might never have been elected.[11] Hitler recognised this at the time, saying that Brüning's austerity 'will help my party to victory'. Brüning's successor implemented fiscal stimulus and the Nazis actually lost seats, but it was too late.

On coming to power, the Nazis immediately set off on an immense public works programme – largely put in place by their predecessors – to galvanise the economy. Recovery was almost inevitable given the extent of the decline, but the effect was dramatic. By the end of 1934, unemployment had fallen from almost 6 million to 2.4 million. The Nazis were quick to take the credit. Roads, public buildings such as stadia, schools and hospitals, rearmament, industry – all saw huge public spending. By 1938, Germany was essentially at full employment,[12] with wage and price controls to prevent inflation. By 1939, there was actually a shortage of as much as a million workers.[13] Slave labour brought in from conquered territories, especially Poland, made up the shortfall.

As national socialists, the Nazis were big believers in welfare. 'We and we alone have the best social welfare measures,' boasted the Minister of Propaganda, Joseph Goebbels – and a plethora of welfare programmes were introduced. The National Socialist People's Welfare was formed in 1933, to promote 'the collectivity of a people's community'. It helped some 17 million people and was deemed the 'greatest social institution in the world'. Provisions included everything you might expect in a generous welfare system: unemployment and disability benefits, rent supplements, day nurseries, healthcare insurance, old age insurance and homes for the elderly. In a similar vein, the German Labour Front, the single biggest Nazi organisation in the country, also undertook numerous programmes for its workers, via the infamous Strength Through Joy system. Education too was provided by the state.

Like all public spending programmes, the intention – to look after the people – might have been benevolent. The problem was how to pay for them.

One of the 1933 campaign pledges that the Nazis most conspicuously failed to fulfil was the promise to reduce taxes. These had been high under the previous regime and they remained so. Turnover taxes accounted for something like 20% of tax revenues; income taxes about a third.

In addition to paying regular taxes, employers and workers also had to contribute to the Labour Front, so that, in total, around 30% of the average wage-earner's income was taken.[14] As the war approached, taxes were kept heavy so as to depress consumption and increase the amount that could be spent on armament.

Hitler himself was above paying taxes. In 1934, the Munich tax office sent him a fine for failing to declare his income and pay his taxes. He was given eight days to settle. After a few words from someone at the finance ministry, the tax office then declared, 'All tax reports delivering substance for a tax obligation by the Führer are annulled from the start. The Führer is therefore tax-exempt.'[15]

Broadly speaking, the ratio of taxation to debt was moderate, and German tax levels were comparable to those of their British and American counterparts. Once the war started, however, taxes did not shoot up in the way they did amongst the Allies.

'Repeatedly,' says historian Götz Aly,[16] 'civil servants tried to raise tax rates, only to find themselves undercut by the Nazi leadership, which intervened to protect lower- and middle-income Germans.' The Ministerial Council for the Defence of the Reich was formed to draw up a blueprint for wartime taxation. It imposed an additional tax of 50% on all wages, but 'promptly excluded all but the wealthiest Germans . . . In the end only 4% of the population paid the 50% surcharge.'[17] Even if total revenue rose by about 95% over the course of the war,[18] taxes made up a smaller and smaller proportion. In 1939, 45% of expenditure was financed by taxation. By 1944, that figure had fallen to 16%.[19] Total tax revenue amounted to less than half of what Germany borrowed.[20]

The Nazis were fortunate in that Germany had a relatively small public debt when they came to power. Memories of hyperinflation still lingered and the country had a cautious attitude to debt and currency expansion. The Nazis also benefited from a deal struck by the previous administration in 1932 to suspend most payments pertaining to the Treaty of Versailles. This left Hitler with a budget surplus in 1933, which he put to work. He then began to borrow. By 1936, the president of the Reichsbank, Hjalmar Schacht, warned that inflation was getting worrying, but he was soon dismissed and his warnings went unheeded.

In 1937, official debt stood at 40% of GDP. Britain's was nominally higher, but large amounts of German debt were kept off official statements.[21] By the end of the war it seems the national debt had increased by 1,000%,[22] but the truth is that German borrowing was a closely guarded secret and Nazi accounts were often fraudulent. Most of this debt was internally levied, and by the end of the war, the practices of so-called secret borrowing and forced borrowing were common.

Debt, taxes and inflation taxes were not enough to fund government spending. Nazi Germany looked elsewhere for its revenue.

## How the Holocaust began with taxes

Though the Nazis considered German Jews both inferior and foreign, they held no such views about their wealth. What they confiscated paid for roughly one third of Germany's war effort.[23]

Nazi tax authorities actively worked to 'destroy Jews financially'.[24] From 1934 onwards, tax laws discriminated against them. Jews were required to register all their property and assets, whether domestic or foreign. If it was discovered that assets had been hidden, they were sentenced to 10 years in jail and had *all* their wealth confiscated. Once the declarations were made, Hermann Göring, president of the Reichstag, then instituted a 20% wealth tax on Jews. The Jews were one of the wealthiest socio-economic groups in Germany, and it raised millions. Even those who managed to escape the country had to pay an exit tax.

Jews were banned from working in certain sectors – the civil service, the law and medicine. Jewish tax advisers had their licences revoked. Decrees restricted Jewish doctors from being paid by public (state) health insurance funds. Jewish actors were banned from appearing on stage and in films.

Entire hierarchies of bureaucrats were formed for the purpose of taxing Jews. They 'discovered dwellings and bank accounts and emptied them', says Christine Kuller of the University of Munich.[25] They then made sure to dispose of any trace of those who disappeared in extermination camps. The Nazis made fortunes selling the possessions not only of those who had been sent to extermination camps, but of those who fled the country. Auctions were held of items looted from Jewish homes. The profits were lodged in a Gestapo bank account and then forwarded to the Reichsbank in Berlin. When homes in the Baltic states and Poland were looted, taxmen made careful inventories of the stolen items, the train wagons in which they were being transported and their destinations. No such careful records were kept for the Jews.

In 1938, with the military budget growing and spending starting to spiral out of control, a law was passed that nationalised all property owned by German Jews. Göring issued them with war bonds in return for their stolen wealth. These would only be honoured if Germany won the war.

As for the territories Germany took – from Scandinavia in the north to Greece and Italy in the south, from France in the west to Russia in the east – the Nazis followed the path of the traditional conqueror. They plundered and then they taxed. Looting was rampant – soldiers stole personal items, equipment, cars; even buses and trains were taken and sent back to Germany. Tax breaks actually encouraged German soldiers to loot and plunder: anything they stole from local homes, farms or businesses that would fit into a postal bag could be sent home with no tax paid. In 1940, during the first six months of the invasion of Russia,

German soldiers shipped 3.5 million bags of stolen property back home.

The Nazis raised the pay of soldiers in conquered territories, while at the same time devaluing the conquered country's currency, so that Nazi soldiers saw their purchasing power increase; they were then encouraged to buy goods (effectively at below market value) and send them back to Germany. Conquered locals would be left with a shortage of goods, leading to higher prices, often starving citizens and bankrupted local economies. Greece suffered hyperinflation as a result.

Conquered peoples had to make large contributions to support any soldiers who were garrisoned nearby. They were forced to remit their gold holdings to the German central bank. In France, the Germans seized the stock market and sold off portions to pay its bills.

As well as their property, so too was the labour of conquered peoples expropriated; even their entire lives. First Jews, political dissidents, homosexuals and other alleged criminals, then prisoners of war and civilians were brought from occupied territories and sent to work in labour camps. It is thought some five million Poles went through the camps, three million of whom died.[26] By 1944, slave labour made up one quarter of Germany's entire workforce, calculates historian Michael Allen, whether in its factories or on its farms.[27]

## The nation that won the war but lost the peace

Britain's taxpayers had a similar experience to their American cousins in the Second World War. Income taxes reached their highest levels ever, as did the number of people paying. In 1938 in Britain, 4 million people in a population of about 47.5 million were paying; by the end of the war, the number had tripled to over 12 million.[28] If you thought a 94% rate for higher earners in the US was punitive, in the UK the top rate reached 97.5%.

The national debt almost tripled, from £8.3 billion in 1939 to £23 billion (around $92 billion) by 1945[29] – nearly 237% of GDP. But while Britain began the war borrowing the money domestically, by the end it was reliant on external credit, mostly from the US.

It was not just the cost of the war itself but the rebuilding effort afterwards that crippled the British. Two million homes, for example, were destroyed during the Blitz just in the south-east. (All Europe suffered from the destruction of its infrastructure in a way that the US and Canada, Pearl Harbor aside, did not. This was especially so for Germany, where, for example, 89% of the built-up area of Würzburg, 83% of Remscheid and Bochum and 75% of Hamburg and Wuppertal was destroyed.)

During the war, the US provided Britain with essential supplies through the Lend Lease Act. After the war was over, the US lent another $586 million and provided a further $3.7 billion line of credit to be paid off in 50 annual instalments. What hurt the British was that the debt was in dollars, so the burden grew as the value of the pound fell. Britain effectively lost its autonomy, as the US insisted it sell down its gold and dollar reserves and subjected it to numerous audits. Britain had to sell off many of its capital assets, particularly those in the US. All in all, the war cost the UK its place in the global world order, as well as its empire.

Inflation too played its role, just as it had done in the First World War. The cost of living increased by 60% between 1938 and 1946. By 1951, it had more than doubled.[30] Put another way, the pound lost over 50% of its value. Inflation's other insidious effect was to push earners into higher tax brackets, so that they ended up paying more tax.

What was so different about the Second World War was that, unlike the wars of previous eras, which were paid for in loot, plunder and the taxing of newly conquered territories, the price fell on the citizens of the victorious nations, especially the British. It might have been on the winning side, but Britain did not enjoy the spoils of victory. Taxes in 1946–47 were three times what they had been in the year before the war.[31] What had only recently been the world's wealthiest nation was still rationing food in 1954. It only settled its debts to its Canadian and US allies in 2006.[32] While Germany had all its external debt written off in 1953, Britain for the most part honoured its war debts. Perhaps that is a major factor in why Germany and Japan are said to have 'won the peace'.

# Chapter 13

# The Evolution of Social Democracy

*A government that robs Peter to pay Paul can always depend
on the support of Paul.*

George Bernard Shaw (1944)[1]

With the hostilities of each world war over, government spending decreased, but taxes never returned to the levels they had been at before the war. Nor even close. Instead, they settled at higher levels.

Income taxes were now a feature of twentieth-century life for everyone. Wars let the tax genie out of the bottle and nobody put it back. The Institute of Fiscal Studies (IFS) calls this process 'the ratchet effect'.[2] The pressure to get re-elected limits the ability of politicians to raise taxes during peacetime, but 'wars ease this constraint',[3] and once new taxes and higher tax rates are in place, they remain, rarely to be removed.

Even today, income tax rates tend to be higher in nations that were involved in the Second World War than in those that were not. Chile, for example, has the lowest income taxes (relative to GDP) of any OECD nation and it had little involvement in the Second World War.[4] This is not a hard-and-fast rule, but worth noting all the same. The OECD nations with the lowest levels of government spending are Chile, Ireland, Costa Rica, South Korea and Switzerland – all of whose involvement in the Second World War was considerably lower than the five highest: Finland, France, Denmark, Belgium and Greece.[5]

High tax rates remained partly because governments had incurred many new obligations during the wars, from debt to rebuilding to looking after the victims. They also remained because politicians the world over, hoping to win popularity or political credit in the present, designed programmes that committed their governments to large spending programmes in the future. A politician who promises better roads, or schools, or welfare, is incurring obligations that cannot easily be abrogated. The more that is promised, the greater the size to which government grows – and thanks to the world wars, the tax structures were now in place to meet those promises. The obligations facing today's taxpayers are the result of decisions sometimes made as much as 100 years ago. Government spending promises made today will impose similar obligations years into the future.

Thus did government spread from traditional areas – the army, the police, infrastructure – into other areas of the economy, education, welfare and healthcare especially. In the table below, courtesy of the Institute of Economic Affairs, you can see the huge increase in government spending that has taken place since 1870.[6] In Australia it has doubled. In Germany, France and the UK it has increased more than fourfold, in the US, roughly five.

| | 1870 | 1913 | 1920 | 1937 | 1960 | 1980 | 2000 | 2010 | 2015 | 2018 |
|---|---|---|---|---|---|---|---|---|---|---|
| **Australia** | 18.3 | 16.5 | 19.3 | 14.8 | 21.2 | 34.1 | 34.6 | 36.6 | 35.6 | 35.4 |
| **France** | 12.6 | 17.0 | 27.6 | 29.0 | 34.6 | 46.1 | 51.1 | 56.4 | 57.0 | 56.2 |
| **Germany** | 10.0 | 14.8 | 25.0 | 34.1 | 32.4 | 47.9 | 44.7 | 47.4 | 44.0 | 43.9 |
| **UK** | 9.4 | 12.7 | 26.2 | 30.0 | 32.2 | 44.7 | 37.8 | 48.8 | 43.2 | 40 |
| **USA** | 7.3 | 7.5 | 12.1 | 19.4 | 30.0 | 35.3 | 33.9 | 43.2 | 37.8 | 37.8 |

Ratios of general government expenditure to GDP at market prices (%)

Though there have been variations along the way, the broader trend is one of growing government. At the turn of the twentieth century, government spending in European countries accounted for around 10% of GDP and taxes were low. A hundred years later, early in the twenty-first, this figure exceeds 50% in many European countries[7] and taxes are high. Income tax, as the largest single source of government revenue, has made much of this growth possible.

In the years after the Second World War, the UK was a relatively high-tax country, and it remained so until the late 1970s. Government spending as a share of GDP rose from 1948 to 1977. The second half of the 1960s saw the most significant and sustained increase in the tax burden of the twentieth century outside of wartime. There was a change in attitude in the late 1970s, which saw Margaret Thatcher become prime minister in the UK and Ronald Reagan president in the US; both leaders believed in low taxes and limited government, and the rate of government spending levelled off. In most other developed nations, the state continued to grow at least into the 1980s and often beyond.

Accompanying Reagan and Thatcher came a trend to reduce the top rates of income tax. This was a global phenomenon. In 1900, top earners faced almost zero taxation on the last part of their incomes. High top marginal rates were introduced after 1910, and they kept rising. In the UK, with surcharges, the top rate was effectively 90% through the 1950s and 1960s (higher during the wars). By 1978, the highest bracket was essentially taxed at 98% (that is not all income taxed at 98%, but all income above a certain level). With the inflation of the period, and thresholds going unchanged, more and more people found themselves caught up in the top bands, paying higher rates.

After about 1980, most countries started reducing the higher rates. Thatcher reduced the top rate to 60% and then to 40% in 1988. Today the corresponding figure is 45%. Germany and France sit a few per cent higher. In the US, it is 39.6%. The lowering of top marginal rates did not lead to shrinking government, just a slowdown in expansion.

## *The slow death of local government*

Not all taxes rose and not all areas of government grew, however. Another common feature of taxation in the twentieth century was that, at the local level, it actually shrank. In the early twentieth century in the UK, local taxes accounted for about a third of total revenue. Now that figure is just 3–4%.[8] Further, as the IFS notes, 'the only significant local tax left – the council tax – finances only around one-seventh of total local spending'.[9]

The same trend is true of the US. At the turn of the century, local government collected more tax than federal.[10] Even on the eve of the Great Depression, local governments raised as much as half of the total US tax revenue, with property taxes alone – collected at the local level – accounting for 40%.[11] These latter fell off a cliff during the Great Depression. By the end of the Second World War, they accounted for just 10% of all government revenue.[12] This is partly explained by the huge rise in taxation elsewhere – income tax especially – with no corresponding rises locally. But there is another factor.

Perhaps the first law of taxation is that governments will collect taxes where they are easy to collect. Taxes on income taken at source by a remote central authority that is hard to hold to account have proved easy. Local taxes, for the most part, do not offer the possibility of straightforward deduction at source. There is more scope for non-compliance. People are more reluctant to pay out from funds they already hold, particularly when they have already paid taxes at the federal level. As the saying goes, 'People pay their taxes to government in sorrow, but to their local councils in anger.' There is more interaction with the tax collector and local authorities are easier to hold to account.

In the UK, of course, Margaret Thatcher's attempt to levy greater taxes at the local level – the poll tax – failed so badly it ended her as a political force. Scandinavia, where a large percentage of tax is levied locally, is the exception to this pattern. But even there the lion's share of taxes is deducted from income, even if at the local level.

In many cases, taxes are collected centrally and then distributed locally. By this process, power shifts to the central authority. He who has the tax revenue has the power. Government has become more centralised, more distant, less local and in many ways less accountable. Central authorities have become so much better at raising revenue than local authorities that the nature of government itself has changed as a result.

## Digital money and VAT = greater tax returns

Another striking feature of latter-twentieth-century taxation is how much more effectively central governments have been able to collect taxes, even when rates are high.

During the Second World War and in the immediate aftermath, most countries put new measures in place to ensure collection at source: the US introduced tax withholding in the Current Tax Payment Act of 1943. The following year saw the advent of Pay As You Earn (PAYE) in the UK. Until this point, taxes were collected annually or twice annually. Now that they were deducted weekly or monthly, government got their money more quickly. The efficiency and speed of collection further increased the potential to spend. The US treasury says that withholding 'greatly eased the collection of the tax for both the taxpayer and the Bureau of Internal Revenue'. It freely also admits that withholding 'greatly reduced the taxpayer's awareness of the amount of tax being collected, i.e. it reduced the transparency of the tax, which made it easier to raise taxes in the future'.[13] The goose, in other words, is less aware it is being plucked. By 1950, just about every developed world nation, and many developing ones besides, had built an administrative system to levy money at source.

Governments effectively used employers as their tax collectors. Non-compliance met with heavy fines and worse. Banks became their henchmen to make sure money was properly collected and suspicious activity reported. The fact that money is issued by government and maintained by the central bank further increased the control. Technological advances in the 1980s and 90s led to money becoming digital and payments electronic. Such automation meant that non-compliance became even more difficult, while collection and compliance rates improved.

A further evolution was the collection of VAT and sales taxes. In 1960, just one country had VAT – France, the country of its origin – although, of course, goods and sales taxes had existed elsewhere previously. By 1980, the number was 27. Today, 166 countries have VAT.[14] Governments are quick to copy an effective tax system – 'There is no art which one government sooner learns from another than that of draining money from the pockets of the people,' as Adam Smith once observed. VAT rates worldwide are fairly constant, between 15% and 20% (24–25% in Scandinavian nations). The EU imposes a minimum rate of 15%. Again business became the tax collector: it is a legal requirement for anyone with turnover above a certain minimum to collect VAT, then submit it to the government.

Effectively governments have outsourced their tax collection and woe betide anyone who doesn't comply.

Some consider VAT unjust because it is not progressive – everyone pays the same rate and so the poor pay more as a percentage of their wealth. Others consider it fair for the very same reason – everyone pays the same rate. One of its side effects has been a reduction in excise taxes. As a tax on consumption, there is a voluntary quality to VAT – you do not have to buy the item and thus pay the VAT if you do not want to, but then it could also be argued that the tax reduces trade. Many governments use VAT exemption to support certain industries.

Wherever you sit on the argument, VAT has become an important source of government revenue. In many countries – Chile,[15] Russia and China, for example – it is the government's largest source of revenue. In the UK it amounts to about 17% of total tax revenue.[16] In mainland Europe the average is 28%.[17] The USA does not have VAT, per se, but taxes on goods and services account for 17% of government revenue.[18]

## Why developed nations are better than developing ones at collecting taxes

A notable difference between developed and less developed nations is how, in the words of data research website Our World In Data, 'developed countries today collect a much larger share of their national output in taxes than do developing countries', even if the tax rates are the same.[19] There are many reasons for this.

Chief among them is that the financial technology, banking and tax infrastructure tend to be more advanced in developed nations. There is often also greater faith in political institutions, which leads to higher levels of compliance. Less developed nations tend to rely more on taxes on trade and consumption. Further, many did not participate as fully in the two world wars, which enabled higher rates of income tax.

Thus do central governments in high-income countries – particularly those in Europe – tend to control a much larger share of national production than governments in low-income countries. While in France, for example, central government spending accounts for almost 50% of all national output, in Nigeria the corresponding figure is close to 6%.[20]

Collection improves as countries develop. Turkey, for example, has more than doubled its tax revenue since 1980. In China, the share of GDP collected by taxing individuals and corporations on income doubled between 2000 and 2012.[21] As a result, the developed world has considerably more to spend on social security than the less developed world. Conversely, the developing world enjoys more growth and less stagnation. Effective tax extraction methods, financial technology and high levels of social security spending are related. As time passes, we can expect the developing world to finesse its collection, just as the developed world has done. In fact, we are seeing that already.

## The big change in government spending

*It used to be that the sole purpose of the tax code was to raise the necessary funds to run government. But in today's world the tax mandate has many more facets. These include income redistribution, encouraging favored industries, and discouraging unfavorable behavior.*

Arthur B. Laffer (2011)[22]

US military spending did not end after the Second World War. There was the Cold War, the Korean War, the Vietnam War. Then America became embroiled in wars in the Middle East, where it remains to this day. The US now spends over $800 billion each year on defence – over 20% of the federal budget.[23] The Department of Defense has become the largest employer in the world, with some 3.2 million people on its payroll. The US military–industrial complex is a frighteningly influential lobbying force.

And yet despite the enormous amounts involved, as a percentage of GDP, US military spending, relative to its other outgoings, is actually in decline. In 1960, defence spending accounted for 8% of GDP, compared to 3% today.[24]

Declines in defence spending are more pronounced elsewhere. The global average in 1960 was 6% of GDP. Today it is 2%. In Europe, barely 1.5% of GDP is spent on defence[25] – on a proportional basis, less than half of what America spends. The UK stands at 1.8% of GDP. Defence accounted for over 25% of UK government spending in 1953; today it is less than 5%.[26]

Spending on infrastructure and capital projects, such as social housing, is also in decline. In the UK, for example, it is roughly half of what it was in the 1960s and 70s.[27] Today the UK ranks 132nd in the world in terms of capital investment as a percentage of GDP, spending less than 17%. Instead it relies on private money and public–private partnerships to raise investment.[28] The USA has slipped from 15th in the world in 1960 to 109th today.[29]

Despite spending less on infrastructure and defence, governments have still expanded. The money is spent elsewhere. After the First World War, the UK government was expected to provide 'a land fit for heroes', and something similar occurred after the Second. The cost of war was replaced by the cost of the huge welfare programmes of the new Labour government, especially the National Health Service. The story was the same across Europe. Public spending grew particularly quickly between 1945 and 1980, with the main areas of spending being welfare, healthcare and education. In the UK, social security spending accounted for 15% of the national budget in 1948. Today it is over 30%.[30] Healthcare has increased from 8% in 1956 to over 20% today. The NHS will account for 38% of GDP by 2023.[31] Education spending increased through the 1940s, 50s and 60s, since when it has broadly remained constant at around 11% of the government budget – ranging between 4 and 6% of GDP.[32] The numbers vary slightly from country to country – for example, the US, to many people's surprise, actually spends more on healthcare (via its insurance system) than most European nations. But the broader trend remains: less on the likes of defence and infrastructure, more on healthcare, welfare and education. The use of taxation to redistribute wealth and 'reduce the inequalities of capitalism' became an ideological weapon in the Cold War and has remained so.

On a day-to-day basis the change is barely noticeable. A few per cent here or there with each budget may seem marginal. But the incremental effects, looked at from a hundred-year view, mean the transformation in the role and size of government is verging on incredible. In much of continental Europe in 1900, social spending accounted for less than 1% of GDP, compared to over 30% today. In countries such as Denmark and Finland, more than 40% of total government spending goes to social protection. In South Korea and the US the corresponding figure is close to 20%. The increase in absolute terms – rather than the relative terms I've described above – is even greater, as GDP per capita has increased so substantially over this period.

## Tax Freedom Day

In 1948, a Florida businessman decided that it just wasn't clear enough how much the average American was paying in tax.

Dallas Hostetler came up with an idea. He would highlight the day of the year when the average person's taxes are paid and their debt to the government met. From that day on, their earnings are theirs to keep and spend as they (rather than the government) see fit.

He called it US Tax Freedom Day.

Every year for the next two decades Hostetler would calculate US Tax Freedom Day. He even trademarked it. When he retired in 1971, he handed the trademark to the Washington DC think tank the Tax Foundation, who picked up where he left off. Various bodies around the world now calculate Tax Freedom Day in their own country. The Adam Smith Institute does it in the UK.

It is, inevitably, an imprecise calculation, because so many averages are involved, but by comparing the Tax Freedom Days of various nations around the world, you gain an idea of how much tax a nation pays, the relative size of its government and the levels of economic freedom people in that country enjoy. It is a simple and easily comprehensible demonstration of the tax burden in the economy.

In the US and Australia, Tax Freedom Day occurs in the final week of April. The British have to wait until June, while for the French and Belgians it is not until the final week of July that their service to the state is complete.[33]

At the turn of the twentieth century, Tax Freedom Day came in early to mid January. That is the extent to which government has grown. Over the course of a lifetime it means that a typical citizen will work for at least 20 years of his life without pay, in many cases more than 25.

The medieval serf had to work three days per week on his lord's land in exchange for the lord's protection and the right to work his own land. In the twenty-first century, between 40 and 60% of the ordinary citizen's labour is taken by the state in exchange for its protection and the right to keep the rest. Today's conditions are nothing like as harsh as they were then. We have more freedom of expression and movement. Benefits far exceed their medieval equivalents. But it's illuminating to see that the time we spend to pay our obligations is essentially the same.

# Chapter 14

## The Unofficial Taxes: Debt and Inflation

*Blessed are the young for they shall inherit the national debt.*

Herbert Hoover (1936)[1]

Even with taxes as high as they are, government spending in most cases outweighs tax revenue. Budget surpluses are rare. The pledges governments have made must be honoured, and so they have to turn to other methods to raise revenue. Chief among these is debt.

Debt isn't literally a tax, of course, but it can be viewed as one, especially in the way governments use it. It is a 'tax on the future'.

During the First World War, the US lent Britain money. Those loans were only finally paid off in 2015,[2] 100 years later. In effect, my generation has been working to service the interest incurred by that of my great-great-grandparents. Future generations will have to service the debts of – and thus pay for – today's far greater fiscal irresponsibility.

As I write, the US national debt stands at $21.5 trillion. It doubled under George Bush. It doubled again under Barack Obama. It will double again under Donald Trump. Apart from the four years of small surpluses between 1998 and 2001 (Internet bubble related), the US has run a budget deficit every year since 1969.

The UK's national debt stands at £2 trillion. The German national debt is currently €2.1 trillion, the French €2.3 trillion, the Italian €2.4 trillion. It is worth reminding ourselves just how big a trillion is. It is a million millions.

These extraordinary debt levels are only going to get more extraordinary. Almost every developed nation in the world has a government debt problem, yet continues to run deficits. Japan has run an annual budget deficit since 1966, France since 1993, and Italy has seen perpetual annual deficits since 1950.[3] As a result, debts grow. UK government debt is over 80% of GDP. France and Spain both top 90%. The US has cleared 100%, Ireland 110%, Portugal and Italy 130%. The crown lies in the Land of the Rising Sun. Total gross Japanese debt as a percentage of GDP is an astounding 230%.[4] Try as they might – and in many cases they don't even try – governments are incapable of reining in spending. Their obligations – based on promises made by previous incumbents – are too great.

'Who is the money owed to?' is a question that is often asked. In the case of the US, about 30% is debt owed to foreign countries, in particular China, and to foreign investors. Another third is owned by the federal government itself, via social security funds, retirement funds and so on. The Federal Reserve Bank, having created the money to buy it via quantitative easing, a form of digital money printing, owns about 12%. Mutual funds, banks, pension funds, insurance companies and other investors own the rest. Anthropologist David Graeber suggests that US debt owned overseas is actually a form of modern tribute, levied to pay for its military presence overseas.[5]

In the case of the UK, about 25% of the debt is owned by the Bank of England (which, like the Federal Reserve, effectively printed the money to buy the debt); 25% is held by foreign countries and foreign investors; the rest is owned by banks and building societies, pension funds, insurance companies and investors.

It is likely that you own some of your government's debt in your pension. Thus, whether you were aware of it or not, you have lent the government money. The government bond market is enormous, worth in excess of $100 trillion. It is perhaps twice as big as global stock markets. Only the foreign exchange markets are bigger.

Currently, the interest payable on the US national debt is around 7% of the federal budget. In the UK, it is closer to 6% (more than half the education budget). As the debt grows, even with interest rates this low, just servicing the debt is going to be a big enough challenge, let alone paying it back. If interest rates return to historically normal levels, between 4 and 6%, there is going to be a critical squeeze on government finances.

Yet much of this money is unlikely ever to be paid back without some considerable devaluation of the currency. It is a problem that is almost unsolvable. Since the situation does not appear immediately pressing, most politicians – like the rest of us – simply ignore it. But deficits continue, and so the debt mounts. The inevitable squeeze on government finances gets incrementally greater.

There are many who are surprised that crisis has not come already. If it does, as in the financial crisis of 2008, perhaps everyone will scratch their heads and wonder how governments could have been allowed to become so indebted. The Queen will ask a group of economists why none of them saw this coming. Some people on the fringe will put up their hands and say, 'We did,' and nobody will take any notice. But, as Deutsche Bank's senior analyst Jim Reid observes, 'periods with a higher number of shocks and crises coincide with higher levels of debt and higher budget deficits'.[6] What we are experiencing now is, outside of wartime, unprecedented.

Whatever the outcome, you can be sure that governments will turn to the taxman to help them out.

Many of those who will face the consequences of today's debt have not even been born yet. In terms of a vote, they have no say on the debts piling up. Yet it is they who will have to pay this money back with their taxes – or, worse, face the consequences of not paying it back. Not only is debt a tax on the future, it is, to use the cry of the American revolutionaries, taxation without representation.

## The inflation tax

*For whosoever hath, to him shall be given, and he shall have
more abundance: but whosoever hath not, from him shall be
taken away even that he hath.*

Matthew 13:12

The Renaissance polymath Nicolaus Copernicus called it 'insidious'[7] – insidious because it is 'hidden'.[8] It happens, said Keynes, in a way 'not one man in a million is able to diagnose'.[9] It goes undeclared, unseen and misunderstood.

Yet it is almost as old as money itself, and throughout history, accidentally or otherwise, rulers have resorted to it when their finances are in trouble: in ancient Rome, in the Ottoman Empire, in Robert Mugabe's Zimbabwe and, though few may understand it, all across the modern world today.

It is inflation.

Like debt, inflation may not be an official tax, but that does not mean it does not exist. Indeed, it is often deliberately propagated, and its effect is the same: it confiscates wealth from one group and transfers it to another – from the salaried or the saver to the state, from creditor to debtor, from employee to employer. It is 'a particularly vicious form of taxation', said economist Henry Hazlitt.[10] Milton Friedman was equally damning: 'It is a hidden tax that at first appears painless or even pleasant . . . It is a tax that can be imposed without specific legislation. It is truly taxation without representation.'[11]

The modern era is anomalous not just for its extraordinary levels of taxation and debt, but also for its inflation. The twentieth century, says statistician Dr Bryan Taylor, who compiles data for the Global Financial Database, produced more inflation and worse inflation 'than any other century in history . . . Every single country in the world suffered.'[12] It has continued into the twenty-first.[13]

Governments inflate when they cannot pay their debt, or, as Friedman observed, 'to acquire resources to wage war'.[14]

Inflation is one of those words the meaning of which has been distorted. Often you will hear people arguing on television about whether we are living through inflation or deflation, and the reason their argument is inconclusive is that they mean different things by the word. Today inflation is defined as 'rising prices' and deflation 'falling prices', but rising and falling prices in what? Central banks mostly ignore inflation in house prices and financial assets in their measures and look at certain consumer prices, which are prone to the deflationary forces of improved productivity.

For the sake of clarity, I stress that I am using the traditional definition of the word: the expansion in the supply of money and credit with the consequence of higher prices. An economist might call it 'expanding the money supply' or 'artificially stimulating credit'; a historian might say 'debasing money'. Whichever words you care to use, the process is the same.

As financial technology has evolved, so have rulers' means to debase money and thereby levy the 'inflation tax'. Roman emperors reduced the amount of gold and silver in coins – so-called coin clipping. Medieval kings did the same. Western European governments went one stage further in 1914 and removed gold and silver from money altogether in order to fund their hostilities. Weimar Germany, post-Second World War Hungary and Zimbabwe simply printed money, unbacked by anything. Today's central bankers suppress interest rates, they use dubious measures of inflation, they employ quantitative easing. The methods may change, but the intention is the same. Devalue money and you devalue debt – and you lighten your obligations. But you also confiscate value from anyone who holds this money.

In the nineteenth century, under a settled gold standard, inflation barely existed. Whether in Europe or the US, prices actually fell over the 100 years leading up to the First World War – by as much as 40% in the US.[15] The UK is the only country for which a complete consumer price record is available, and at the end of the nineteenth century prices were 30% lower than at the beginning.[16] In both countries there were periods of moderate inflation and deflation, but no lasting trend. In the US, for example, during the civil war, there was some inflation, and deflation followed to bring the economy back onto a gold standard. The Confederate states, who printed money to pay for the war, suffered high inflation and then the eventual collapse of their currency, as often befalls the losing side.

Ignoring debt, the amount of money a nation could print was tied, at least loosely, to the value of the gold or silver it had in its vaults (though ways round this were often found). Thus the only way to increase the base money supply was to mine more precious metal or to conquer somebody else and take theirs. It put a cap on money supply, which meant that prices crept higher only very slowly over time (often depending on the availability of credit) and were often flat or falling for long periods. It is extraordinarily empowering for consumers and workers to see the purchasing power of their money increase.

In the 100 years since 1914, however, so much money has been created that most currencies have lost over 95% of their purchasing power, in many cases over 99%. In the UK, one decimal penny would have had more purchasing power in 1914 than a pound does today.[17] In general, say Professors Carmen Reinhart and Kenneth Rogoff, average prices worldwide are at least 30 times higher than a hundred years ago.[18]

The change in dynamic began shortly after 1910, mainly due to the First World War. In 1914, the UK, France and Germany came off their metallic standards to print the money they needed to pay for the war. Had those countries not done this, the Great War could not have gone on for as long as it did. There was not the metal to pay for it. Isn't that an incredible thought? Monetary debasement – or inflation – made that war possible. Few people realise the terrible and far-reaching consequences of that decision to debase the currency. In the UK, we have only just finished paying off the debt. But that is trivial compared to the cost of human life.

The UK went back on the gold standard in 1925, only to abandon it for a second time in 1931. The nadir of the Great Depression came two years later, in 1933. Prices in the UK have risen every year since, with the only exception being 2009, so that by the beginning of this decade they were over 60 times higher than in 1934.[19]

The US dollar remained tied to gold, and other currencies were pegged to the dollar under the Bretton Woods Agreement of 1945. That kept something of a lid on things until 1971, when the US finally abandoned the gold standard.

As for actual money supply, at the turn of the twentieth century, there was some $7 billion in existence. In 1971, US money supply stood at $480 billion. Today it is $15.5 trillion, over 30 times higher than in 1971, and 2,200 times higher than in 1900.[20] Yes, American GDP has grown by about 16 times since 1971, and the population has increased by 60% (from 207 million to 325 million), but money supply growth has far outstripped both.

In the UK in 1971 there was £31 billion in circulation. Now there is over £2.8 trillion.[21] That is a 90-fold (8,900%) increase. Over the same period, UK GDP has grown by about 17 times while its population has gone from 55 million to 65 million. Increases in the money supply have eclipsed both economic and population growth.

One of the most insidious manifestations of UK inflation has been in house prices. In the 649 years from 1290 to 1939, UK house prices rose 887%. This sounds like a lot, but given that it is a 650-year period, it works out at just 0.4% annualised and roughly reflects the amount of newly mined gold over the time. Adjusted for inflation, house prices actually fell by 49%. But since 1939, house prices have risen 41,363% (8% annualised).[22] The cause of this inflation is the same as everywhere else: money supply growth.

Many people blame high house prices on lack of new-build, and population growth. But in the 10 years between 1997 and 2007, though the population grew by 5%, the housing stock grew by 10%.[23] If house prices were a simple function of supply and demand, they would have fallen slightly over the period. Instead, they tripled.[24] Mortgage lending over the same period went up by

370%²⁵ – a commensurate amount. It was the increased supply of money, through the issuance of debt, that caused house prices to rise. The effect of it all has been an enormous but subversive transfer of wealth.

A whole generation now refers to itself as Generation Rent, because they believe they will never be able to afford to buy a house. This is an absurd situation. Houses do not cost a lot of money to build, and over 95% of the UK is not built on.²⁶

When looked at that starkly, the amount by which the purchasing power of money has fallen is astonishing. But this is the effect of inflation compounded over time. The process, however, is gradual, and so goes almost unseen. Your money has lost 3–5% of its value each year, even after interest, since 1914. So excluding interest, $10,000 in year one is worth $9,600 in year two, and $9,216 by year three. After five years it is closer to $8,500, and after seven closer to $7,800. Every year, your money buys you less.

The currency that best maintained its purchasing power in the twentieth century was the Swiss franc. That is the currency that remained pegged to gold for the longest (until 1999).

'It may not feel like it,' says Deutsche Bank's Jim Reid, 'but we live in inflationary times relative to long-term history.'

Average wages have risen as well, but not by as much as the purchasing power of money has fallen. So each year, effectively, you make less money. The difference is covered up by more debt, longer working hours, both parents working when previously only one had to to maintain a middle-class lifestyle, fewer children and so on. Thus we have carved out a situation in which many, especially the lower and middle classes, are growing increasingly stretched and each generation is poorer than the last, ground between the millstones of taxation and inflation.

Central banks have a remit to curb inflation, and this they will usually do by raising interest rates. But their measures of inflation – RPI and CPI – only measure the prices of certain everyday goods. They ignore other sectors of the economy altogether: property prices, for example, and financial assets. It means they can then declare that inflation is low and set low interest rates, thus stimulating debt and creating more inflation.

If interest rates in the 2000s had reflected money supply growth, they would have been double what they were and it would not have been possible for the housing bubbles to take hold. This was taken one stage further after the 2008 financial crisis, when interest rates were slashed close to zero and quantitative easing was introduced. The episode shows the instinct in current authorities to inflate in the face of a crisis.

These are the means by which currency is debased and the inflation tax is exacted today. The ultimate purpose, almost invariably, is to erode the value of debt, particularly government debt, and to enable government spending. The effect is to transfer the value of that money – i.e. people's wealth – to the state. 'By a continuing process of inflation,' said Vladimir Lenin, 'governments can confiscate, secretly and unobserved, an important part of the wealth of their citizens.'[27]

Some sectors of society actually benefit from the process of inflation. If you own the assets or operate in the sectors that profit from all this newly created money – the financial sector, for example, or the New York or London property in which it mostly lives – you make spectacular gains. But if you don't own these assets – and most young people don't – you get left behind. And the wealth gap gets bigger. The worst inflation usually manifests itself where government spending is greatest, with the miserable irony being that governments that spend most looking after their poor end up making them poorer. 'There is no subtler, no surer means of overturning the existing basis of society,' said Keynes, 'than to debauch the currency.'[28]

Consider again Jean-Baptiste Colbert's 'The art of taxation consists of so plucking the goose as to obtain the most feathers with the minimum amount of hissing.' Undeclared, unseen and not properly understood, the inflation tax means that the goose is plucked noiselessly. It is, as Copernicus said, insidious – the stealthiest of stealth taxes.

# Chapter 15

# *The Future of Work*

*The robot that takes your job should pay taxes.*

Bill Gates (2017)[1]

Until this point we have been looking at the past, and the surprising ways in which tax has affected both history and the present day. Over the next few chapters we turn our attention to the future, a much more problematic subject.

We are in a period of great economic change, and so the way we are taxed will have to change. This means the way we are governed will change too. Let us consider some of what is coming. We start with work.

Income taxes, as we have seen, are governments' largest source of revenue. But just as governments' need for revenue grows more pressing, whether it is to cover their spending programmes or service their debts, income tax in its current form is going to get harder to collect. The relationship between employer and employee is changing. Traditional employment is waning. The gig economy is waxing.

Estimates of the number of workers operating in the gig economy – people working on short-term contracts or as freelancers – vary wildly. In the US, the Bureau of Labor Statistics says 10% of its workforce is made up of contingent workers.[2] Other studies show that number to be much higher. According to the Gig Economy Data Hub, 27% of US workers 'participate in independent work'.[3] McKinsey's estimates tally. The Federal Reserve puts the figure at

31%; the Freelancers Union says it is 36%.[4] A recent study by LinkedIn shows it will be 43% by 2020.[5] This variation in estimates can be put down to differing definitions of what the gig economy actually is. If you add illegal and unregistered workers to the mix (these are even harder to quantify accurately), the numbers get more hazy still. Ernst & Young's Contingent Workforce Study of the US perhaps best illustrates the situation, projecting that by 2020, one in five US workers will be contingent; include part-time workers and '40% to 50% of the workforce will be in non-permanent employment by 2020'.[6] Whichever figures you look at, one thing is for sure: the gig economy is growing, and growing rapidly – by 66% in the 10 years to 2015, according to one Harvard study,[7] and no doubt by more since.

This is a global phenomenon. In the UK, the number of people working for themselves has grown by half since 2000,[8] versus a roughly 6% rise in employees over the same period.[9] London is the UK's most modern city – where it goes, the rest of the UK usually follows – and its gig economy has grown by 73% since 2010.[10] In 2017, over 15% of the UK workforce was self-employed,[11] but factor part-timers into the mix and the number is much higher. In Europe, Australia and all across Asia there are similar levels of growth.

Some have criticised the gig economy, saying it exploits people and does not give them the employment protection they deserve. Others like it. In general, surveys show higher satisfaction levels among the self-employed than the employed. LinkedIn's surveys show that 67% of freelancers are either satisfied or highly satisfied with their work,[12] and the large majority of giggers want to stay in contingent work to progress their careers.[13] Many workers like it because it enables them to take on multiple smaller jobs with greater flexibility. The rights and wrongs of the gig economy are irrelevant here, however. The point is that it is a growing trend. Whether because there are no other options available to them, or because they prefer the lifestyle, or both, more and more workers are embracing it. According to LinkedIn, 81% of freelancers will continue to work in the gig economy. By 2030, says Ernst & Young, a full 50% of full-time US workers will be contingent.[14] We can expect similar numbers around the world.

Employers also like the gig economy. Without being tied into long-term contracts, there is more flexibility. Gig workers dramatically reduce the costs (mostly in the form of taxation) and other burdens of employing staff. These savings can then be passed on to the consumer. Thus their customers like it too, in that it results in lower prices. Uber embraces (or exploits, depending on your view) the gig economy, and so we have cheaper taxis, providing a higher level of service. Amazon does the same, and so we have cheaper products delivered to our door. Lower prices and superior service are why companies that encourage and exploit the gig economy tend to be so much more successful than older models.

In 1990, the three biggest companies in Silicon Valley had a market capitalisation (cap) of $36 billion and employed over a million people. Today, the three biggest – Facebook (25,105 full-time employees),[15] Google (88,000)[16] and Apple (123,000)[17] – employ about 25% as many people, yet their combined market cap, as I write, is around $2.2 trillion, over 60 times higher. Uber, the world's largest taxi company, has only 16,000 employees.[18] Airbnb, the world's largest accommodation provider, has 9,053.[19] Compare that to the traditional employers of the old world. Walmart employs over 2.3 million people, the US Department of Defense over 3 million, Volkswagen over 600,000.

The traditional, easily taxable employer–employee relationship is fading. This means, first, the loss to the government of employment and payroll taxes. Then there is the problem that income taxes will become harder to collect. At present there are no systems in place to deduct tax at source from contingent workers. There is considerable scope for non-compliance, whether accidental or deliberate. The IRS already attributes 44% of its $450 billion annual tax gap to the improper compliance of individual business income.[20] In the US, 69% of freelancers surveyed said that in regard to their tax affairs, they received no help from the 'shared economy platform' they are working with, 36% did not know what records needed to be kept and 34% did not even know they had to file quarterly returns.[21]

'The huge rise in insecure work isn't just bad for workers. It's punching a massive hole in the public finances too,' according to Frances O'Grady, general secretary of the UK Trades Union Congress (TUC). 'Zero-hours contracts and low-paid self-employment are costing the economy billions every year in lost tax revenues. That's money that could be spent on stopping the crisis in our schools and hospitals and making sure every elderly person gets decent care.'[22]

She's right, at least in part. However, it is not the economy that is losing billions in tax revenues, but the government. Gig work is actually saving the economy billions in that it enables companies to bring cheaper, better products to market. It is growing because it bypasses government costs.

Prime Minister Theresa May appointed the strategist Matthew Taylor to review modern employment practices, and Taylor has since declared that self-employed workers typically pay £2,000 a year less in tax than employees doing equivalent jobs.[23] Given that someone on the UK average salary of £27,500 would pay about £5,300 in income tax and National Insurance, this is no small loss to the Exchequer.[24] Then there's the additional loss of revenue in employer contributions. More people working from home means smaller business premises are required and there will be an ensuing decline in revenue from business rates.

In short, the rise of the gig economy means a fall in government revenue.

The response will be to raise taxes for the self-employed, and to re-regulate those who employ them. Already in the UK those freelancers who hire themselves out through limited companies have had their tax rates increased. The rates of VAT payable by the self-employed have also been altered. Meanwhile, employers such as Uber and the courier Hermes have come under pressure through the courts by those seeking to redefine full-time employment and gig work.

I suspect tax authorities may eventually try to find ways to deduct presumed income at source from the platform that provides the work, and then leave it to the individual business to submit their expenses and claim back the difference – much as withholding currently works in the US. This will place the burden of tax collection on the 'shared economy provider', who will, no doubt, look for ways to resist. If it works in one country, others will try to follow suit. However, this will be no easy task, and a large part of the gig economy does not go through the large platforms. Maybe automated systems will be set up to deduct presumed taxes owed at the point when payment for that labour takes place, but again this will not be easy, and it raises all sorts of issues about infringing personal liberties.

Even if such measures are enacted (and there is no guarantee they will be), it will be messier than regular income tax deduction at source from traditional employers. Governments will have to look to other areas where taxes are easier to collect.

## Digital nomads are the new non-doms

*What knight errant ever paid a tax, a queen's levy, a tribute,*
*a tariff, or a toll?*

Miguel de Cervantes, *Don Quixote* (1833)[25]

They might be web designers or developers, graphic designers, coders, traders, bloggers, content creators, teachers, translators or consultants. They are 'the new elite with no fixed abode', says the BBC,[26] members of the growing class of sovereign individual that is the digital nomad. By 2035, there will be one billion of them,[27] according to Pieter Levels, an entrepreneur and digital nomad himself. One billion seems an absurdly high number, but if you follow Levels' logic, the estimate seems conservative. There are several conspiring factors at work here.

First, there is the fact that it has become hard for young people, especially graduates, to find jobs with good prospects at home. Meanwhile, the cost of home ownership has grown so extraordinarily high across the developed world that many, particularly anyone born after about 1985, are excluded. The gap between what they are able to earn, after taxes, and the houses they are able to buy is so painfully large that many can't or don't even bother attempting to bridge it. They rent instead. Home ownership levels are falling across the developed world. But a European digital nomad living in, say, South America or South Asia can enjoy a lifestyle twice as nice on half the salary. Given the choice between debt slavery for not particularly pleasant accommodation and an exciting life on the road, many choose the latter.

Values have changed. This is the age of the asset-light generation, which prizes experience over material things. Generation Rent will hire the Rolls-Royce, they won't buy it. 'Most people who own homes are like rich people or old people,' says Levels disparagingly. 'We don't want homes. We don't want the hassle.'[28] Stuff is not an asset; it's a burden. They want wealth, but they are less bothered about possessions. They don't work in the 'real world' economy; they work in the digital economy, where the opportunities are far greater. You can work in the digital economy from anywhere. And the digital nomad moves about the globe with little more than what he can fit in his backpack.

Not only are home ownership rates falling, so are marriage rates – from over 70% in the 1960s to the high 60s in the 1990s to around 50% today. Whether it is a job, a home or a family, there is less to commit the younger generation or tie them down to a place.

House prices may be extortionate, but the cost of travel has fallen dramatically, and keeps falling. International air travel is about a twentieth of the price it was in the 1940s, and about a quarter of what it was in the 1980s.[29] Even with jet fuel prices almost ten times higher than in 1998,[30] air travel is still roughly 50% cheaper.[31] Not only is it getting cheaper all the time, it is getting better. Soon we will be able to fly from Europe to the Far East in four or five hours.

Internet speeds are also improving around the world, while getting cheaper. We will soon have 5G and 6G. More and more people can work remotely from more and more distant places. Globally, 70% of people now work remotely, or telecommute, at least once a week, according to a recent study by Swiss office provider IWG[32] (and the study was for full-time employees, not the self-employed). Over 70% of people who work remotely only began doing so in the last four years.[33] More than 80% like working remotely[34] (90% according to some studies)[35] and want to continue working this way for as long as possible. Interestingly, some 94% of remote workers advise others to do the same.[36] This has directly affected the growth of the gig economy. 'First, they work from home,' says Levels. 'They get bored there, or lonely, so they go to the coffee shop, then they travel.'[37]

Over half the world is now middle class or richer, a study from the Brookings Institution has revealed.[38] Just as the European or North American in his twenties or thirties might pass through Asia, Africa or South America, so are Asians, Africans and South Americans passing back the other way, motivated by the same exciting possibilities of travel. The rise of the digital nomad is a growing global phenomenon.

Author Tim Ferris's self-help book on the subject, *The 4-Hour Work Week: Escape the 9–5, Live Anywhere and Join the New Rich*, spent more than four years on the *New York Times* best-seller list, has been translated into 35 languages and has sold close to 1.5 million copies worldwide.[39] Those numbers give you an idea how desirable this life is becoming. There are already entire social networking sites specifically for digital nomads, with millions of subscribers, crowd-sourced databases and comparison sites measuring up the best places to go at any given moment. It is only going to get bigger.

The global population is projected to be nine billion in 2035. Of this the workforce will be some six billion, says Levels, and of that six billion roughly half will be freelancers.[40] One in three of those freelancers will be a nomad. Thus does Levels arrive at his projection of a billion nomads by 2035.

And why wouldn't this demographic be growing? The life of a nomad is a good one. It beats being a slave to wages, taxes and a mortgage. It's one I am planning for myself once my kids are grown up. Who doesn't want to see the world?

The digital economy itself is growing, and at a far faster rate than the real economy. That is creating the possibilities for nomads that don't exist elsewhere. People follow opportunity, they always have. The rise of the digital economy began in the 1980s and 90s, but the Internet is what has really kick-started it all. Today valuations of digital companies dwarf their analogue rivals. Walmart may have greater revenues, but Amazon has the greater market cap. Major developed economies are investing more in intangible assets – design, branding and software – than in such tangible ones as machinery and buildings. Assets one can neither see nor touch are where future wealth lies. The digital economy is where the action is. That's where the digital nomad finds his employment.

Just as the gig economy offers more flexibility and lower costs, so does the life of a digital nomad: no mortgage, no premises and lower day-to-day expenses compared to the developed world. In addition, the single biggest expense of your life is removed: that of the state. The digital nomad pays no council tax, for example, no payroll tax, no National Insurance. The amount of VAT he pays is also likely to be lower, depending on where he is. And how much income tax does he pay? And to whom?

Tax laws were written in another age, before this new economy existed. Technically, you pay tax to the country in which you are resident. To be resident in a country you have to spend more than 183 days a year there. Many nomads are on the move long before that.

Some will pay taxes to the country where they are citizen. The US citizen who lives abroad is obliged to file a tax return at home (a law that goes all the way back to Abraham Lincoln and his unwavering ambition to protect Union tax revenue). However, most countries have no such law. The UK national, who no longer lives in the UK, was, while in Thailand, hired to do a job by a company in Israel; he then did the job while in Brazil and was paid when in Mexico. The tax obligations here are not entirely black and white, nor are the expenses.

Income tax is one of the most problematic issues facing the digital nomad: how to pay, how much and to whom. Some pay as though they are still nationals of their country of birth. Some find the process so onerous they do not. Some deliberately avoid paying, if they can, and find ways of legitimately doing so. The digital nomad often feels little obligation to his or her country of birth, its high house prices and lack of opportunity. He does not live there, and has little intention of returning for any great duration. He makes no use of his country's social services. He has no children there, no marriage, no home, no investment nor ownership to commit him. Why should he pay taxes?

As taxes go up at home, the unintended consequence might be to drive more people into digital nomadery. Just before the last general election, I stumbled across the following comment on Twitter from one @paulypilot: 'I do my work from home, on the Internet. I'm happy to pay UK taxes, as they are fair. If they increase tax, I'll leave. They'll get 0%.'[41]

He received a flurry of replies – 'My thoughts exactly' and so on – before he then outlined various ways in which he could 'leave'. 'It's not necessarily about physically moving, just ensuring that taxable income leaves the UK,' he said. Or, 'I'd spend a few months in UK, Denmark, Norway, France, then winter in the Far East.' The scope for non-compliance by digital nomads is considerable. Both reporting and payment are much harder to enforce on someone who is not there; who is constantly on the move.

The life of a non-dom was once the preserve of the super rich, residing in Panama, Monaco or Switzerland to lower their tax obligations. The revolution in tech, especially fintech, means it is now a possibility for ordinary people too.

Cities may actually start competing to attract digital nomads. In China, one city, Tianfu – 609 square miles of it – has actually been built specifically with this in mind: to attract the mobile digital elite. Levels points out that international cities like London, New York and Tokyo have more in common with each other than, say, London and Birmingham or New York and Philadelphia. He envisages a world in which cities start enacting their own special nomad taxes and tax breaks to attract this new, mobile workforce. This points towards a situation in which international cities begin detaching from their nation states.

As they grow older and start families, nomads will settle, runs the thinking. But it is not so black and white. Digital nomads are having fewer kids and they are having them later in life. Even when they do start a family, says Levels, many of them keep to the nomadic life they know. They remain self-reliant. The Internet and home schooling become the primary sources of learning – and this in itself brings into question factors on the other side of the tax equation: the future role of government services. And if they do settle, where will that be? Somewhere taxes are high and the cost of living expensive? Or somewhere taxes are low?

## Will robots take our jobs?

It's the Fourth Industrial Revolution, says Klaus Schwab, founder and chairman of the World Economic Forum.[42] Nobody quite knows what the impact will be, but as robots and artificial intelligence (AI) increasingly take on the tasks that previously fell to workers, especially blue- and white-collar workers (even those definitions are out of date), one thing is for sure: there will be further disruption to easily taxable, traditional employment.

Whether it is AI, machine learning, faster and more powerful computers, robots or algorithms, 3D printing, biotech or blockchain, tech is becoming increasingly capable and increasingly integrated. Some argue that millions will lose their jobs and find no others to replace them. A debilitating life of unemployment lies ahead. Others argue that machines will boost productivity and wealth, and create better employment prospects. Just as the Industrial Revolution meant that machines could undertake the brutal work of low-level factory workers, farm labourers, indentured servants and slaves, so will tech create similar economic improvement today. Will there be more work, less work or simply different work?

A 2013 study by Oxford University concluded that '47% of US employment was at risk'.[43] The Bank of England announced in 2015 that 'half of all British jobs' could be lost to 'smart machines', along with 80 million jobs in the US.[44] In 2017, McKinsey used rather more balanced wording when it estimated that 51% of activities in the US were 'susceptible to automation', representing $2.7 trillion in wages.[45] It estimated that 800 million jobs – 30% of jobs worldwide – could be 'displaced', and that around 14% of people might have to change 'occupational category'.[46]

The problem with forecasting of this kind, even if data-driven, is that it involves making predictions about things that have not been invented yet. If we look to the effect on employment of the most recent sweeping technical innovation – the Internet – we can see that many jobs disappeared, but as many, if not more, new ones were created. Most jobs have changed. There are some things we have to do at work that we didn't have to do 20 years ago, and other things we no longer have to do.

In Geoffrey Chaucer's *Canterbury Tales*, written around 1390, we hear the stories of 24 different pilgrims, told as they travelled from London to the shrine of St Thomas Becket in Canterbury Cathedral. There is a knight, a merchant, a clerk, five tradesmen, a sergeant of the law, a miller, a cook, a shipman, a physician, a reeve (magistrate) and many more besides. Over 600 years later, all those professions still exist in some form or other, despite all the advances that have been made since. Of course, the nature of the work has changed, but the roles still exist. There is going to be upheaval, no doubt. The Industrial Revolution meant more jobs ultimately, but there was enormous displacement of the agricultural workforce in the meantime.

It's easy to see drivers, for example – whether taxi drivers, coach drivers, truck drivers, even airline pilots – facing declining demand for their labour in the years ahead as self-driving vehicles enter the mainstream. The transportation industry is changing. Though the change has been coming for some time, the actual adoption of automated self-driving systems could happen quite suddenly – the main barriers seem to be regulatory. But the impact will be considerable. Roughly 3% of American workers – over 4.4 million people – work as drivers of some kind.

Other sectors face a similar upheaval. Restaurants are replacing waiters with tablets that make recommendations and explain the menu. In Tokyo recently I was served by a robot bartender. Stores have replaced staff with self-checkout. The day is already here in some stores where you can pick stuff off the shelves and just walk out with the item billed to your account. The US military is the world's largest employer. From soldier to pilot to surveillance officer to bomb disposal expert, you can see robots replacing humans. Warehousing and manufacturing face major change. Already 80% of a car is built by robots. Healthcare, data entry, paralegal work, tax preparation, accounting, banking, fund management and financial trading can all be done better by robots. AI already outperforms humans in translating, facial recognition, mimicking speech, driving, writing articles, trading financial products and diagnosing cancers.

Robots make fewer mistakes. Machine intelligence is such that they learn from them when they do, as well as from the mistakes of others. They work longer hours. They don't require pensions, holidays or insurance. They don't take sick leave or play truant, they don't have domestic issues or mental health problems, or suffer from any other human failing. It's not hard to see why their use will increase.

But new jobs will also appear. These are hard to enumerate because we don't know what they are yet. Nor do we know where they will be – it is not much good to the people of Newcastle if all the job creation is in Oklahoma.

Meanwhile, the nature of many jobs and the duties they entail will simply change. There will still be soldiers, but fewer may be fighting in the front line. There will still be accountants, but the grind of data entry and processing will be performed by machines. More and more people and goods are going to be transported in the years ahead, but there may be less work for drivers. With the rise of the gig economy, it may be that many people have multiple smaller jobs, rather than one full-time position.

In 2016, PricewaterhouseCoopers, like the Bank of England, was very bearish about the prospects for workers. AI would see about 30% of UK workers lose their jobs to automation, it said. In 2018, that stance softened. Even though 20% of jobs would be affected, as many would be created as would be lost. The overall effect on UK employment would be 'broadly neutral'.[47]

Measures to protect labour from automation will not be the answer. In recent years, they have backfired. Increased demands for workers' rights have actually accelerated the adoption of machine replacements.

Bill Gates and others have called for taxes on robots to replace lost income tax. This sounds like a nice idea, but it will be fraught with practical difficulties. The definition of what a robot is is unclear. Is it a visible machine performing tasks? Is it an algorithm analysing data? Where is the machine? Where is the IP? How do you tax an inanimate object? How do you measure the tax payable? By hours worked? By productivity? You can't do it on the basis of what somebody used to earn, as the nature of the job will have changed – how would you tax a car on the basis of a horse-drawn carriage driver's earnings?

Presumably a notional salary paid to the robot would have to be calculated (this is a minefield in itself) and then the company would have to pay a corresponding tax, but unless this is done on a global basis, companies will simply relocate their robots to low-robot-tax jurisdictions. To make this work will require a lot more than political will, and it is not even clear that there is that. As a tax on capital rather than labour, proposals might run into the resistance of considerable corporate lobbying.

That said, taxes on some robots quite obviously located onshore will come. Taxes on self-driving vehicles, for example (are these robots?), are almost inevitable. They cannot be relocated elsewhere, even if the IP can. They will be too easy a target to ignore. Some sort of mileage tax – with higher prices per mile in cities and, especially, city centres – is most likely, I expect. Mileage can be tracked in real time and payment can be deducted automatically. It might even be that these taxes can be levied by local authorities.

One of the few certainties in this enormous economic upheaval is that income tax, governments' largest source of revenue, will be affected.

## Chapter 16

# *Crypto Money: The Taxman's Nightmare*

It's winter 2018. I'm having dinner with Roger Ver, perhaps the most well-known early champion of bitcoin. His impassioned advocacy of the new technology earned him the nickname 'Bitcoin Jesus', and his canny investments in the sector turned him into a millionaire hundreds of times over. He is now the CEO of bitcoin. com. I'm trying to impress on Roger just how big the 'digital nomad' workforce is going to get, and just how much it is going to upset government revenue streams, but it is old hat to him.

'You don't have to tell me. I'm seeing it every day,' he says. 'I'm one of the ones giving them work.'

'How many people work for bitcoin.com?' I ask.

'Maybe a hundred and thirty, hundred and forty,' he says. 'And they're all nomads one way or another. I have no idea where many of them are much of the time. Could be Lisbon, Chiang Mai, Medellín next week.'

'And where are they all from?'

'Oh man, everywhere. I've got Americans working for me, Europeans, Asians – Chinese, Korean, Japanese, Indians, Indonesians – South Americans. Must be at least twenty different nationalities.'

'How do you pay them all?' I ask.

'Bitcoin cash,' comes the immediate reply (bitcoin cash is an offshoot of bitcoin, designed for quicker payments). 'Logistically, it'd be too difficult, too expensive to pay each one in their national currency. They're providing a borderless digital service; we pay them with borderless digital money. It's the only thing that would work. Anyway, they want to be paid in bitcoin cash. That's why they want to work for us.'

Cryptocurrency is notoriously volatile. 'What about the exchange risk?' I ask.

'They're happy to take it on. They can convert into their own national currency as soon as they get paid if they want to, but as far as I know, most don't. They believe in bitcoin cash. They want to get as much exposure as they can.'

'What about taxes?'

'Oh man, organising the tax affairs for every different nationality, hiring the expertise, some of them work part-time, some are full-time, the cost of that – I don't even want to think of what it would be. These are nomads. None of them work nine to five. They organise their own time schedules. They organise their own tax affairs.'

'Do you think they all pay taxes?'

'You'd have to ask them that. It's their responsibility – between them and their governments. I would have thought some do, but there are some who haven't been home in years and have no intention of going home; they don't like what their countries have become; they don't support their governments; they think what their governments are doing is wrong – so they might be against the idea of funding that with taxes. And also there are some, you know, who might want to stay compliant, to stay legal, but the tax laws don't cater for their situations. Their status is unclear, and the bureaucracy can be so complicated, often it's just easier to put it off.'

Not only does this rapidly growing workforce operate beyond borders, the money that it uses is beyond borders – non-government currency outside of traditional banking. It will make trade even harder to monitor, control and tax.

Remember that Pieter Levels calculation that there will be a billion digital nomads by 2035? 'Of all the nomads I meet,' says Levels, 'at least half work in the crypto economy.' If current trends continue, that would mean as many as 500 million people operating outside government money systems by 2035. Such a thought may seem ridiculous, but crypto advocates with their finger on the pulse of what is going on will tell you the number will likely be much higher.

## Crypto activism

Of all the emerging threats to government revenue, crypto technology is perhaps the greatest.

The twentieth-century large-government model was accompanied by – indeed, has been made possible by – fiat money. Control of money gives governments immense power. If a government feels it needs more money – to pay for a war or some other specific purpose, such as, in recent years, bailing out the financial sector – it can simply issue more of it. Non-government systems of money undermine that. Governments cannot debase money over which they have no control – there is no inflation tax. Deduction at source, VAT, sales or transaction taxes are harder to enforce and monitor, as is reporting. As more and more people use alternative currencies, particularly online and abroad, taxes will become harder to collect.

Many who don't understand or don't want to understand bitcoin and crypto currencies – including notable economists (Paul Krugman to Nouriel Roubini) and bankers (Jamie Dimon) – have simply dismissed them. In doing so they dismissed perhaps the most powerful technological breakthrough since the Internet, while those who listened to them missed out on what was the greatest money-making opportunity any of us ever will see in our lifetimes. From its first recorded exchange price in October 2009[1] of $0.001309 to its December 2017 high at around $20,000, bitcoin rose over 15 million-fold, with at least five corrections of 80% or more along the way. If bitcoin was going to die, it would have died years ago. Instead it has grown into a near-trillion-dollar industry, with a frenzy around the possibilities of the tech the like of which has not been seen since the Internet arrived in the 1990s.

Systems of money and technology have always evolved together, one pushing the other forward. The mud of ancient Mesopotamia first baked into tokens to record debts was then inscribed with pictures instead – and humans developed their first systems of writing. The metal casting of coins, which could ensure the weight of metal contained, made shells, whales' teeth and other such primitive forms of cash redundant. The printing press did the same for precious metals and we started using paper money instead. Electronic banking put paid to the cheque, in some countries faster than others (the USA has been one of the slower nations on the uptake). Contactless payment is now doing the same to cash, which is becoming less and less convenient. In the marketplace, convenience usually wins. Money is tech. Bitcoin and its many offshoots are the latest evolution, specifically designed to be cash for the Internet. It is unlikely that the large majority of people will ever use bitcoin to do their weekly shop at the supermarket, but crypto's use in online transactions will continue to grow.

With this in mind, many cryptos have been designed for specific purposes. There are coins for where total anonymity is desired (monero, grin); coins for where speed of transfer is important (litecoin, dash); coins specifically designed for tipping and small payments (stellar, dogecoin); coins to build apps on top of (ethereum, cardano, EOS), and so on. There are more than 3,000 different altcoins already. They make fiat money look backward.

The day is not far away when it will be normal to have several different wallets on your computer or phone, just as you have several different apps, each wallet containing a coin for a specific purpose – from tipping blog posts or videos you like, to trading shares, precious metals or bonds, to buying black-market goods. How effectively and efficiently will governments be able to monitor all these transactions and levy due taxes, without massive violations of privacy?

The subversive possibilities of this non-government crypto money are quite deliberate. The technology was born out of the cypherpunks, a dissident group of coders that emerged in the 1990s. They had banded together because of shared concerns about the new technology that was the Internet. While they could see its potential, they also saw the possibilities it would open up for corporate and state invasion of privacy. They were deeply apprehensive – and given what has happened since, their apprehension was well founded. Their solution lay in developing open-source technologies, especially around cryptography, to defend privacy.

The cypherpunks' politics were deeply libertarian, if not anarchic. Their distrust of the state was considerable. The group's founder was a Californian computer scientist by the name of Tim May. Cryptographic developments will, he wrote in his Crypto Anarchist Manifesto of 1988, 'alter completely the nature of government regulation, the ability to tax and control economic interactions, the ability to keep information secret, and will even alter the nature of trust and reputation'.[2]

He went on: 'Just as the technology of printing altered and reduced the power of medieval guilds and the social power structure, so too will cryptologic methods fundamentally alter the nature of corporations and of government interference in economic transactions. Combined with emerging information markets, crypto anarchy will create a liquid market for any and all material which can be put into words and pictures.'

The key to realising the cypherpunks' dream was a system of anonymous Internet cash – that is, a system by which any amount of money, large or small, could be sent directly from A to B over the Internet with no middleman (usually a bank) processing the transaction. But for all Tim May and the cypherpunks' bold words, there was a technological problem that stood in their way. It was known as double spending, and was, essentially, the problem of preventing people from copying and pasting digital money as you would any other type of digital code, be it text, image or video. For 20 years or more that problem remained unsolved, so much so that many computer scientists deemed it unsolvable without a central body to process transactions. Many cypherpunks gave up on their anarchic dream. Then along came Satoshi Nakamoto with his invention bitcoin. The rest is history.

Encryption now allows people to communicate, browse and transact away from the prying eyes of large corporations or government. As a result, information, and thus people, will be harder to control and to tax. It is extremely easy to encrypt something, extremely hard to decrypt it. 'It is like an egg,' says tech writer Jamie Bartlett, 'a lot easier to crack than to put back in its shell.'³ 'The universe believes in encryption,' said another cypherpunk, Julian Assange. It is a direct challenge to state authority, one that will be used for foul means as well as fair. Above all, it is a challenge to the state monopoly on money, and its ability to enforce taxes.

As the technology has proliferated, so has the cypherpunks' worldview. Throughout the cryptographic community there is a deep mistrust of government. They believe its rules are wrong and they do not want to play by them. Just as a growing left-wing authoritarian worldview is taking hold (over half of US millennials now have a positive view of socialism), so is there an equally passionate libertarian belief system emerging. Its ideological beating heart is in crypto. As *Sapiens* author, anthropologist Yuval Noah Harari, would attest, do not underestimate the impact of narrative on human evolution. It is my view, though beyond the scope of this book, that just as religious doctrines provided the guiding narrative for many centuries, to be followed by the varieties of secular socialist and social democratic thinking that dominated the last century, so libertarianism is one ideology that will dominate the next.

In his 2009 essay 'The Education of a Libertarian',⁴ PayPal founder Peter Thiel makes the argument that capitalism and democracy are incompatible. Capitalism is not 'popular with the crowd', he says; the masses demand greater concessions from capitalists in the form of redistribution and regulation. He maintains that it is not possible to achieve meaningful political change through political activism, saying, 'I have changed radically on the question of how to achieve these goals.' Instead, he says, the way to achieve political change is through technological advancement. 'The mode for escape must involve some sort of new and hitherto untried process that leads us to some undiscovered country. And for this reason I have focused my efforts on new technologies that may create a new space for freedom.' Thiel's 'undiscovered country' lies in cyberspace, outer space or on the oceans.

Thiel's essay was born in part out of frustration and the establishment's reaction to the global financial crisis of 2008 – bailing out banks, slashing interest rates and so on. He was not alone in his anger and he was not alone in his desire to fix things. Bitcoin's creator, Satoshi Nakamoto, was driven by precisely the same motivation, announcing his invention just a few months before Thiel wrote his essay, and then developing it with a reference to a *Times* headline of the day announcing another bail-out of the banks. Satoshi later urged adopters to 'Escape the arbitrary inflation risk of centrally managed currencies!'[5] Bitcoin is just the sort of 'technological advancement' Thiel was describing, by which political change might be achieved.

The belief of libertarians such as Thiel and Nakamoto in small government, low taxes and individual responsibility has a lot of sympathisers operating in the Wild West of new technology. Their aim is to disrupt and improve. They know government is behind the curve. Many call themselves ancaps – anarcho-capitalists. This is a growing movement of like-minded, extremely competent people working in the realms of computer code, whose aim is to disrupt and improve the world order. Their means are not political activism but technological advancement. The tax and other implications are enormous.

## What Coinbase's run-in with the IRS tells us about the future of crypto and governments

The bitcoin community has invented its own word to describe critics who refuse to see bitcoin's enormous potential – nocoiners. Nocoiners make the argument that if bitcoin becomes 'too big', governments will just make it illegal. Given bitcoin's potential use in money laundering and black markets, there are plenty of reasons by which a government could justify such a decision. On a practical level, a government could close down major exchanges, ban banks from hosting accounts of bitcoin companies and make it illegal to use bitcoin. But it could not close down bitcoin. This was built into bitcoin's essential design – it is a distributed network with no central point of failure. It is not linked to any territory or organisation. What's more, making something illegal does not stop people using it. The war on drugs showed that. Attempts to shut down other peer-to-peer networks – the torrent websites of yesteryear – did not work. If governments try to stop people using bitcoin, individuals will just use VPNs and Tor to transact, or move their coins offline.

But crypto is now an established multi-billion-dollar industry. A ban would meet with multiple legal suits. Blockchain tech has a myriad of applications beyond an alternative system of cash for the Internet – there are no good grounds to shut many of these down. I've no doubt more authoritarian governments will ban it nonetheless, but this new economy will simply relocate to jurisdictions where it is welcome, and those jurisdictions will enjoy the economic growth that comes with new tech, while the authoritarian economies get left behind. Even if all the governments of the world united (impossible, I would have thought) in making cryptocurrency illegal, it is unlikely they could stop it. They could drive it underground, but you cannot uninvent something. The cat is out of the bag.

Governments will, however, force reporting requirements on major crypto exchanges. In 2016, the IRS tried to compel the US's largest crypto exchange, Coinbase, to hand over records for some 500,000 customers, as it sought to collect back taxes. Coinbase fought the summons in court. The IRS subsequently lowered its demand to ask only for details of accounts with bitcoin transactions worth $20,000 or more. Coinbase tried to argue that the narrower request was still an illegal imposition, but the court ruled in favour of the IRS. 'The summons,' wrote US District Judge Jacqueline Corley, defending the ruling, 'serves the IRS's legitimate purpose of investigating Coinbase account holders who may not have paid federal taxes on their virtual currency profits.' The resulting order meant that the details and historical transaction records of a much lower 14,355 accounts were handed over, along with records of over nine million transactions.

What drove the demands in the first place was non-payment of taxes. Between 2013 and 2015, the value of a bitcoin went from $13 to over $1,100, yet only 802 Americans filed the correct tax forms.[6] This is probably a tiny percentage of those who made considerable capital gains.

There are several morals to this tale. First, tax evasion in crypto currency, especially of capital gains, is commonplace. Second, governments will come after unpaid gains where they can. If crypto gets bigger, they will be even more likely to come after unpaid taxes, and more aggressively. Third, exchanges such as Coinbase, centralised in one jurisdiction, are vulnerable, even if they try to fight back through the courts. The requirements of the tax collector will trump them. Those who take their crypto trading elsewhere, however, to exchanges in safer jurisdictions, or to decentralised exchanges, will be harder to impose requirements on. Particularly if they are nomads.

### The predictions of two 1990s fund managers that came true

In their 1997 book *The Sovereign Individual*, James Davidson and William Rees-Mogg made the argument that the nation state is in its final days. Five hundred years ago, the church was the regulator. It looked after many of the public services – education and care, for example – which today fall to government. The word 'politics' did not even exist. But with the invention of the printing press and other developments, information was liberated and slowly the church's power began to fade. The nation state filled the vacuum. Today, with the invention of the Internet, the nation state and its politics are beginning a similar decline.

From a tax perspective, it is easy to agree. The system is increasingly demanding; the taxes needed to fuel it are drying up.

A citizen gives up certain freedoms and pays taxes, the authors argue, to secure certain rights. The state needs control to maintain the belief of citizens, but if it loses control of money, borders, information, business, crime and, most of all, trust, the myth is broken. The transaction ceases. The shift from an industrial to an information-based society will liberate individuals and reduce the power of government. The nation state will not endure in its present form. The winners will be the smart, the enterprising and the mobile. Cyberspace creates opportunities regardless of location. Borders are irrelevant. It will become easier to create assets beyond the reach of typical government coercion. Unprecedented financial independence will become possible. If money can be earned anywhere, there is no need to live somewhere with punitive taxation or limited freedoms. If conditions in one location become onerous, the individual who is nimble enough can up sticks and move to another. The sovereign individual can pack up and relocate tomorrow. So can the software company. The industrial manufacturer cannot.

Governments that charge too much will effectively drive away their best customers. Sovereignty will be commercialised. People will choose their jurisdictions the same way they might choose an insurer. Those jurisdictions that fail to provide a suitable mix of services at a good price will face the same insolvency pressures as a bad business.

As more business and wealth moves online into borderless, intangible digital assets, governments will experience a steep decrease in taxation revenue. For those that have obligations based on much higher revenue projections, this will be problematic. It will likely lead to financial crisis and then political upheaval. This in itself will prejudice the future of these nation states.

The digital nomad is, surely, Davidson and Rees-Mogg's sovereign individual. His money is crypto currency. The future they outlined is proving prophetic.

## The smartphone and the scalability of tech

Whenever there is a terrorist attack, or any kind of panic, somebody always seems to video it on their phone. Within a few minutes those images are uploaded and spread across the net for all to see. A passer-by with a smartphone is ahead of professional news teams, which take longer to mobilise. It means that the world, or that part of it with Internet access, can be right on top of what is going on at any time.

Imagine if, in the trenches of the First World War, soldiers had had smartphones. Just as people do now, they would have filmed what was going on. Thousands, perhaps hundreds of thousands of videos of the unspeakable atrocities would have been shared across the net every day. The people of Europe would surely have demanded an immediate end to the conflict.

Technology is empowering people, enabling them to hold their leaders to account. The smallest detail is scrutinised, the whitest of lies exposed; even the slightest transgression is brought to the public eye.

We are now able to do millions of things that we were not previously able to do. We have instant access to unlimited information for free. We can communicate with almost anyone in the world at zero cost. We can make films that 20 years ago would have required multi-million-dollar budgets. All you need is a phone.

Walking past the homeless charity at St Martin-in-the-Fields by Trafalgar Square the other morning, I saw a queue of 20 or so people sitting on the ground up against a wall with their sleeping bags and other accoutrements, waiting to be given breakfast. A good 80% of them were playing on their phones. Even the homeless now have smartphones. Knowledge, communication and media have been socialised – far more successfully than healthcare and education – in that they have been made widely available to all for almost (not quite) zero cost – and with zero government involvement.

More people in the world now have a mobile phone than have a toilet, according to a 2013 UN survey.[7] By 2023, that mobile phone will mostly be a smartphone, according to Sony Ericsson:[8] there will be over seven billion smartphones in a global population of eight billion.[9] (Although not every subscription equates to a user, it's not unreasonable to assume that something like 70% do.) Meanwhile, global mobile broadband subscriptions will reach nine billion by 2023 – *more* than there are people. The vast majority of the population will soon be online with a smartphone. That smartphone will be the first way by which many of the world's poor will experience the Internet.

Suddenly those in the developing world are gaining access to vast amounts of information – information we in the developed world now take for granted – from which they were previously excluded by their lack of connectivity. How will they use that new-found knowledge? Thousands of apps will enable them to do things they were not previously able to do. The Internet is opening up to them. What will they do with all the new contacts they are about to make and networks they are about to join? Perhaps, more significantly, there is now the opportunity for financial inclusion.

A stroll through any developing-world city shows there is no shortage of people who want to talk to you, to sell you stuff, to trade and exchange with you. The world is full of people who want to learn, communicate, do business and, generally, improve their lot. But financial exclusion – not having a bank account and thus a means to accept or make payment – means that many are prevented from engaging in any sort of commerce beyond their immediate vicinity.

Financial exclusion is a major reason why landlines could not grow (the peak was 1.26 billion landlines in 2006; the number has been falling ever since)[10] where mobile telephony has. You need a bank account to get a landline. Most in the developing world do not have one. The telephone companies cannot justify the investment and the infrastructure was never built. But you do not need a bank account to get a mobile phone, just cash. More people are able to get one, and supply has increased to meet that demand. As a result, it is not just information that such people are starting to experience for the first time, but financial inclusion. Though even today over 30% of the global population – two billion people – remains unbanked,[11] just three years ago it was closer to half. Thanks to fintech and Internet connectivity, that number is rapidly falling.

So many new possibilities are opening up to the world's poor that did not previously exist – to educate themselves, to make new contacts, to create, to buy and sell. Meanwhile the developed world will have several billion potential new people to outsource jobs to, to sell products to and to receive products from. That is a lot of new trade. Trade and exchange is how we progress.

However, for the person coming online with his or her first smartphone, the quickest way to any kind of financial inclusion is via crypto currency. You can get a wallet in a few seconds, and are immediately in a position where you can accept crypto as payment for your goods or services. The implications of a developing world coming online for the first time going straight to crypto are enormous. Great marketing steps are being taken to get, for example, central Africa trading via crypto. The potential international scalability of crypto currency dwarfs the scalability of national currencies, which are limited by their borders.

Exciting times lie ahead. The smartphone is the portal. It and its associated tech will do more for global poverty than any amount of government aid, in that it will enable people to trade and exchange their way to prosperity – and, eventually, be able to afford the sanitation and other basic services that have previously been unavailable to them.

When you consider the sheer weight of numbers, the possibilities are quite daunting. My view is that we are at the early stages of a global economic boom of historic proportions. Rather as the Industrial Revolution enabled many to escape rural poverty and, within a generation, form a new middle class, so is something similar about to happen, but on a much bigger scale. This boom will take place largely in cyberspace, trading intangibles, hard-to-tax digital goods and services, often using non-government currencies, in a world where national borders are not so clear.

Not all developments will be 'good', of course. Many people will use their new-found power for nefarious purposes. But the greater flow will be positive and progressive. Nor will progress be equal. Many will be held back, perhaps by tyrannical or censorious governments, or by unfortunate geographical circumstances. The process will be slower for them. But the sheer weight of prosperity and progress elsewhere means this is a war that those who would hold their people back will eventually lose. Nor will this prosperity be instantaneous. It will take time. It is a generational shift. But it is still an inevitable tide in the affairs of men.

A global economic boom implies greater tax revenues, but not if a large portion is taking place in the intangible, borderless digital world. A global economic boom also implies technically empowered, better-informed people, more trade across borders, higher expectations of government and greater ability to hold it to account.

# Chapter 17

## *Digital Breaks Free*

*The avoidance of taxes is the only intellectual pursuit that*
*still carries any reward.*[1]

John Maynard Keynes

Amazon became the West's biggest retailer without owning a single shop. It upended traditional retail by delivering products to your door for less money than you would pay in store. It avoided the cost of retail premises and the property taxes and business rates that come with them. In employing gig workers, as we have seen, it avoided many of the tax costs of employment. With operations in different jurisdictions, Amazon minimises corporation taxes too. And with its merchants dispatching products in one country for delivery in another, it often doesn't pay VAT either.

Amazon is not alone. The success of so many Internet giants has been their ability to offer a superior product or service at lower prices than competitors. They are able to sell at lower prices because their business models avoid 'traditional' costs altogether. Cost of government, be it via regulation or taxation, is one of the biggest outlays a business faces. If a company can avoid it legitimately and without reputational loss, it will. That extra cost can often mean the difference between success and failure.

China's Alibaba is now the world's largest retailer and it carries no stock. Uber is the world's largest taxi firm and it owns no cars. Facebook is the largest media company yet it creates hardly any content. Airbnb owns no property. TripAdvisor does not own a hotel. They are all 'platforms'. In an online digital world without borders, where exactly are these platforms based? Where is the intellectual property? Where is the service they deliver? Which of the company's subsidiaries actually makes the money? Who then should they pay tax to? How much, and why?

The iPhone has parts manufactured all over the world; it is assembled in China and sold somewhere else. Apple can pretty much choose how much tax it wants to pay and to whom. One EU estimate was that it paid less than 0.01% tax on profits of over $100 billion.[2] Tax systems have not kept up with the innovation.

Amazon famously exploited a 1992 ruling by the US Supreme Court that a company does not have to pay state taxes if there is no physical store or other tangible presence in the state. Even though people in, say, Arkansas can buy things from Amazon, the company has no store there and so does not have to pay taxes.[3] In a world in which one business model pays taxes and another does not, it is obvious which will succeed.

But not only are these platforms bypassing existing tax structures, they are putting companies that abide by them out of business. Uber put paid to the local minicab office. Goodness knows how many high street shops have gone out of business thanks to the likes of Amazon. As these local companies fold, so are the taxes they once paid lost to the government. Meanwhile the revenues of the platforms make their way to company HQ in Unknownland.

## Why companies avoid making money

Once upon a time, companies existed to deliver some desirable product or service, and make money by doing so. Today, largely because of high corporation taxes, profit has almost become a liability.

The 1970s and 80s saw the emergence of the cable television giants in the US. As they built up audiences and attempted to dominate regions, unknowingly they also set out the template for today's multinational tech platforms. Profits meant taxes, and taxes, according to John C. Malone, the billionaire boss of Tele-Communications Inc. (TCI), were 'leakage'[4] – unnecessary and to be avoided where possible. To avoid them, he made expansionary acquisitions and leveraged up the company with debt (to be written off against profit), declaring he'd rather pay interest than taxes. It might not have had profits, but all the while TCI had cash flow. The term EBITDA (earnings before interest, tax, depreciation and amortisation), now a standard business valuation model, only came to be as Malone sought to educate his investors.

Uber, Facebook, Netflix and many other minimal-tax-paying expansionary giants do the same thing today, only on a much greater, international scale. Even when they are not making taxable profits, they are expanding their businesses, growing their user bases and generating huge revenues. Business is good, as is evidenced by their performance in the stock market and the statements their CEOs make to investors, but many are paying as little tax as they can get away with. As I write, it has just been announced that Facebook's 2018 UK tax bill will be less than 1% of its £1.3 billion in UK sales. There might be legitimate write-offs, but deep down everyone knows Facebook makes more money than its tax bill suggests.

Despite being multi-billion-dollar international corporations, many of these businesses remain deliberately unprofitable in order to reduce tax obligations. Acquisitions, research and development, and other forms of expansion are undertaken so as to have more to write off against taxes. Vast swathes of would-have-been profit is owed to offshore structures in low-tax jurisdictions for supplying the brands, trademarks, patents and intellectual property. Starbucks, for example, argues that the lion's share of its profits is generated by its brand. While its onshore operations may make little profit, despite huge turnover, the Starbucks subsidiary, which owns the brand and to whom onshore operations must pay brand rights, is located elsewhere, and so taxes are avoided. Rupert Murdoch's media empire does something similar. Even the

*Guardian*, bastion of moral superiority that it professes to be, uses an offshore vehicle in the Cayman Islands to reduce its tax bills – thus did it avoid tax on the £302 million profit it realised for the sale of *Auto Trader* in 2008.

Though many might see this tax strategy as abhorrent, it is entirely legal. Such strategies will continue for as long as we live in a globalised world with different tax laws in different countries, even with all the tax shaming that goes on. The shortcoming is in the law. If such practice is to be prevented, then laws must adapt, which they have hitherto failed to do. Meanwhile, those who are unable to engage such strategies in their own tax affairs pay a disproportionate amount and grow increasingly discontent with the blatant injustice.

Value is determined by market share as much as it is by profitability. Tomorrow's profit potential is more important than today's profit. Disney has something like 30 times as much revenue as Netflix and yet both have similar market caps. The market will wait for profit, even earnings; today it wants market share.

But if a company is not profitable, there is no tax revenue to government.

With this focus on market share, many tech companies offer their services for free, and we have seen the emergence of a sort of digital barter. As the saying goes, 'When the Internet is free, you are the product.' Tech giants have created entirely new markets in the valuable commodity that is data, especially your personal data – almost a currency in itself. You get Gmail, Google Maps or Google Search for nothing. In exchange, Google gets information about you. Its domination of the Internet increases and its valuation increases with this expanded market share. The taxman gets nothing.

If Google then sells that data, or uses it to sell advertising space, there is a taxable transaction, but not if it sells it in a different jurisdiction.

Soon these tech giants will begin issuing their own private money systems, likely based on some kind of cryptographic model similar to bitcoin, although more centralised. These coins will be exchangeable for goods and services, even data, as platforms become self-sufficient economic communities, with people trading amongst themselves using Uber dollars or Airbnb coin. How to tax these? Taxing the content creators of the future, who do not take payment but accept 'rewards' in Facebook or YouTube coin, is not so straightforward. Entirely new economies will emerge that bypass existing tax structures, because money itself is changing. Will governments take tax payments in Facebook coin, and then use Facebook coin to make their own payments?

If a business wants to compete, it will also have to find ways to keep the cost of government down. Money that in another time might have made its way to the state via the taxman no longer does so. Governments are going to have to rethink the way they tax people.

You can be sure that this innovation will continue. On umpteen different fronts, technology is doing to the twentieth-century large-government model exactly what the Internet did to media and publishing in the 2000s. Just as the music and newspaper industries were unprepared, so have governments been shown to be now, only more so.

There is a battle brewing between tech and government. Different jurisdictions are taking different approaches. The solution of the Donald Trump administration in the US has been, generally speaking, lower taxes and amnesty. To encourage companies back onshore, Trump slashed corporate taxes by 40% from 35% to 21%. In addition, companies with overseas operations will not pay corporation taxes at the US rate in that jurisdiction, but at the local rate in which that operation is based. So if a US corporation has a Mexican and a UK subsidiary, its Mexican subsidiary will pay the Mexican corporation tax rate and its UK subsidiary will pay the UK rate.

In addition, to encourage the repatriation of money held abroad, companies with offshore capital have eight years to pay a one-off tax on cash and cash equivalents (bonds, usually) of 15.5% and 8% (previously they would have had to pay 35%).

It is estimated that some $3 trillion was held overseas at the time the new tax laws were brought in. Eight firms (the likes of Apple, Microsoft and Google) hold about two thirds of that. After two quarters, some $460 billion has come back onshore.[5]

The EU, on the other hand, perhaps more than any other jurisdiction, has taken the fight to the tech giants. This fight could have grave repercussions for Ireland. What's more, it could change the constitution of the EU itself.

## *The EU's war on tech*

In the 1990s, Ireland deliberately imposed low levels of corporation tax to make the country attractive to multinationals wanting access to the EU. It was a successful decision that led to Ireland, with its English-speaking, educated workforce, becoming the most attractive place in the world for foreign direct investment[6] – the so-called Celtic Tiger. Apple was perhaps the most notable company to base itself there, but it was by no means the only one. Over a thousand multinationals in a wide variety of different businesses made Ireland the hub of their European operations, including Google, Hewlett Packard, IBM, Facebook, LinkedIn, Twitter, Pfizer, GlaxoSmithKline and Genzyme.

After around three years of investigations, in 2017 the EU demanded roughly €250 million in back taxes from Amazon and the extraordinary sum of €13 billion from Apple. Apple has since paid, and Ireland is holding the money in escrow while the decision is appealed – a process that will take several years. The inference is that Ireland no longer has the power to enforce its own rates of corporate tax (the EU has long disliked Irish corporate tax rates). Without such low rates, and with the tax changes afoot in the US, the attractiveness of Ireland as a base falls and its business model is jeopardised. The outcome of the Apple appeal has major constitutional implications for both Ireland and the EU. Who has the power?

The EU is also trying to institute a 3% revenue tax on digital services provided by large corporations. This idea has been gestating for some time. It has met with support in some quarters and criticism elsewhere (turnover taxes are highly problematic – profit and turnover are very different beasts – so they affect different businesses' models inequitably). For any tax legislation at the EU level to be adopted, however, there must be unanimity among member countries, so it is far from certain that such a tax could be enacted. As a result, the EU is trying to change its laws.

In 2017, European Commission President Jean-Claude Juncker said that a 'qualified majority' – 55% of member states representing at least 65% of the EU population – should be enough to ensure 'fair taxes of the digital industry'. But he also wants this 'qualified majority' to enable other taxation, including 'simpler decision-making' on VAT, 'a common consolidated corporate tax base' and a financial transactions tax. Majority rather than unanimity will 'improve our ability to speak with one voice', he added in 2018.[7] Such legislation would effectively give Brussels greater licence to impose taxes. It would sideline any smaller countries that might oppose any such rulings, and centralise power in Brussels away from nation states. This would be a major constitutional change to the EU. The implications are tremendous.

It is one example of the changes to international and national power dynamics that are coming in the years ahead, as inevitable changes to tax laws are implemented.

## How to tax 3D printing and the Internet of things

The taxing of tech is only going to get more complicated. Tax laws have not kept up with the value chains, so even if a company wants to be compliant (and most do; they don't want to break the law), it is often hard to do so. With servers in multiple jurisdictions delivering remotely into other jurisdictions, where is the profit? Where are the costs? Where is the IP? Where is the value created? Where is the VAT payable? What about the risk of double taxation? These and many other such questions remain unanswered.

There will be similar problems with 3D printing (assuming it takes off). You might have a 3D printer in your home, or somewhere nearby. When you buy a product, instructions will be sent to your printer by a server in another jurisdiction (likely somewhere secure but remote, where land and energy costs are cheap), using code from another and IP from yet another. Again, where is the value created? Where is the profit? Who is making the money? How do you tax it? Who taxes it? There are all sorts of geographical challenges. Meanwhile, manufacturing will be turned on its head as existing factories, warehouses and transportation systems – as well as customs – get bypassed. Long-standing protocols to tax the movement of goods and the supply of services will no longer apply. Government income is jeopardised.

The Internet of things (IOT) will see more and more devices at home and work connected to the Internet. Sensors of different kinds will be everywhere. They will then exchange data with each other. In simple terms, the heating in your home might know you are coming home because it is linked to the location tracker in your smart watch, and so it will switch itself on to ensure your house is the right temperature when you get back. The lights will come on as you arrive. The same principle will be applied to energy management at the metropolitan level. If there is nobody walking down a street, there is no point lighting it. IOT will have applications in transportation, manufacturing, agriculture, medicine, care, education, asset management, environmental monitoring – in fact it is hard to find areas where it won't.

Often this exchange of data will involve the easily taxable sale of goods or a service. Your fridge detects you are out of milk or cheese and orders a delivery. A flying drone shows up 30 minutes later with the goods. Often, however, there will not be such a transparent sale, just an exchange of information or data. Even if that exchange might build wealth of some kind, there may not necessarily be a taxable financial transaction. Often the definition of what are goods and what is a service will be blurred. Transactions might not take place in government currency. There will be the same cross-border geographical challenges we have been discussing. Quite how governments will tax it all is not yet clear. There might be sales or transaction taxes, some kind of communications, telecoms or Internet tax – though the latter will be difficult in the US since Congress declared a 'permanent moratorium on Internet access taxes and on multiple and discriminatory taxes on electronic commerce'.

'Governments of the Industrial World, you weary giants of flesh and steel,' wrote Grateful Dead lyricist John Perry Barlow, in his 'Declaration of the Independence of Cyberspace'. 'I come from Cyberspace, the new home of Mind. On behalf of the future, I ask you of the past to leave us alone. You are not welcome among us. You have no sovereignty where we gather . . . Cyberspace does not lie within your borders.'[8] This widely circulated paper, written in 1996, has no legal backing, of course, but it captured an essential aspect of the Internet that has created a major problem for governments: how to tax multinational digital intangibles.

This disruption to the tax model will continue. In the 2020s we will see the emergence of decentralised autonomous organisations (DAOs). DAOs have no company HQ, no formal organisation at their heart, no base in any jurisdiction and no central point of failure. Like bitcoin, they are distributed networks, with no main body to close down or tax. Their currency is their own issued tokens, outside of existing fiat economies. Their platforms and businesses are automated by code, often written on an open-source basis. Many DAO developers have crypto-activist or libertarian worldviews, and have stated that their intention is to replace the state altogether. If you thought governments were unprepared for the disruption brought to their revenue models by the tech giants of the 2000s and 2010s, they are even less prepared for DAOs.

New technology has put governments in their current predicament. Tax laws were written in a non-digital age for a physical world with clearly defined borders. Unless governments can figure out a way to tax the intangible digital world fairly – in other words, in a way that doesn't kill trade – then the large-state social democratic model will fail. There will not be the revenue for it to survive. The economic inequality of one group being heavily taxed while another makes itself exempt will be unsustainable: there will be too much popular anger.

When William the Conqueror wanted to value England, he sent out surveyors to inspect the country. Their findings were compiled in the Domesday Book – a tax survey of the country. Assessing value has always meant measuring, counting and valuing tangible things. There is a story of British inventor Michael Faraday explaining electricity, and the discoveries he had made about it, to the then Chancellor of the Exchequer, an increasingly impatient William Gladstone. 'But, after all, what use is it?' Gladstone asked petulantly. Faraday's response was immediate: 'Why, sir, there is every probability that you will soon be able to tax it!'[9]

The challenge for governments will be to find a way of taxing the borderless digital economy. Even stock markets struggle to value intangible tech companies on traditional measures, leading to the constant accusation by traditionalists that such companies are bubbles. Economies have changed. Tax systems must change too.

'Governments can most effectively collect taxes on things that can't move,' said Milton Friedman with great foresight. 'Cyberspace is going to make it very much more difficult for government to collect taxes, and that will have a very important effect on reducing the role that governments can play.'[10]

What governments have on their side, as this story unfolds, is swathes of data to process. Tech may be the problem, but it is also the solution.

# Chapter 18

## *Data: The Taxman's New Friend*

'Digital technology is the cause, and it's the remedy,' says Melissa Geiger, KPMG's head of international tax. I'm meeting with Melissa and her colleague Chris Downing, partner in tax, specialising in tech. Chris agrees. 'Tax administrations love digital and they hate digital.'

I've come to their impressive offices in Canary Wharf, London, to seek out answers as to the future of tax, and specifically governments' increasingly vexing problem of how to tax the intangible economy. At present there does not appear to be any silver bullet. But if there is one, it lies somewhere in the haystack of technology – especially data analysis.

First up, digital technology will improve the efficiency of existing collection.

'It's an unprecedented answer to what they call the tax gap – the gap between the amount of tax they think they should be collecting and what they actually do collect,' says Chris. 'It's not just the grey economy or the black economy, or cash transactions. It's things like the errors that occur with a guy going to see his accountant with a bag of receipts. Now we capture information digitally. Electronic invoicing, blockchain, real-time reporting – all of these types of things are putting governments in a position now where they can maximise revenue in a way that they could never do before. We don't necessarily need to disrupt the tax base or make major policies about new taxes if we can collect the right amount that's owed. If we can generate an extra 2%, 3%, or 4% of tax revenues by doing that, then some of the other stuff is less important.'

Digital technology will also improve the efficacy of collection itself. It's easy to see the computer in that driverless car making automated payments for every mile it covers. The digital database that is blockchain, visible for all to see, used to record information and transfer anything from currency to data to assets, also has implications for tax collection. One example might be, say, in the large container ship and its contents passing into port. Insurance, duties, fees and taxes, based on that ship's contents, can all be automatically tracked and paid without any human involvement. The system is cheaper and more accurate.

Many central banks around the world have made noises about eventually putting their own national currencies on a blockchain. Estonia will likely be the first. Blockchain tech is already in use on a number of its registries – national health, judicial, legislative, security and commercial. If central banks do adopt blockchain tech – and that is a big if – every transaction will be recorded, with the provenance and destination fully auditable. Non-compliance, whether by error or design, will get that much harder and the tax gap will shrink dramatically.

Tech will do the work of officials: if you do something where a tax or a fine is payable, tech will automatically remove the money from your wallet. Everything can be coded.

Electronic invoicing is also coming into the mainstream. 'In Brazil, they have digitised almost all of their processes around tax collection,' Chris tells me. 'Invoices must be submitted electronically in real time, so data is provided in real time. You have to provide electronic versions of ledgers at the end of periods. Thus the government has a "3D view" of any business activity taking place at any given moment. It will know your likely tax liability almost before you do. They levy 100% fines on you for everything you have got wrong. So unless you are on your game, the risk is your tax liability is worse.'

This is all rather too authoritarian and Orwellian for my liking, and I say so.

'It's funny. If you look at the most technologically advanced tax administrations, they are probably now in emerging markets,' he observes. 'Because I don't think public opinion stops them from getting things done. They don't have to worry about public consensus, they just go and do it. We have seen it in Brazil, we have seen it in Mexico, we are seeing it in China. In Mexico, they have an electronic invoicing system too. Every time you raise an invoice to a customer it has to go through a government portal and be registered.'

'Every invoice?' I say.

Chris and Melissa both nod. 'Every invoice. Even if you are a tiny business,' says Chris. 'If you claim a VAT credit back on something, that invoice has to go through that government portal and be certified. If it isn't, you don't claim it back. They are the central hub of information and can certify everything. Errors from the biggest corporations down to the smallest businesses, whether deliberate or inadvertent, will get caught.'

'Do you think other countries will go that way?' I ask.

'They already are,' says Melissa.

Italy is introducing electronic invoicing. There is an EU directive for business-to-government invoices. Even if laws remain backward, reporting requirements and collection methods are advancing all the time. Tax authorities are demanding more and more information from companies: data about their suppliers and customers, digital invoices, transaction times, accounting entries. They are using AI and robotics to check and cross-check that information with other tax records. Armed with better information, they can get more aggressive in their collection.

'If I have fifteen plumbers and I can see that they pay this amount of tax and they get this amount of revenue, I can immediately see a stand-out one,' says Melissa, 'but it has got much more sophisticated than that. In one country – I am not going to say which – they were able to generate what they thought a company's tax liability should be from some numbers they saw on spending and R&D in a newspaper article.'

We are just beginning to witness the power of data, data analytics and machine learning. Already Amazon seems to know, based not only on my past buying habits, but on other unlikely connections, what I want to buy before I have even begun typing. As early as 2012, Target knew a teenage girl was pregnant before she did. In 2015, researchers found that based on just 300 Facebook likes an algorithm could predict a subject's answer better than their spouse.[1] Now your sex, race and political party affiliation can be worked out just by your Facebook likes. The Donald Trump election campaign was able to win the key swing states of Pennsylvania, Florida, Ohio, Michigan and Wisconsin by analysing data drawn from multiple different sources to target 'persuadable voters' and then personalise ads to them.[2] Mums, for example, would be targeted with gentler ads with soft voices expressing concern about the future; young men with something more brash and aggressive. The company hired to do the work, Cambridge Analytica, found that a preference for American cars was a strong indication of a potential Trump voter. If data records then showed somebody who had bought, say, a Ford or a Chevrolet in recent years but had not voted, they were a 'persuadable voter' and specifically targeted. Bots and algorithms did all the legwork.

Something similar is happening in tax. HMRC, for example, has a powerful computer program called Connect, which already has more information than all the data in the British Library. At the same time, it has extended its data-gathering powers. It can force platforms such as Amazon, Apple, Airbnb and PayPal to hand over data, including the names and addresses of sellers and advertisers.[3] It can already put together a detailed picture of most taxpayers, and can purchase more data if necessary. Just as Amazon knows what you might want to buy, so will the taxman have firm ideas of how much tax you should be paying.

One early success for Connect was when it noted a string of credit card transactions at a private London address. The house was worth millions of pounds, yet was owned outright by someone with no tax history. His only visible income was a state pension. A routine Internet search found an escort agency advertising from the address. An HMRC investigation followed, and the owner admitted to having been trading there for over six years.

Tax authorities know that certain habits are indicative of a person avoiding tax, and so machines will trawl data for behavioural patterns. Put crudely, the guy who does Google searches about tax havens, buys expensive champagne and opens accounts with bitcoin exchanges in Liechtenstein is worth greater investigation than the civil servant with an interest in model train sets. Bots will scrape social media for evidence. If a trader is declaring low income, but on Facebook he is posting pictures of himself on expensive holidays, then that tells you a story. Several individuals from the TV show *My Big Fat Gypsy Wedding* were seen on camera spending thousands on lavish family weddings. HMRC realised it was undeclared income and soon came knocking. Ranking tax returns by risk enabled the IRS to get 25 times more tax evaders without increasing the number of investigations.[4] Signs of ghosting and moonlighting will be looked out for. Landlords worldwide are increasingly being required by local authorities to register their properties. If this results in a system of licensing, part of that will require registration for tax. If a company fits a certain trade profile where there is a history of evasion, they will also face greater scrutiny. Again, bots will be doing the work.

As machines learn more and more, not only will you be scrutinised, you will also be increasingly quantified and ranked. This will affect decisions about the jobs you are offered, the loan deals you qualify for, the price of insurance you must pay, the level of service you are able to get. Everything will be rateable. Tech will make informed predictions about you: when you are likely to die or become ill; how hard you are likely to work; how successful you are likely to be at a job; how faithful you are likely to be to your spouse; how likely you are to commit a crime; how much money you are likely to earn; whether you are likely to go bankrupt or commit tax fraud. Accurate profiles can be built using qualitative methods such as psychographics. Platforms will not necessarily treat people equally: those with the right qualities will get better treatment than those without. Machine learning, one company claims, can already predict if a person is a criminal with 90% accuracy using a single photograph of their face.[5] It can predict crime on the basis of circumstantial evidence. The moral implications of predictive probability in collecting taxes are considerable.

The authoritarian will argue that if you have nothing to hide, then there is nothing to worry about. The libertarian will argue that this kind of activity violates both privacy and freedom. No matter where you stand on the argument, this is what is coming, pretty much wherever you are in the world. Both technology and unbalanced government finances make it inevitable.

'The digital lifeworld will bring about a transformation in the capacity of humans to scrutinize each other,' writes Jamie Susskind in his book *Future Politics*.[6] 'First, whole swathes of human life that were unrecordable or too complex to be grasped in their entirety will be seen and understood by those with the means of scrutiny. Second, this scrutiny will be increasingly *intimate*, taking place in spaces we previously thought of as "private". Third, the information gathered through scrutiny may be increasingly *imperishable*, outlasting our memories and even our lives. Fourth, our behaviour will become much more *predictable* to machines tasked with looking to the future. Finally, our lives will be increasingly rateable, subject to scores, ratings and rakings . . . The cumulative result will be scrutiny beyond anything we've experienced in the past, and a corresponding increase in the power to which we are subject.'

Tax collectors will use every tool available to them – from scrutiny to automated payment at source. Right or wrong, this is where we are going.

Tax authorities will make no secret of how much data they have, using fear and guilt to deter evasion and avoidance. There will be the threat of prosecution for evaders, with lower penalties for those who come forward.

'A country like Brazil,' says Chris, 'may have the most digitally enabled tax administration. It's also the country where you will probably find the businesses with the biggest tax teams, because you are employing armies of people to try and comply with regulations and deal with them. Could you see a scenario in the future where you have got a company with two people earning the money and ten managing the regulatory chaos that follows behind it? I think you generally could if you don't find alignment and consistency in how these things work.'

The dance goes on: between collector and payer, between freedom and taxation, between collecting as much as you can and not hampering business activity. The tools may have changed. But the dance is eternal.

## This is an international effort

Data sharing and analysis is becoming an international effort. Tax authorities are already sharing their data and more besides. The Common Reporting Standard enables details of bank balances, interest, dividends, capital gains and income in 47 different nations worldwide to be shared with home governments. Another sign of cross-border collaboration came when Swiss bank Credit Suisse was recently subject to simultaneous investigation by the UK, France and the Netherlands.

Nevertheless, tax systems themselves remain unhomogenised. 'Regulation is so fractured and fragmented – it's crazy,' sighs Melissa. 'That's the thing that most of our clients struggle with – how do you go about complying with so many different regulations.'

'The thing that almost everybody craves,' says Chris, 'is greater certainty. And yet every time I see the OECD coming out with something big, country-by-country reporting, for example, everybody interprets it differently, so you end up with 57 different varieties, none of them saying the same thing.'

Both Chris and Melissa see greater fragmentation in the years ahead. Competition is the cause. It's almost certainly going to drive corporate business taxes down, they say.

There is the role of so-called tax havens to consider in all this, although the definition of what a tax haven is varies according to political alignment. One person's competitive rate of tax is another's haven. But as long as the option remains for different nations to offer different tax rates to attract international business and invest-ment, competition will remain and it will drive down corporate rates. Some tax campaigners have called for a global concerted effort to clamp down on tax havens, penalising them with trade embargoes and so on, but such aggressive measures, coordinated internationally by the major economies of the world, look unlikely. Is France going to stop trading with Switzerland? The United Kingdom with Ireland? The US with its own state of Delaware? More than 50% of global trade passes through tax havens, says Nicholas Shaxon in his book *Treasure Islands*.[7] Some $7.6 trillion of private wealth is stored in offshore tax havens, according to Gabriel Zucman in his *Hidden Wealth of Nations*, amounting to 8% of global household wealth.[8] It would be quite some embargo.

There is also the strong argument that tax havens play an import-ant international role, checking governments that might be inclined to more punitive levels of taxation and providing a means for indi-viduals to escape authoritarian states that have little respect for private property. No matter what the political consensus of the time, your wealth, you might well argue, is not public property.

'I wonder if you are going to end up with two types of tax,' suggests Melissa. 'One for tangibles, where you say they have got to be here, so we are taking 20 or 30%. And one for intangibles. You can go anywhere in the world, so come to Ireland for 12.5%, come to the UK for 10%. You'd then be promoting a two-tier system between old-world physical interaction and new-world intangible interaction.'

Some have deemed Ireland a tax haven because of its 12.5% corporation tax. Its workers, who pay a rate of 40% on earnings above €38,500, might not see it that way. And therein lies another problem: the economic distortion created by taxing different areas of the economy at different rates. Taxing income so heavily but capital so lightly is a major factor in the rising economic inequality we have seen in recent years, and the ensuing political unrest, as we shall see in the next chapter.

Perhaps, I suggest, standardisation might come by the back door. Multinationals almost all use robot process automation (RPA) in their accounting. It works 24 hours a day, unlike humans, analysing every transaction the company makes, automating payments, sales and business tax returns and other routine activities, all the time making increasingly informed decisions and judgements as the machines rapidly learn. Data from every region, every arm of the corporation is fed into central repositories – effectively data warehouses from multiple spreadsheets around the world. Analytics match invoices with accounting data and information from suppliers and clients in order to increase efficiencies as well as, as accountants put it, 'identify tax planning opportunities'. Data and data analytics are being improved all the time. This is the digitisation of tax administration. Despite widely varying tax systems, there is conformity in the software. Such centralised data can then be used to settle different audits in different jurisdictions. If one nation sees an audit deal reached in one country, they will expect the same in theirs or better. Thus we stumble to 'one global tax' by the back door.

'Maybe one day,' says Chris. 'But we are a long way from that. You'll see more fragmentation first. Any new leader who comes in, or an old one who wants re-electing – they're going to think, "I'm going to reform the tax system to help investment – just like Trump did." The desire to get elected or re-elected will outweigh some directive from the OECD.'

'We will get to a consensus phase,' says Melissa. 'But we have to get through the disruptive phase first.'

## How tech is enabling the tax justice warriors

While tax laws may not have kept up with technology, many in the media have. They are using both new technology and their platforms to attack and expose what they consider to be malpractice by individuals and corporations.

Neither Chris nor Melissa seems to buy into the idea that multinationals are deliberately trying to outwit the taxman so as to avoid taxes. Compliance is often not as easy as it sounds. 'That's an interesting debate,' says Melissa, 'because with the majority of businesses that I work with it is all about paying the right amount of tax, so if that tax is due by law it's about paying that tax. I don't believe that it's about the outwitting position. Public opinion is important to business. It knows that data and technology give more visibility and lots more transparency to what's happening.'

While business will want to pay as little tax as it legally can – and has structures in place to ensure this – nor does it want scandal. Many major accountancy firms now have entire departments set up specialising in 'managing tax controversy' in order to address the reputational risk to companies. The net result of tax shaming is often a reorganisation of tax affairs. Today, even if the entity in question has conducted their affairs according to the letter of the law, legal compliance is often not enough, and an unwanted media spotlight is shone on their affairs.

International companies such as Apple, Google, Facebook, Amazon, Starbucks and Vodafone seem perennially in the news for the ways in which they arrange their tax affairs. They are far from alone. Tax scandal has become a corporate constant the world over, but it is by no means confined to corporations. High net worth individuals and families are being subjected to similar kinds of journalistic investigation into their tax affairs. Footballers Lionel Messi and Cristiano Ronaldo, singers Shakira, Justin Timberlake and Madonna, actors Keira Knightley and Amitabh Bachchan, even the Queen and Prince Charles are just some of those who have found themselves under unwanted scrutiny.

There was the Swiss Leaks scandal of 2015, in which the details of 100,000 accounts and 20,000 offshore companies alleged to have been involved in a giant tax evasion scheme were disclosed. Then the Panama Papers scandal of 2016, when an anonymous source, who went by the name of Joe Doe, leaked to journalists from the German paper *Süddeutsche Zeitung* some 1.5 million documents detailing private financial and legal information about 214,488 offshore entities going all the way back to the 1970s.

Go to Amazon and type in the word 'tax'. You will find very few, if any, books about such important subjects as the past, present and future of taxation, but plenty on the outrage that is offshore banking. There have been numerous film, TV and radio exposés. Entire blogs are devoted to it. Those conducting the investigations are deeply persistent, perhaps because they have an extremely powerful motivation: the sense that they are crusading against an injustice, that they have the moral high ground in a battle between right and wrong. Tax shaming has become a weapon in an already heated political and ideological war. This motivation is only going to grow more intense as government services face further cutbacks due to insufficient revenue.

The trend of tax shaming is growing, and it will be a major theme in the years ahead. In 2016, the *International Tax Review* ranked the International Consortium of Investigative Journalists second in its Global Tax 50 – a list of the most influential individuals, organisations, events and trends in the tax world (the EU's Margrethe Vestager, European Commissioner for Competition, came first, for taking on, among other multinational enterprises, the tax affairs of Apple). In 2017, tax-shaming investigative journalists were banded together as a group under the banner The Fifth Estate. They were ranked fourth.

As those who 'efficiently manage their tax affairs so as to minimise payment' are named and shamed, so ordinary people get more heated. It is a major factor in the growing tide of political discontent the world is experiencing, a manifestation of the inequality that so many are angry about: that the playing field is not level, that it is one rule for some, another for the rest. It will remain a major feature in the inevitable discontent of the years ahead.

HMRC is playing a similar game of name and shame. Every three months it publishes a list on its website with the details of anyone who has evaded taxes over £25,000. It publishes their name or the name of their business, the amount of tax they evaded and the penalty for that evasion. Meanwhile, tax authorities encourage individuals to report any form of fraud or evasion. Individuals often use it as a means to exact revenge. HMRC received more than 113,000 reports last year, and paid out over £500,000 in rewards.

But the big problem remains.

If a company or an individual is legally compliant, no matter how much outrage a certain sector of the media or populace may feel, that body is still legally compliant. The fault is with the law. Digital technology may have given governments great power, but the underlying problem – of how to tax the intangible online digital world – remains unsolved. There are visible transparent supply chains all over the world – tantalisingly out of the taxman's reach – but nobody has yet figured out a way to tax the value.

How right John Perry Barlow was in his 'Declaration of the Independence of Cyberspace'. Governments, he said, do not 'possess any methods of enforcement we have true reason to fear . . . Cyberspace consists of transactions, relationships, and thought itself, arrayed like a standing wave in the web of our communications. Ours is a world that is both everywhere and nowhere, but it is not where bodies live . . . Your legal concepts of property, expression, identity, movement, and context do not apply to us. They are all based on matter, and there is no matter here.'[9]

Homogenisation of international tax will only come if a practicable solution to the problem of taxing the globalised, intangible digital economy is found. Until then, fragmentation remains likely as different nations try different approaches.

Tax collection itself will become more ruthless, invasive and aggressive, as existing systems are enforced. Disclosure will be demanded of everyone, from accountants to lawyers to financial advisers, in the hunt for taxes. Governments are broke. They have no choice. But it's likely treatment will not be equitable, as some targets (the tangible economy) are easier than others. Perhaps the focus should be less on the cheats, and more on finding a system that works. If such a system cannot be found, the role of government will have to change.

Government will have to do less.

# Chapter 19

# The System is Broken

*When there are taxes, the just man pays more than the unjust man
on the same income. When there are refunds, the just man takes nothing,
while the unjust man profits.*

Plato (380 BC)[1]

Today's social democracies are founded on the principle that government's role is not just to provide for the protection of the people, but also to redistribute wealth and equalise life chances – to balance out the inequalities of the market economy.

Taxation was supposed to be the means to achieve that.

Yet society has remained deeply unequal, by some measures as unequal as ever in the free world.

There is extraordinary inequality of wealth. Every year Oxfam puts out a list of alarming statistics that demonstrate this. Among this year's were that a US CEO earns in a day what an ordinary American worker makes in a year;[2] that billionaire wealth rises at six times the speed of an ordinary worker's;[3] and that the combined wealth of the world's richest 1% is greater than that of the other 99%.[4]

But there is also great and growing inequality of health. Good health is notoriously difficult to quantify, but the most commonly used measures are life expectancy and infant mortality. In Britain, the difference in life expectancy between the richest and poorest is now at its widest ever,[5] while the gap in infant mortality rates between the poorest and the national average has also grown.[6]

Such health inequality is by no means unique to the UK. In the US, life expectancy in a neighbourhood where the median household income is less than $25,000 a year is about 14 years shorter than a neighbourhood where the median annual household income is more than $53,000.[7] Even if two districts border one another, residents of the richer districts can have a life expectancy over 30% longer than those of the poorer one.[8]

There is also inequality of opportunity. Across the globe, the privately educated outperform the publicly educated. In the UK, just 7% of students are educated privately, but they occupy the vast majority of top jobs, comprising, for example, 61% of doctors and 74% of judges.[9]

So much of this disparity can be traced back to systems of tax and money.

Take wealth inequality. For those who have very little, especially the young starting out, the only resource available to them is their labour. Yet we tax labour heavily and constantly, largely because income tax has proven easy to collect. In taxing labour so heavily, however, we restrict the possibilities of those who rely on their labour to advance.

The super rich, however, hard though they may have worked, are unlikely to be where they are as a result of their paid labour, except in the rare cases of those on extraordinarily high salaries, such as multinational CEOs, sports players and so on. More are there through the expansion of their businesses, the appreciation in the value of their assets – their houses, their land, their companies, their stocks, shares and bonds, their fine art and so on. These are not taxed year in, year out in the way that income is (and I am not saying they should be). Even at the point of sale (assuming there is one), if there is a gain, the rate payable is usually lower. Many simply avoid selling where they can, or employ avoidance and reinvestment schemes before gains become taxable profit.

In short, one group – workers – pays a higher rate of tax. Income and capital are not taxed equally, hence the inequality. The ratio of capital to labour in the US has fallen from 67:33 in the 1960s to 56:44

in the post-financial-crisis period. In other words, the relative value of labour has fallen dramatically. It will only fall further if jobs are lost to automation. The inherent inequity of a two-tier tax system is obvious.

The inflation tax also creates winners and losers. It actually *benefits* those who own assets – land, property, companies, stocks, shares, even fine art and antiques – as these tend to rise in price as the value of money falls. At the same time it hurts those who rely on salaries or savings, in that it erodes the value of the money they earn while pushing the price of the assets they want to buy, especially houses, out of reach. The salaried classes are hit on both sides.

The tax system does not treat people equally. Some are penalised, others benefit. It's why so many economies have become geared around asset ownership. Our systems of tax and money actually *cause* inequality.

In the years ahead, it seems unlikely that the increasingly disenfranchised middle and working classes will be happy to shoulder an increasingly unbalanced tax burden. It points to even greater social and political unrest.

As for inequality of health and education, a proper examination of both is beyond the scope of this book. You can find examples of state education or healthcare working well; you can find as many of them disappointing. But the endless arguments over both show how high levels of dissatisfaction are – much higher than in areas of the economy such as food, clothing or tech, where government is less involved in provision. The most commonly proffered solution is to spend more on health, education and welfare. It might be coincidence, but since the Second World War, health inequality in the UK actually grew most during the period (1997–2007) when the NHS had most, as a proportion of GDP, spent on it, suggesting that simply spending more might not be the answer.[10]

What if we went the other way and stopped funding services such as healthcare and education via taxation? If we left money in people's pockets and allowed them to decide how to spend it?

Healthcare, welfare and education are essential human needs. They are not going to disappear. The friendly societies of the nineteenth century were terrifically successful in the context of the period. They rose quite organically without government sponsorship. It is possible that a twenty-first-century version of the friendly societies could emerge.

## Adam Smith's four canons

In his *Inquiry into the Nature and Causes of the Wealth of Nations*, Adam Smith laid down four general principles that any tax system should follow. They apply as much today as they did when they were published in 1776.

His first was that taxes should be fair. Citizens should 'contribute towards the support of the government, as nearly as possible, in proportion to their respective abilities'. With income and inflation taxes so high, as outlined above, this principle is not being adhered to.

The inflation tax and other stealth taxes besides breach Smith's second principle too, which was that 'the time of payment, the manner of payment, the quantity to be paid, ought all to be clear and plain to the contributor'. Even ignoring inflation, modern tax systems – with some notable exceptions such as Hong Kong and Singapore – are neither clear nor plain. They are blighted with complexity. The UK, with the longest code in the world, at 10 million words and 21,000 pages, is the worst offender.[11] To put that in some kind of perspective, it is about 12 times the length of the Bible. At 1.26 million words, Marcel Proust's *À La Recherche du Temps Perdu* holds the Guinness World Record for the longest novel ever written. The UK tax code is eight times as long. Ten million words is more than most people read in their entire lifetime.

However, it is one thing reading the UK tax code, another understanding it. Much of the language is notoriously incomprehensible.

Nigel Lawson, who was Chancellor of the Exchequer between 1983 and 1989, made it his policy to remove a tax every budget, and did so six times. He also reduced the number of income tax bands to two. But since then the amount of tax legislation has ballooned. Gordon Brown was the worst offender. The tax code trebled in size while he was Chancellor. George Osborne came to power promising radical simplification, saying the UK tax code was 'one of the most complex and opaque' on earth. He even set up the Office of Tax Simplification. The tax code doubled again under his tenure.

This complexity is not confined to the UK. It is the curse of the West. The US Internal Revenue Code – at 2.4 million words – is roughly six times as long as it was in 1955 and twice as long as in 1985. Another 7.7 million words of tax regulations have been promulgated by the IRS to clarify how these statutes work in practice. In addition there are a further 60,000-odd pages of tax-related case law, essential for accountants and tax lawyers trying to calculate what their clients owe.[12] Confounded by his tax forms, Albert Einstein once famously declared, 'The hardest thing in the world to understand is income taxes.'[13]

The Hong Kong tax code, meanwhile, comes in at 276 pages. It is about 1.5% the size of the UK's.

Complexity compounds inequality. Some, whether individuals or corporations, hire experts to find and exploit the loopholes, of which there are many. The rest don't have the resources to do this and end up paying more on a proportional basis. The many tax reliefs, tax breaks and subsidies tend to be the reason tax codes are so complicated, and this in itself creates inequality. Lobbying for a subsidy or a relief – whether based on financial interests or belief systems, or a bit of both – has become the norm. Again, some have the resources to lobby, but others do not. Certain businesses are granted special favour; others are not. Surely the rules should be the same for everyone.

Complexity also creates error, something for which the bodies in charge of administering tax, such as the IRS and HMRC, are notorious. Remove the complexity, simplify the system and you remove much of the scope for error and avoidance, as well as making the playing field more level.

Smith's third principle was that taxes should be levied 'at the time, or in the manner, in which it is most likely to be convenient for the contributor to pay it'. Taxes levied at source or at the time of payment mostly fit the bill here, though they are levied not for the convenience of the payer but to maximise takings.

Fourthly, Smith suggested that taxes should cost as little as possible to collect. If it costs 50 cents to collect a dollar in tax, there is little justification for the tax to exist. The way current tax systems are geared, this cost usually falls to the payer. The employer must collect income tax. The seller must collect VAT. In the US, tax compliance costs the economy some $409 billion per year.[14] That is equivalent to the gross product of 36 states combined. Americans will spend some 8.9 billion man hours complying with IRS tax filing requirements.[15] That is equivalent to 4.3 million workers doing nothing but tax return paperwork – 4.3 million is roughly the same number as there are Americans who work as drivers.

In the UK, despite all the advances in financial and other technology, the cost to the government of collecting taxes remains as expensive as it was 50 years ago.[16]

It is not hard to see that in most parts of the globe, things are not right.

## 'Rage, rage against the dying of the light'

In the years since the global financial crisis of 2008, a rising tide of anxiety and dissatisfaction has spread across the West, manifesting itself in many different ways – the surprise election of Donald Trump, Brexit, the *gilets jaunes* riots in France, Catalonian independence. Strong-man politicians, whether of the right or the left, are gaining prominence and popularity all over the world, while centrists are rejected. Authorities have been at a loss to deal with it. The media has been at a loss to explain it.

The discontent is nothing new. It is the same discontent that was felt by the followers of Urakagina in 3,000 BC Lagash, the English peasants in 1381 or the French revolutionaries in 1789. Many feel unrepresented in a tax system that perpetrates so much economic injustice. The difference is that today many of the contributing factors are so much harder to diagnose, because so many taxes are concealed and not directly and immediately felt. Income taxes are deducted at source, before pay is received. VAT and sales taxes are included in the purchase price, as are fuel duties and sin taxes (taxes on 'sins' such as drinking, smoking and gambling). Stealth taxes go unseen. The inflation tax happens, as Keynes said, in a way that 'not one in a million is able to diagnose'. The tax that is debt is cast into the future.

But as the saying goes, 'You can avoid reality, but you cannot avoid the consequences of avoiding reality.' The discontent may be harder to articulate, but the consequences of such heavy taxation are still felt.

Many families struggle to get by. Both parents must work in order to enjoy the middle-class lifestyle that little more than a generation ago was affordable on just one salary. They put off starting a family until later in life, they have fewer children, they have more debt and they live in smaller homes. Buying a house has become a near impossibility. The same is true across the West. My generation is poorer than its parents'. The next generation is poorer than mine. It is the opposite of progress and evolution. Such occurrences are rare in history, outside of times of war. You perhaps have to go back to the Dark Ages to find the last time it happened in Europe.

At the same time as being squeezed, they see the money they have earned being spent in ways with which they do not agree – on wars, welfare or waste. And yet they have little say, bar a vote of dubious impact every five years for parties that for the most part represent different shades of grey. 'Taxes are the price we pay for a civilised society' are the words inscribed on the outside of the IRS building in Washington DC. I'm not sure having to work in such an inequitable system to fund things with which we do not agree is civilised. If any of the things you get for your money are unsatisfactory, you cannot demand a refund, nor can you take your custom elsewhere, unless you leave the country. If you don't pay, you end up in jail. In fact, with so many taxes deducted at source, even the option to not pay and risk jail has largely been removed.

By 2030, man will be living a life of leisure, working just three hours per day, free 'from pressing economic cares'.[17] This was the famous 1930 prediction of perhaps the most influential economist of the twentieth century, John Maynard Keynes. Keynes was right about improving productivity. Food, clothing, technology, even the cost of building houses (excluding the land) – all these things have quite dramatically both fallen in price and risen in quality over the last hundred years. In 1900, 80–90% of a worker's earnings went on food, clothing and shelter.[18] Now it is just 40%. But he was wildly wrong about the amount of time we would spend working, because there is one enormous cost he overlooked. It is ironic that he of all people, such an advocate of state spending, should have missed it. Across the West, it is the biggest expense in anyone's life, costing more than a house, a car, a pension or an education: the cost of the state itself. Government does so much – and we accordingly must pay so much – that it has now grown to become, pretty much wherever you are in the developed world (there may be one or two exceptions), the most expensive purchase you ever make over the course of your life.

But today, while some seem to enjoy extraordinary wealth and opportunity, many feel disenfranchised and unrepresented. Revolution is in the air once again.

## The end of the nation state?

Perhaps the defining feature of the international history of the past 200 years has been the emergence of the state as supreme political body.

Until the nineteenth century, the world was, in the words of tech author Jamie Bartlett, 'a sprawl of empires, unclaimed land, city-states and principalities, which travellers crossed without checks or passports'.[19] Wars, revolutions, industrial progress and socialised welfare altered that. But over time, borders change. We may have grown up thinking of certain countries with certain borders, but in the context of history, the nation state is a relatively recent model, born in large part out of the tax revolutions of the seventeenth, eighteenth and nineteenth centuries. Its survival will depend on being able to raise sufficient taxes to cover spending.

While already running deficits, many leaders are trying to offset the rising tide of political discontent with greater spending programmes. Trump has promised huge outlay on infrastructure. In the UK, Chancellor Philip Hammond's pledges to increase NHS spending will mean the NHS will account for 38% of GDP by 2023.[20] This will increase the need for tax revenue when it is by no means certain these revenue sources will remain.

Perhaps the beginning of this threat to the nation state model can be traced back to the mid to late 1990s, when, for the first time, investment in intangibles overtook investment in physical assets.[21] For centuries economies had revolved around the production and consumption of physical things – from cars to cows to grain to gold. Today the most valuable assets are non-physical and intangible – software companies, brands, intellectual property, operating systems, unique supply chains. Even money itself is no longer tangible. Companies built around intangibles grow faster. If a system – Google's search engine, for example – works, it can scale much more rapidly than anything a 'physical' company can offer. An app need only be uploaded once, but it can be downloaded millions of times. This potential speed of growth attracts investment, and so the process accelerates.

At the same time, the new 'non-profit' business models of tech companies and their ability to locate themselves anywhere have given them the ability to pay less tax, where others pay more, and so tech has advantage there too. Low taxes mean more capital to invest and grow. So tech advances and becomes more capable. Even computer power itself grows exponentially, doubling roughly every two years, as costs fall. The power that technology companies wield within our society grows at a similarly extraordinary rate. As Karl Marx famously observed, when the dominant mode of production changes, so do the political and social structures.

The nation state and its tax systems were built up around a physical world. Even today, the UK does not include spending on market research and branding in its GDP.[22] Unless nations adapt to the new world around them and the transition to digital, the very model of the nation state is brought into doubt. Either they must find a way to tax intangibles, while remaining competitive with other nations, or they must cut their spending. Otherwise insolvency looms.

Government insolvency, disruption of tax revenue, a potential crisis in the bond market, a loss of faith in national currencies – these are all very real possibilities in a world already awash with political discontent and desire for change. They are also recipes for revolution and civil war. Such a fate will be avoided by those nations that act first and adapt best to the realities of the new economic world around us. This also means adapting the way they govern and the services government provides.

Smaller nations tend to be more nimble. Already signs of adaptation are apparent. We see nations such as Iceland (which actually crowd-sourced its constitution), Estonia and Malta, even various Caribbean islands, embrace blockchain technology, for example, in both their tax laws and their government services, while others look on baffled. Smaller nations outperform larger rivals. Of the ten richest nations in the world on a per capita basis, none has a population of more than 10 million.[23] Of the 20 richest nations in the world, just two (the US and Germany) have a population larger than 20 million. In 1950, however, the story was rather different. The US was probably the richest nation on earth. Purchasing power parity data is inaccurate, but there would have been at least four countries in the top ten with populations over 10 million – the

US, Venezuela, Australia, Canada and possibly the Netherlands, with Belgium, France and Argentina just missing out.[24] Small has become economically beautiful. It was not always so.

The trend towards smaller states, with people wanting more local rule, is politically apparent as well. The UK voted to leave the European Union. Catalonia wants independence from Spain. In the last 25 years, Yugoslavia has become Bosnia and Herzegovina, Croatia, Kosovo, Macedonia, Montenegro, Serbia and Slovenia. We will see many more incidences, though the path towards smaller states will not be easy. Spain has shown it will not allow Catalonian freedom lightly. Brexit has turned toxic, with the main areas of dispute – customs union and access to the single market – both being, of course, tax issues. History has shown that it often takes some kind of revolution, insolvency crisis or war to achieve change and the meaningful tax reform that comes with it. Governments rarely offer it voluntarily. But dwindling tax revenue will force hands.

As nations fragment, the tax systems that follow will be determined by the chosen systems of rule. But every state will be competing for business. Those that will attract the most business will be the ones with strong private property laws and the most attractive tax rates to the new global citizens and companies. This competition will put further pressure on other nations to adapt their ways.

As tech starts to replace government services (many are turning to tech for their education, healthcare and transport), so does it open the door to lower government spending, but one suspects some kind of fiscal pressure will force it on most, rather than it being chosen voluntarily. In cultures where high levels of spending are entrenched, there will be great resistance to lower taxes. Many will try to implement higher rates of tax, and new taxes – perhaps wealth taxes, mansion taxes, vacant homes taxes or turnover taxes. More inflation taxes, which are not directly felt by a voting electorate, at least not at first, are inevitable. For example, the doctrines of modern monetary theory (MMT) and so-called people's quantitative easing (PQE), in which governments create money to fund spending and thereby manage the economy, are gaining traction.

Attempts to clamp down on tax evasion, tax avoidance and tax havens will become more strident. The collection of taxes will grow more aggressive, and will include a growing moral argument – already at work – that you are somehow a bad person if you don't agree with high taxes or how they are spent. The same moral arguments were used on the medieval knights who did not want to go to war with their king and had cowardice taxes levied on them. History shows these cycles do not usually end well.

Damage could be mitigated by early and meaningful tax reform. But history also shows that this does not happen easily. Such reform is normally precipitated by some kind of crisis. All but the strongest politicians take the path of least resistance, which is to tinker round the edges while heading in the general direction of more taxes, greater complexity and higher rates. It takes a politician of rare strength and fortitude to attempt such reform, and win a mandate for it, without the weight of extreme circumstances on his side. But as Asia marches relentlessly forward, the West, particularly Europe, must change the way it taxes its people if it does not want to get left behind.

The ideological struggle between large government and small, between authoritarian and libertarian, between old business practices and new tech, between more taxes and fewer taxes will continue. Neither side will roll over voluntarily. But those nations that opt for low, fair and simple systems of tax will be the ones that thrive. Where taxes are lowest – and thus where people are most free – is where we will see the most invention, the most innovation and the greatest wealth creation. This has been the case throughout history, and it will always be the case.

# Chapter 20

## *Designing Utopia*

*I am in favour of cutting taxes under any circumstances and for any*
*excuse, for any reason, whenever it's possible.*

Milton Friedman (2003)[1]

There has never been a civilisation without taxation.

Much as we may loathe taxes, it is inevitable that some of our
labour and property will be taken for the 'common good'. The
question is, how much? Freedom and taxes are antithetical. How
you tax is ultimately a question about your values. What kind of
nation do you want Utopia to be?

Do you want the social democratic model of much of Europe
today, with high taxes, and government the main provider in areas
such as welfare, education, pensions and healthcare, resulting in
low levels of economic freedom and individual responsibility?

Would you prefer higher taxes, an even more pervasive state and
less freedom?

Or would you prefer lower taxes, greater economic freedom and
more individual responsibility, with a belief that government is not
the best means to provide education, welfare and so on?

If you prefer what we have, or want more of it, the argument is
about how those resources are then spent. In my Utopia, based
loosely on Hong Kong, we go the other way.

Let's start with the top line. If you remember, in the developed
world, between 40 and 60% of GDP goes on tax. In Utopia, we
return to a number closer to the ancient traditions of the tithe. The

overall tax burden – including debt and inflation – should be around 15% of GDP. That's about a third of what we currently pay. Government spending should not exceed that figure. Although if you offered me 20%, I'd still bite your hand off.

There are income taxes in Utopia, there is VAT, but these never exceed 15% and, in the case of VAT especially, there are few exemptions. We also have some Pigouvian taxes – so named after early-twentieth-century British economist Arthur C. Pigou – on activities that have negative outcomes: industry or activity that creates pollution, for example, or leads to increased public healthcare costs (smoking especially). Pigouvian revenue, like fines, is channelled directly into the public activity where the damage is caused. For example, tobacco duty is channelled directly to the health service. Narcotics are legal in Utopia, and these too are taxed at the flat rate of 15%, with levies also going directly into healthcare and treatment for addiction.

There is no corporation tax. There is no need for it. Dividends are taxed at the same rate as income and the income of corporate workers is taxed too. Zero corporation tax will attract considerable investment from abroad. In addition, corporations will pay a location usage tax – more on this in a moment.

There is no National Insurance, no capital gains tax, no inheritance tax, no council tax, no stamp duty, no tariffs, no business rates, no television licence fee, no vehicle excise duty. Airport passenger duty and fuel taxes are both halved and any revenue generated is spent solely on related infrastructure.

The tax code dramatically shrinks in size. Instead of being 21,000 pages, as we now have in the UK, it is around 300 pages, like Hong Kong.

One practical consequence of lower taxes is that there is less evasion – there is less incentive to take the risk, while lower taxes tend to inspire greater loyalty. As the experience of Hong Kong shows, lower taxes also bring in increased investment from abroad.

## *Location, location, location: One new tax Utopia needs*

You might think that my Utopia is all about reducing the number of taxes, not introducing any new ones.

But there is one new tax I think is essential. It's a tax based on the location of any ground that you own. I like to call it location usage tax (LUT). It's one of the fairest taxes I can think of, and it would help in shifting the burden of taxation from labour to capital, thus helping to encourage productive activity.

The idea dates back to the physiocrats of the seventeenth century. Physiocracy means 'government of nature'. There are two types of wealth: that which has been made by man, and that which has been given to us by Mother Nature. A house is made by man, but the land underneath it, the airspace and broadcast spectrums around it, and any mineral wealth nearby have all occurred as a result of nature. Man-made wealth should belong to those who made it, but natural wealth should be shared. If you build a house on a plot of land, you are improving it, and the results of your endeavour should be yours to keep. But the plot of land itself was always there, and some of its 'unimproved' value should be enjoyed by all.

'Men did not make the earth,' wrote the Enlightenment philosopher Thomas Paine in 1797. 'It is the value of the improvement only, and not the earth itself, that is individual property . . . Every proprietor owes to the community a ground rent for the land which he holds.'

Imagine two identical plots in a city centre. One is undeveloped scrub, the other has a magnificent building on top. They would both be taxed at an identical rate. The only thing that is considered is the value of the land in its unimproved state. It could be a $10 million house, but we are only concerned with the unimproved value of the land beneath. The wealth that has come as a result of building should be kept by the developer who took the risks, or the new owner. But if the undeveloped plot appreciates in value due simply to the fact that the city is growing and more people want to live in the area, then that appreciation is unearned wealth and some of it should be shared. Often land appreciates because taxes have been spent building a superfast railway nearby. That gain is not due to the endeavour of the owner of the plot, but because of some kind of communal activity, so the unearned gain should be shared.

If you want exclusive use of a plot, and you want the government to protect your title to that plot, then a fee based on the plot's unimproved value should be paid to the community. You would pay a percentage of the annual rental value of that plot in an unimproved state. A house might cost $400,000 to build. The land itself might be worth $100,000. Thus to buy the house on the open market would cost $500,000. The annual rental value of that $100,000 plot in its unimproved state might be $10,000. The fee payable for the exclusive use of the land would thus be a percentage of $10,000. If a train station is built nearby, the value of the plot might increase to say $200,000. The annual rent might now be $20,000. The fee payable would be a portion of that.

The nineteenth-century economist Henry George popularised the idea of this tax. He called it 'the single tax', because, he argued, it should replace all other taxes. His 1879 book on the subject, *Progress and Poverty*, sold millions of copies to become the best-selling American book of all time (at that point). A fan of his even invented a board game to educate people about the dangers of the current system of land ownership. We know the game as Monopoly.

Today George's single tax is known as land value tax. I do not like this title as it suggests rural landowners will pay large amounts when in fact the tax falls most heavily on those corporations or individuals who own prime real estate in city centres. That's why I prefer the term location usage tax. Effectively, it's a consumption tax. The more valuable the land you use, the more tax you pay.

This is not some whimsical idea dreamt up by seventeenth-century philosophers or nineteenth-century economists. It has been put into practical effect. And where else but Hong Kong? Roughly 40% of Hong Kong revenue accrued from land value. The city state owned all the land and leased it. In this way some of the increase in the value of the land, which came as a result of the industry of its people, was shared, rather than expropriated by the lucky few who owned the prime sites. The government was also able to preserve 75% of Hong Kong land as open space – only 25% is built up.[2]

Singapore, Taiwan and South Korea too have found ways to tax site value. It assisted their economic growth as it enabled them to reduce taxes elsewhere. Sun Yat-Sen became the first provisional president of the Republic of China in 1911. The 'Father of the Nation' spent many of his formative years in Hong Kong and was a confirmed believer in this same principle. Today China could be following this lead, as it appears to sell little land outright.

Unfortunately, the practicalities of getting such a tax implemented are hellish.

David Lloyd George and Winston Churchill tried it in the UK in 1909. 'Roads are made, streets are made, services are improved, electric light turns night into day, water is brought from reservoirs a hundred miles off in the mountains – and all the while the landlord sits still,' Churchill thundered in the House of Commons. 'Every one of those improvements is affected by the labour and cost of other people and the taxpayers. To not one of those improvements does the land monopolist, as a land monopolist, contribute, and yet by every one of them the value of his land is enhanced. He renders no service to the community, he contributes nothing to the general welfare, he contributes nothing to the process from which his own enrichment is derived.'[3] But the House of Lords, largely made up of landowners, blocked the Act. It's likely that any attempts to introduce it today would be similarly unsuccessful, unless it can clearly be shown to replace other taxes.

But this is Utopia. We can do what we like. We do not want a society of homeowners sitting idly by while their houses go up in value, at the expense of the next generation. We are designing a society in which productivity is rewarded and unearned wealth is not. In

Utopia, there is no room for landlords who, as John Stuart Mill put it, 'grow richer in their sleep, without working, risking, or economizing'.[4] The increase in the value of land, he argued, as it arises from the aggregated efforts of an entire community, should belong to the community – and not to the individual who might hold title.

Here is how it would work.

Every parcel of land in the country is assessed for its unimproved rental value – that is, the value of the land as if it had not been developed in any way: no building, no farm, no factory – just the land. We are not assessing the value of Harrods or Bloomingdale's, but the land beneath. Thus the location of the land will tend to be more significant in terms of rental value than the amount. Undesirable scrubland in a remote location with no planning permission will have very little rental value. Prime sites in city centres, with good infrastructure nearby, will have a very high rental value.

The Land Registry will have a record of who owns each plot of land.[5] The owner then pays an annual fee, which would be a percentage of the unimproved rental value. What percentage? That depends on the type of society you want. If you want large government and large spending, the percentage will be high. If you want small government and minimal spending, the percentage will be low. The percentage to be levied can be debated by political parties and determined by the electorate at the ballot box.

Milton Friedman, a man who, if ever there was one, espoused low taxation, called it 'the least bad tax'.[6] It is easy to see why. LUT does not tax productivity, but instead captures unearned wealth. It is simple to administer – once the system is in place, the only issue is annual revaluation. It is an impossible tax to evade. You can't hide land. Land cannot be based offshore. The owner's name is on the Land Registry. They are liable. The tax is transparent. Unlike debt, inflation or other stealth taxes, government spending is directly felt by the taxpayer, which forces accountability onto government. It is the ideal solution to the problem of taxing multinational digital intangibles. It does not matter if the intellectual property of your software is registered to a company in Panama, or your server is in Iceland; if you are using this land here for your data centres, or you are making use of this bandwidth, or you have headquarters in this prime city location, you must share some of the unimproved value of the community's natural wealth that you are exclusively using (location usage tax does not just apply to land, by the way, but to any asset granted by nature – the airspace, the mineral wealth, even the broadcast spectrums).

What's more, the tax tends to make for more efficient use of land. Those who are holding undeveloped land waiting for its value to appreciate – a practice known as land banking – are compelled to either put the land to immediate use, or to sell it on to someone else who will. For the same reasons, it disincentivises speculation in real estate, something that, over the years, has caused many economic crashes.

Land is the most basic wealth of all. It is also the most unequally distributed. Throughout the world, a few select individuals, corporations and government departments own disproportionately large amounts of land – both in cities and in the countryside. Brazil, Spain and the UK are where land is most unequally distributed.[7] Not only do many large landowners pay no tax on the land they use, they actually receive subsidies of one kind or other for it, especially in Britain and Europe. The money for that subsidy comes predominantly from taxes paid by workers. I'm sure that in most cases workers would like to become landowners, but instead their taxes contribute to the landowners' subsidies. The worker indirectly funds the asset owner. No wonder there is such a gap between the two.

Location usage tax will not only change the way we think about land and land ownership, but it will change the way a society thinks and acts, because the rewards and incentives are different. In Utopia, endeavour is rewarded. Land banking is not.

No nation has employed location usage tax in its purest form – at the expense of *all* other taxes. But where nations have employed it at the expense of *some* other taxes – not only Hong Kong, Taiwan and South Korea, but also Denmark, New Zealand, Botswana, Estonia and parts of Australia – there is economic outperformance.

In Utopia we advocate that location usage tax should amount to around a third of government revenue, the rest made up by income taxes, VAT and other taxes, including the Pigouvian taxes outlined above. Nevertheless, should one region want it, it will be possible for that region to employ location usage tax and no other taxes, because different regions are going to be able to set their own tax rates. We are decentralising power and devolving it to the regions.

Here we are borrowing from the Swiss and Scandinavian models, where a much higher portion of taxes is both determined and collected at the local level. This brings both greater accountability to those collecting and spending tax revenue and greater transparency to those paying the taxes: they are able to monitor how their money is spent, rather than watching it disappear into a central pot – they are closer to the results. In Utopia, cities and regions are able to set their own tax policies and their own tax rates. A large portion of tax powers will be devolved to the regions.

The effect will be to create regional tax competition. Adam Smith's invisible hand can thus be brought to government as competition, accountability and choice play out. Those regions with the best tax rates will thrive. Those policies that work best will be copied, those that don't will be abandoned. If one region wants high taxes and high spending when another doesn't, such an outcome is possible. Future outcomes will show which policies work best. Accountable local government will be better able to change and adapt than central government.

Utopia will also incorporate the modern business model of subscription.

## How subscription could work for public services

Until the 1990s, you could only buy newspapers, music and films in physical form. The move to digital meant that media could now be reproduced quickly and cheaply with no loss of quality (a far cry from vinyl to cassette or TV to VHS) and then freely and instantly distributed. People have since gradually stopped buying newspapers, CDs, DVDs or other kinds of 'physical' media. Yet a paradoxical situation emerged in which people actually consumed more content – they read more articles, listened to more music and watched more video than ever before – but revenue for the creators collapsed. The value of content fell, close to zero in some cases. What saved many businesses was subscription.

In 2010, *The Times* became the first mainstream newspaper in the UK to erect a paywall. Shortly afterwards, its website experienced a decline in visitors of over 90%. It was derided. Yet in 2014, *The Times* recorded its first profit since 2001. Of the major broadsheets in the UK, only the *Guardian* remains open to all. Its writers might like the free platform that gives them greater prominence than other journalists, but for many years it was haemorrhaging money. It was only in 2019, after huge cuts and by asking readers for donations and subscriptions, that it was able to turn a small profit. The voluntary subscriptions made up for the loss of advertising revenue to Facebook and Google. Many smaller publications have actually thrived thanks to the subscription model, particularly anything selling advice.

The music industry has also had to remodel. Live gigs helped it survive (and live events have also become a valuable income stream for many newspapers), but subscription has also helped, whether it's YouTube channels or streaming services such as Spotify, where people pay a monthly fee in exchange for access to a wide range of music.

Subscription has probably worked best of all in television, starting with the likes of Sky and HBO, and then followed by Netflix, Amazon Prime, BT and Now TV, bringing Hollywood production standards to the small screen. TV is now responsible for some of the best video of our times.

In the space of around 20 years, these industries followed a journey from 'paid' to 'free' to 'crisis' to 'subscription'. Journalist Andrew Willshire suggests we are on the same path with our public services.[8]

Until the National Insurance Act of 1911 and the First World War, education and healthcare were paid for directly by individuals, often via the friendly societies. Charities and churches helped, subsidising care, welfare and education for the poorest, but everyone was expected to contribute as best they could. As the state became responsible for the provision of care and education, the connection between what an individual paid and the service he received in return was broken. We went from 'paid' to 'free'. Today demand for these services, and expectation of standards, is high. Both far exceed the ability of governments to cover the cost via taxation. Few want higher taxes (at least not those who must pay them), yet most services are severely stretched. Almost every week there seems to be some story or other about a public service being in crisis. The extraordinary levels of public debt owed means no solution is in sight. We are now at the 'crisis' stage of Willshire's cycle.

In other areas of the economy, subscription is commonplace. We choose who we want to follow on Twitter, Facebook or Instagram. We can choose which TV programmes we want to watch or which podcasts we want to listen to. We choose our provider, then pay our monthly mobile phone tariff, our broadband tariff, our TV tariff, our music tariff, our news tariff, our gym tariff, our insurance tariff and so on. Even if we don't actually use the service that month, in most cases we don't expect our money back. Subscription is now normal. Behaviour has changed.

In most subscriptions there is a flat rate to pay for the basic service – often the basic model is even free. Then there are optional extras. We can go to the gym at an off-peak time, but pay extra if we want to go when it's busy. If we need extra data on our phone one month, or there is a specific sports game we want to watch, we pay a little bit extra. Sometimes that 'little bit extra' can be quite a lot, even if the cost to the supplier is low. A good example of this might be first-class tickets on a plane or train, compared to standard class. In many cases these extra payments are where the bulk of the profits are made.

So that is how the subscription model works. Here is how we introduce subscription to Utopia.

Income tax will incorporate all forms of income – dividends, salaries, rents – and will be applied at a flat rate of 15%. This single income tax is easy to administer. At such low rates, avoidance falls. All personal allowances are removed. Instead everyone receives universal basic income, which is taxed as part of the single income tax. This will also thus bring simplification to both welfare and taxation.

The revenue from single income tax is divided into multiple subscriptions, with specific revenue dedicated to specific expenditure. Economists call this 'hypothecated taxes'. As we will know that 'this money will be spent on that service', greater clarity is brought to public spending. The allocations will be determined by the Chancellor, and will thus be an issue debated by political parties and voted on at elections.

The first subscription is 'membership of society' to cover basic costs of government – defence, infrastructure, police, etc. The second is for redistribution – welfare and pensions. A third is for education. A fourth for healthcare and related social services.

For each, there must be a clear statement of what is provided – what size of army, what NHS treatment or drugs, what schooling and so on. Anything additional to the basic stated levels of provision should be paid for. Transparent tax returns show that all citizens are nominally charged the same for each service, though low earners are effectively subsidised. Higher earners will explicitly see their extra contribution.

Payment for services at the point of use is encouraged at every stage. You might not want to pay higher taxes, but would happily pay extra for yourself, friends or family to get a private room in a hospital, say, or better food. Extra revenue then goes back into the service, wherever funds are needed. Willshire calls this 'co-payment'. To work, the price of this additional level of service must be well above the cost of providing it – e.g. a first-class train or air ticket often costs the passenger more than double the standard ticket, though it does not cost the carrier double to provide. Thus those who choose to (usually those with more money) are volunteering payment, for which they get tangible benefit, while subsidising the service for others. If income from co-payments is considerable, it may even be possible to reduce the single tax rate. A voluntary, progressive tax system is thus created.

Co-payment also restores the buyer–seller dynamic, which is missing from many public services. At present, an NHS user can, for example, not turn up to appointments or behave rudely to staff, with very little comeback. On the other side of the coin, a doctor can provide a suboptimal service and not be held to account.

Compare this to the commercial sector. In most shops and restaurants you are given good, quick service by somebody who wants to please. The service provider is accountable to you, the customer. In order to boost sales, manufacturers try to produce the best product they can. If you don't get good service, or a good product, you don't go back, you leave bad reviews and so on. On the other side of the trade, if a customer behaves badly, they are not always welcomed back, they might get bad feedback and have their reputation affected. This dynamic forces good behaviour on participants. Buyer regulates seller and seller regulates buyer. It happens quite naturally and incentivises constant improvement.

The subscriptions and co-payment system can also make space for contributions from charities and the private sector. A local charity could offer to make co-payments for certain disadvantaged people, insurance could be sold against the cost of top-up services and so on. It will be flexible enough to incorporate into the future world, in which tech usurps existing government services.

The subscription model simplifies tax and welfare, and brings greater transparency to government; it raises more revenue from higher earners, but by their own choice, and thus we have natural rather than arbitrarily imposed levels of progressive tax.

## *Fix tax and you fix society*

No single tax or tax system is going to tick every box all of the time. But I hope this Utopian system, based on Hong Kong, comes close.

I think it's essential that we bring the subject of tax back to the fore: that we study, discuss and debate tax, as people did during the Enlightenment. I hope the ideas I've presented in this book will get things going.

Tax is the way we will shape the world in which our children will live.

History has shown time and time again the terrible consequences that misguided, poorly thought through or outdated tax legislation can have. We need new and better tax systems to reflect the new economy of the twenty-first century.

Tax reform is one of the few ways by which politicians really can change the world. Fix tax and you fix society. Tax is the zero patient.

Let's get started!

# Acknowledgements

This book started life in 2016 as a comedy (sort of) show at the Edinburgh Festival called *Let's Talk About Tax*. I thought transposing it into a book would be easy and quick – a formality. It ended up taking the best part of three years. Taxation is as old as civilisation, and I have found myself at times rewriting the entire history of civilisation from the perspective of taxes. Oof! In that regard, I would like to start by thanking my editor, Martina O'Sullivan, for her endless patience. She did not get cross with me once, despite deadline after deadline passing quietly in the night. Martina also has to be both thanked and admired for the incredible vision she showed in commissioning this book in the first place.

I would also like to thank and commend Celia Buzuk and Jane Selley for their outstanding contributions during the edit.

Thanks also to Toby Bray, formerly my boss at *MoneyWeek*, who goes through all my books, ruthlessly identifies the boring bits and then scythes them down like a militant hedge-trimmer.

Thanks to Roger Ver, Darren Jones, and KPMG's Melissa Geiger, Chris Downing and Ed Fotheringham Smith for their help with my research.

Someone else who needs to be thanked and admired for their visionary greatness is my literary agent, Sally Holloway, of Felicity Bryan Associates. She signed me on the strength of a speculative email sent the day after Boxing Day. (If any budding writers are reading this, send out your solicitations in the quiet week between Christmas and New Year. There's a better chance they might get noticed.)

This book would never have been written without my comedy agents, Christian Knowles and Vicky Matthews, getting that

Edinburgh show on in the first place, so big up to the CKP massive.

I don't know who is doing the PR for this book yet, but thanks in advance for the HUGE amount of work you put in.

Special thanks to Sophie Taylor for her patience too.

And I would not be the writer I am were it not for my dad, Terence Frisby, the most overlooked playwright of his generation, so big up to the dad massive as well.

I can't thank my dad and not thank my mum, so thanks also to Mum, who has been through hell these last two years, courtesy of her lying cheat of an ex-husband (not my dad). There's another book in that story, but that is for another time.

Finally, there is one man to whom this book owes more than anyone. He inspired my interest in this subject in the first place and I have drawn constantly on his research. That is the American tax historian Charles Adams. Adams passed away in 2013, and we never met, but I hope our paths will cross in the great tax haven in the sky.

# Bibliography

Abrahamlincolnsclassroom.org (2018). *Abraham Lincoln and the Tariff*. Available at: http://www.abrahamlincolnsclassroom.org/abraham-lincoln-in-depth/abraham-lincoln-and-the-tariff/ (accessed 16 April 2018).

Abrahamlincolnonline.org (2018). *Abraham Lincoln's 1855 Letter to Joshua Speed*. Available at: http://www.abrahamlincolnonline.org/lincoln/speeches/speed.htm (accessed 3 May 2018).

Abrahamlincolnonline.org (2018). *Lincoln's Eulogy on Henry Clay*. Available at: http://www.abrahamlincolnonline.org/lincoln/speeches/clay.htm (accessed 26 April 2018).

Adams, C. (1993). *For Good and Evil*. Lanham, Md.: Madison Books.

Aeon.co (2018). Sheri Berman, *It wasn't just hate. Fascism offered robust social welfare*. Available at: https://aeon.co/ideas/fascism-was-a-right-wing-anti-capitalist-movement (accessed 30 June 2018).

Ali, I. (n.d.). *Imam Ali's Letter to Malik al-Ashtar, the Governor of Egypt, Revenue Administration*. Al-Islam.org. Available at: https://www.al-islam.org/richest-treasure-imam-ali/revenue-administration (accessed 8 December 2018).

Allen, G. (2012). *Inflation: the Value of the Pound 1750–2011* (ebook). London: House of Commons Library, pp.6, 17. Available at: http://researchbriefings.files.parliament.uk/documents/RP12-31/RP12-31.pdf (accessed 24 September 2018).

Allen, J. (2017) *Technology and Inequality: Concentrated wealth in a Digital World*. Cham: Springer.

Allen, M. (2002). *The Business of Genocide*. Chapel Hill: University of North Carolina Press.

Aly, G. (2016). *Hitler's Beneficiaries: Plunder, Racial War, and the Nazi Welfare State*. London: Verso.

Api.parliament.uk (2018). *The Financial Statement – the Budget (Hansard, 6 March 1854)*. Available at: https://api.parliament.uk/historic-hansard/ commons/1854/mar/06/the-financial-statement-the-budget (accessed 9 June 2018).

Archive.org (1860). *The address of the people of South Carolina assembled in convention, to the people of the slaveholding states of the United States: South Carolina. Convention (1860–1862): Free Download, Borrow, and Streaming: Internet Archive*. Available at: https://archive.org/details/addressof peopleooosout (accessed 6 May 2018).

Archive.org (2018). *Full text of 'Interview between President Lincoln and Col. John B. Baldwin, April 4th, 1861: statements & evidence'*. Available at: https:// archive.org/stream/interviewbetweenoobald/interviewbetweenoobald_ djvu.txt (accessed 7 May 2018).

Archive.spectator.co.uk (2018). *House-Tax v. Income-Tax*. Available at: http://archive.spectator.co.uk/article/13th-september-1873/8/house-tax-v-income-tax (accessed 28 March 2018).

Archives.gov (2018). *The Magna Carta*. Available at: https://www. archives.gov/exhibits/featured-documents/magna-carta (accessed 1 April 2018).

Ash.org.uk (2018). *Large national survey finds 2.9 million people now vape in Britain: For the first time over half don't smoke*. Available at: http://ash.org.uk/media-and-news/press-releases-media-and-news/ large-national-survey-finds-2–9-million-people-now-vape-in-britain-for-the-first-time-over-half-no-longer-smoke/ (accessed 25 October 2018).

*The Assyrian Dictionary of the Oriental Institute of the University of Chicago* (1958). Chicago, Ill.: Oriental Institute.

Austen, J. (1870). *Pride and Prejudice*. Wordsworth Classic Edition.

Avalon.law.yale.edu (2018). *Avalon Project – Constitution of the Confederate States; March 11, 1861*. Available at: http://avalon.law.yale.edu/19th_ century/csa_csa.asp (accessed 3 May 2018).

Avalon.law.yale.edu (2018). *The Avalon Project: First Inaugural Address of Abraham Lincoln*. Available at: http://avalon.law.yale.edu/19th_century/ lincoln1.asp (accessed 11 April 2018).

Balderston, T. (1989) 'War Finance and Inflation in Britain and Germany, 1914–1918'. *The Economic History Review*, 42(2), pp.222–44.

Bank, S., Stark, K. and Thorndike, J. (2008). *War and Taxes*. Washington: Urban Institute Press.

Barlow, J. (1996). *A Declaration of the Independence of Cyberspace*. Electronic Frontier Foundation. Available at: https://www.eff.org/cyberspace-independence (accessed 24 October 2018).

Bartash, J. (2018). *Repatriated profits total $465 billion after Trump tax cuts – leaving $2.5 trillion overseas*. MarketWatch. Available at: https://www.marketwatch.com/story/repatriated-profits-total-nearly-500-billion-after-trump-tax-cuts-2018–09-19 (accessed 12 October 2018).

Bartlett, J. (2018). *The end of a world of nation-states may be upon us*. Aeon. Available at: https://aeon.co/essays/the-end-of-a-world-of-nation-states-may-be-upon-us (accessed 31 October 2018).

Bartlett, J. (2018). *The People vs Tech*. 1st edn. London: Ebury.

Basler, R. P. ed. (1955). *Collected Works of Abraham Lincoln*, Vol. IV. New Brunswick: Rutgers University Press.

Bbc.co.uk (2018). *Government to pay off WW1 debt*. Available at: https://www.bbc.co.uk/news/business-30306579 (accessed 19 June 2018).

Bbc.co.uk (2018). *Vaping – the rise in five charts*. Available at: https://www.bbc.co.uk/news/business-44295336 (accessed 25 October 2018).

Belloc, H. (1913). *The Servile State*. Edinburgh: T. N. Foulis.

Benedictow, O. (2005). *The Black Death: The Greatest Catastrophe Ever*. Historytoday.com. Available at: https://www.historytoday.com/ole-j-benedictow/black-death-greatest-catastrophe-ever (accessed 16 September 2018).

Benson, W. (2010). *A Political History of the Tariff 1789–1861*. USA: Xlibris Corporation.

Bestvalueschools.com (2018). *Understanding the Rising Costs of Higher Education*. Available at: https://www.bestvalueschools.com/understanding-the-rising-costs-of-higher-education/ (accessed 22 October 2018).

Bevan, E. R. (1927). *The House of Ptolemy*, pp.263–8, via: http://www.allaboutarchaeology.org/rosetta-stone-english-translation-faq.htm (accessed 15 February 2017).

Bibula.com (2018). *Straty ludzkie poniesione przez Polskę w latach 1939–1945 – Bibula – pismo niezalezne*. Available at: http://www.bibula.com/?p=13530 (accessed 30 June 2018).

Bloom, E. (2017). *Here's how much money the average first-time homebuyer makes.* CNBC. Available at: https://www.cnbc.com/2017/04/25/heres-how-much-money-the-average-first-time-home-buyer-makes.html (accessed 4 September 2017).

Bloom, J. (2018). *The digital nomads wandering the world.* BBC News. Available at: https://www.bbc.co.uk/news/business-43927098 (accessed 5 October 2018).

Bloomberg.com (2018). *These Are the Economies With the Most (and Least) Efficient Health Care.* Available at: https://www.bloomberg.com/news/articles/2018–09-19/u-s-near-bottom-of-health-index-hong-kong-and-singapore-at-top (accessed 21 December 2018).

Bloy, M. (2019). *The Campaign for the Repeal of the Corn Laws.* Historyhome. co.uk. Available at: http://www.historyhome.co.uk/peel/cornlaws/c-laws2.htm (accessed 11 March 2019).

Bls.gov (2018). *Contingent and Alternative Employment Arrangements Summary.* Available at: https://www.bls.gov/news.release/conemp. nro.htm (accessed 1 October 2018).

Bluche, F. (1990) *Louis XIV.* Paris: Franklin Watts.

Booth, P. and Bourne, R. (2017). *Taxation, Government Spending & Economic Growth: In Brief.* Iea.org.uk. Available at: https://iea.org.uk/publications/taxation-government-spending-economic-growth-in-brief/ (accessed 3 June 2018).

Boyce, M. (2001). *Zoroastrians: Their Religious Beliefs and Practices.* London: Psychology Press. p.148.

Bridge, M. (2018). *The sci-fi future where tech is everywhere . . . and inside us.* Thetimes.co.uk. Available at: https://www.thetimes.co.uk/article/the-sci-fi-future-where-tech-is-everywhere-and-inside-us-sps78rm79 (accessed 27 October 2018).

Brown, J. (2018). *Cash Flow.* The Reformed Broker. Available at: https://thereformedbroker.com/2018/04/24/cash-flow/ (accessed 27 September 2018).

Browne, R. (2018). *70% of people globally work remotely at least once a week, study says.* CNBC. Available at: https://www.cnbc.com/2018/05/30/70-percent-of-people-globally-work-remotely-at-least-once-a-week-iwg-study.html (accessed 5 October 2018).

Burgan, M. (2003). *The Louisiana Purchase*. Minneapolis, MN: Compass Point Books.

Burlingame, M. (2012). *Abraham Lincoln*. Baltimore: Johns Hopkins University Press.

Burns, D. (1992). *Poll Tax Rebellion*. Stirling: AK Press.

Cahill, K. (2010). *Who Owns the World*. New York: Grand Central Pub.

Capella, R. (2012). *The Political Economy of War Finance*. Publicly accessible Penn. Dissertations. 1175. Available at: http://repository. upenn.edu/edissertations/1175.

Carswell, D. (2012). *The End of Politics*. London: Biteback Publishing.

Cato Unbound (2009). Peter Thiel, *The Education of a Libertarian*. Available at: https://www.cato-unbound.org/2009/04/13/peter-thiel/education-libertarian (accessed 11 September 2018).

Cazel, F. A. (1955). 'The Tax of 1185 in Aid of the Holy Land', *Speculum*, Vol. 30, No. 3, pp.385–92, University of Chicago Press.

Cbsnews.com (2018). *How would you feel about a 94% tax rate?* Available at: https://www.cbsnews.com/news/how-would-you-feel-about-a-94-tax-rate/ (accessed 28 June 2018).

Center on Budget and Policy Priorities (2018). *Policy Basics: Where Do Federal Tax Revenues Come From?* Available at: https://www.cbpp.org/research/federal-tax/policy-basics-where-do-federal-tax-revenues-come-from (accessed 28 March 2018).

Cervantes, M. (2011). *Don Quixote*. London: Vintage, p.397.

Cesarani, D. (2015). *Nazi Underworld*. National Geographic – Videos, TV Shows & Photos – Asia. Available at: http://natgeotv.com/asia/nazi-underworld/about (accessed 23 September 2018).

Chanel, G. (2016). 'Taxation as a Cause of the French Revolution: Setting the Record Straight'. *Studia Historica Gedanensia*, 6.

Chesky, B., Gebbia, J., Blecharczyk, N., Johnson, B., Axelrod, B. and Chesnut, R. (2018). *Airbnb*. Craft.co. Available at: https://craft.co/airbnb (accessed 27 September 2018).

Ching, F. (1974). *The Population of Hong Kong*. Hong Kong: Department of Statistics, University of Hong Kong.

Chodorov, F. (2017). *Income Tax: Root of All Evil*. Aubum, Ala.: Dead Authors Society.

Chu, B. (2016). *The charts that shows how private school fees have exploded.* Independent.co.uk. Available at: https://www.independent.co.uk/news/uk/home-news/the-charts-that-shows-how-private-school-fees-have-exploded-a7023056.html (accessed 22 October 2018).

Churchill, W. (1909). *Land Monopoly.* Landvaluetax.org. Available at: http://www.landvaluetax.org/current-affairs-comment/winston-churchill-said-it-all-better-then-we-can.html (accessed 23 December 2018).

Cia.gov (2017). *The World Factbook – Central Intelligence Agency.* Available at: https://www.cia.gov/library/publications/the-world-factbook/rankorder/2186rank.html (accessed 5 September 2017).

Civil War Trust (2018). *Civil War Facts.* Available at: https://www.civilwar.org/learn/articles/civil-war-facts (accessed 7 May 2018).

Civilwarcauses.org (2018). *Robert Toombs's Speech to the Georgia Legislature.* Available at: http://civilwarcauses.org/toombs.htm (accessed 2, 4 May 2018).

Clark, T. and Dilnot, A. (2002). *Long-Term Trends in British Taxation and Spending.* Ifs.org.uk. Available at: https://www.ifs.org.uk/bns/bn25.pdf (accessed 27 June 2018).

Clarke, D. (2017). *Poll shows 85% of MPs don't know where money comes from.* Positivemoney.org. Available at: http://positivemoney.org/2017/10/mp-poll/ (accessed 11 September 2018).

Cobbett, W. (1803). *Cobbett's Parliamentary History of England: From the Norman Conquest, in 1066 to the Year 1803. Comprising the period from the battle of Edge-Hill, in October 1642, to the restoration of Charles the second, in April 1660, Volume 3.* London: Bagshaw.

Coffield, J. (1970). *A Popular History of Taxation.* London: Longman.

Collins, P. (2014). *Virtue and vice: Labour needs to shift tax burdens to unearned wealth.* Fabians.org.uk. Available at: http://fabians.org.uk/virtue-and-vice-labour-needs-to-shift-tax-burdens-to-unearned-wealth/ (accessed 30 September 2018).

Cooper J. S. (1986). 'Clay Cones La 9.1 Presargonic Inscriptions'. The American Oriental Society, New Haven, Connecticut. See: http://www.humanistictexts.org/sumer.htm#4%20Praise%20of%20Uruk-agina.

Cooper, W. J. (2001). *Jefferson Davis, American.* New York: Vintage.

Copernicus, N. (1526). *Monete cudende ratio (Essay on the Minting of Money)*.

Cosgrave, J. (2018). *UK finally finishes paying for World War I*. Cnbc.com. Available at: https://www.cnbc.com/2015/03/09/uk-finally-finishes-paying-for-world-war-i.html (accessed 24 September 2018).

Costly, A. (2018). *BRIA 26 2: The Potato Famine and Irish Immigration to America*. Crf-usa.org. Available at: http://www.crf-usa.org/bill-of-rights-in-action/bria-26–2-the-potato-famine-and-irish-immigration-to-america.html (accessed 2 May 2018).

Cottrell, L. and Davidson, M. (1962). *Lost Worlds*. New York: American Heritage, p.154.

Dailymail.co.uk (2017). *Six of the world's seven billion people have mobile phones but only 4.5 billion have a toilet says UN report*. Available at: http://www.dailymail.co.uk/news/article-2297508/Six-world-s-seven-billion-people-mobile-phones–4-5billion-toilet-says-UN-report.html (accessed 11 June 2017).

Danesi, M. (2007). The Quest for Meaning. Toronto: University of Toronto Press.

Danziger, D. and Gillingham, J. (2004) *1215: The Year of Magna Carta*. London: Hodder Paperbacks.

Data.worldbank.org (2018). *GDP per capita (current US$)*. Available at: https://data.worldbank.org/indicator/NY.GDP.PCAP.CD (accessed 21 December 2018).

Data.worldbank.org (2018). *GDP per capita, PPP (current international $)*. Available at: https://data.worldbank.org/indicator/NY.GDP.PCAP.PP.CD?year_high_desc=true (accessed 5 November 2018).

Data.worldbank.org (2018). *GDP per capita, PPP (current international $)*. Available at: https://data.worldbank.org/indicator/NY.GDP.PCAP.PP.CD?locations=HK-US-GB&year_high_desc=true (accessed 21 December 2018).

Data.worldbank.org (2018). *Military expenditure (% of GDP)*. Available at: https://data.worldbank.org/indicator/MS.MIL.XPND.GD.ZS (accessed 10 July 2018).

Davidson, I. (2010). *Voltaire: A Life*. London: Pegasus.

Davies, L. (2011). *UK National Ecosystem Assessment Technical Report* (ebook). Cambridge: UNEP-WCPC, Chapter 10, p.368, Table 10.3.

Available at: http://uknea.unep-wcmc.org/LinkClick.aspx?fileticket= u6oUgtegc28%3d&tabid=82 (accessed 11 September 2018).

Delaney, K. (2017). *The robot that takes your job should pay taxes, says Bill Gates.* Qz.com. Available at: https://qz.com/911968/bill-gates-the-robot-that-takes-your-job-should-pay-taxes/ (accessed 7 January 2019).

Dell, S. (2016). *Let there be light! Candles in the time of Jane Austen.* Jane-austens-house-museum.org.uk. Available at: https://www.jane-austens-house-museum.org.uk/single-post/2016/1/12/Let-there-be-light-Candles-in-the-time-of-Jane-Austen (accessed 24 February 2019).

Deloitte Czech Republic (2018). *This Year's Tax Freedom Day Falls on 23 June 2018.* Available at: https://www2.deloitte.com/cz/en/pages/press/articles/cze-tz-den-danove-svobody-letos-pripadne-na-23-cervna-2018.html (accessed 15 September 2018).

Demographia.com (2019). *Greater London, Inner London Population & Density History.* Available at: http://www.demographia.com/dm-lon31.htm (accessed 4 January 2019).

Dennett, Jr., D. C. (1950). *Conversion and the Poll Tax in Early Islam,* Harvard, p.10, citing *History of the Patriarchs of the Coptic Church of Alexandra,* ed. Evetts (1910), pp.189–90.

Denning, T. (1965). 'The Magna Charta Ceremonies in England'. *American Bar Association Journal,* 51(10).

Desjardins, J. (2018). *The Buying Power of the US Dollar Over the Last Century.* Visualcapitalist.com. Available at: http://www.visualcapitalist.com/buying-power-us-dollar-century/ (accessed 26 September 2018).

Dickens, C. (1850). *Household Words.* London: Bradbury & Evans.

Dickens, C. (1861). 'The Morrill Tariff'. *All the Year Round, A Weekly Journal by Charles Dickens,* Vol. 6 (September 1861–March 1862), pp.328–31. Available at: https://ia600208.us.archive.org/29/items/allyearround-06charrich/allyearround06charrich.pdf (accessed 12 September 2018).

Dickens, C. (1863). *David Copperfield.* London: Sheldon, p.137.

Dilnot, A. and Clark, T. (2002). *Long-Term Trends in British Taxation and Spending* (ebook). London: Institute of Fiscal Studies. Available at: https://www.ifs.org.uk/bns/bn25.pdf (accessed 3 July 2018).

Dobson, R. (1970). *The Peasants' Revolt of 1381.* London: Macmillan.

Dowell, S. (1888). *A History of Taxation and Taxes in England from the Earliest Times to the Present Day*. London: Longmans, Green and Co.

Downing, C. (2017). *The future of finance and tax: It's all about the data*. Kpmg. com. Available at: https://home.kpmg.com/uk/en/home/insights/2017/05/the-future-of-and-tax.html (accessed 30 September 2018).

Dunn, A. (2002). *The Great Rising of 1381*. Stroud, Gloucestershire: Tempus.

Dyer, C. (2000). *Everyday Life in Medieval England*. London: Hambledon and London.

Dyson, B. (2012). *Full Reserve Banking Is No Bailout*. Positivemoney.org. Available at: http://positivemoney.org/2012/10/full-reserve-banking-does-not-mean-a-bank-bailout/ (accessed 14 September 2018).

East_west_dialogue.tripod.com (2018). *Henry VII's Reign*. Available at: http://east_west_dialogue.tripod.com/europe/id4.html (accessed 21 September 2018).

Ebenstein, A. (2012). *The Indispensable Milton Friedman*. Washington DC: Regnery Pub., p.251.

Edwards, H. and Edwards, D. (2018). *Your primer on talking about the AI-led 'fourth industrial revolution'*. Qz.com. Available at: https://qz.com/1090176/how-to-think-about-job-automation-studies/ (accessed 9 October 2018).

Elliott, A. (2018). *How far have fares really fallen since the golden age of flying?* Telegraph.co.uk. Available at: https://www.telegraph.co.uk/travel/comment/how-airfares-have-fallen-since-golden-age-of-flying/ (accessed 5 October 2018).

En.wikipedia.org (2019). *American Civil War*. Available at: https://en.wikipedia.org/wiki/American_Civil_War (accessed 13 January 2019).

Encyclopedia Britannica (2017). *Ancient Greek civilization*. Available at: https://www.britannica.com/place/ancient-Greece/Classical-Greek-civilization#ref298204 (accessed 17 February 2017).

Encyclopedia Britannica (2018). *United States – World War II*. Available at: https://www.britannica.com/place/United-States/World-War-II#ref613137 (accessed 13 June 2018).

Encyclopedia.1914–1918-online.net (2018). *War Finance (Germany)*. Available at: https://encyclopedia.1914–1918-online.net/article/war_finance_germany (accessed 13 June 2018).

Entin, S. (2018). *Tax Incidence, Tax Burden, and Tax Shifting: Who Really Pays the Tax?* (ebook). Washington DC: Institute for Research on the Economics of Taxation. Available at: http://iret.org/pub/BLTN-88. PDF (accessed 28 March 2018).

Ericsson.com (2018). *Mobile subscriptions worldwide outlook.* Available at: https://www.ericsson.com/en/mobility-report/reports/june-2018/ mobile-subscriptions-worldwide-outlook (accessed 21 October 2018).

Europa.eu (2016). *State aid: Ireland gave illegal tax benefits to Apple worth up to €13 billion.* Available at: http://europa.eu/rapid/press-release_IP-16-2923_en.htm (accessed 28 June 2019).

Europa.eu (2018). *State of the Union 2018: Making the EU a stronger global actor – European Commission proposes more efficient decision-making in Common Foreign and Security Policy.* Available at: http://europa.eu/ rapid/press-release_IP-18–5683_en.htm (accessed 11 October 2018).

Faber, M. (2018). *110: Bryan Taylor* (podcast). Mebfaber.com. Available at: https://mebfaber.com/2018/06/27/episode-110-bryan-taylor-at-some-point-the-stresses-are-going-to-be-so-great-that-some-of-the-countries-in-the-european-union-are-eventually-forced-to-leave/ (accessed 26 September 2018).

Fahey, M. (2016). *Driverless cars will kill the most jobs in select US states.* Cnbc.com. Available at: https://www.cnbc.com/2016/09/02/driver-less-cars-will-kill-the-most-jobs-in-select-us-states.html (accessed 10 October 2018).

Fairchild, F. R. (1922). 'German War Finance – a Review'. *American Economic Review*, 12(2), pp.246–61.

Feldman, G. (1993). *The Great Disorder: Politics, Economics, and Society in the German Inflation, 1914–1924.* New York: Oxford University Press.

Fhwa.dot.gov (2018). *The Reichsautobahnen.* Available at: https://www. fhwa.dot.gov/infrastructure/reichs.cfm (accessed 30 June 2018).

Finance.co.uk (2018). *How Much Tax Will I Pay On £100 Earned?* Available at: http://www.simplefs.co.uk/press-release/how-much-tax-on-100-pounds.asp (accessed 3 June 2018).

*First [and Second] Report[s] of the Commissioners for Inquiring Into the State of Large Towns and Populous Districts*, Vol. 2, Part 2, Appendix (p.2010). William Clowes and Sons, 1845.

Founders.archives.gov (2018). *Founders Online: Rules by Which a Great Empire May Be Reduced to a Small One*. Available at: https://founders. archives.gov/documents/Franklin/01–20-02–0213 (accessed 27 May 2018).

Franklin, B. (2007). *Poor Richard's Almanac*. New York: Skyhorse Publishing, p.28.

Fred.stlouisfed.org (2018). MZM *Money Stock*. Available at: https://fred. stlouisfed.org/series/MZMNS (accessed 26 September 2018).

Freehling, W. H. (1990). *The Road to Disunion: Secessionists at Bay 1776–1854*. New York: Oxford University Press.

Friedman, M. (1976). *Monetary Correction: A Proposal for Escalator Clauses to Reduce the Costs of Ending Inflation*. London: Institute of Economic Affairs.

Friedman, M. (1978). *Milton Friedman Interviewed*. Cooperative-individualism. org. Available at: https://www.cooperative-individualism.org/the-times-herald_milton-friedman-interviewed-1978-dec.htm (accessed 23 December 2018).

Friedman, M. (1998). *The Hong Kong Experiment*. Hoover.org. Available at: https://www.hoover.org/research/hong-kong-experiment (accessed 16 December 2018).

Frisby, D. (2013). *Life After the State*. London: Unbound.

Fritschy, W. (1997). 'A History of the Income Tax in the Netherlands'. *Revue belge de philologie et d'histoire*, 75(4), pp.1045–61.

Ft.com (2017). *No country for young men – UK generation gap widens*. Available at: https://www.ft.com/content/60d77d08-b20e-11e4-b380-00144feab7de (accessed 23 August 2017).

Galofré-Vilà, G., Meissner, C., McKee, M. and Stuckler, D. (2018). *Austerity and the rise of the Nazi party*. Nber.org. Available at: http://www.nber. org/papers/w24106 (accessed 1 July 2018).

Gaunt, R. (2014). *Sir Robert Peel*. London: I. B. Tauris.

George, H. (1879). *Progress and Poverty*. New York: D. Appleton and Company.

Giandrea, S. (2018). *Estimating the US labor share*. Bls.gov. Available at: https://www.bls.gov/opub/mlr/2017/article/estimating-the-us-labor-share.htm (accessed 29 October 2018).

Gibson, M. (2018). *Searching for New Atlantis in China*. Reason.com. Available at: https://reason.com/archives/2018/12/07/searching-for-new-atlantis-in-china/3 (accessed 21 December 2018).

Gigeconomy.ey.com (2018). *Global Contingent Workforce Study*. Available at: https://gigeconomy.ey.com/ (accessed 1 October 2018).

Gigeconomydata.org (2018). *MBO Survey*. Available at: https://www.gigeconomydata.org/research/data-sources/mbo-survey (accessed 1 October 2018).

Graeber, D. (2011). *Debt – The First 5,000 Years*. New York: Random House Publisher Services, p.6.

Graetz, H. (1873). *History of the Jews*. American Jewish Publication Society.

Greenslade, R. (2017). *Times Newspapers posts £1.7m profit, first in 13 years*. Theguardian.com. Available at: https://www.theguardian.com/media/greenslade/2014/dec/02/times-newspapers-posts-17m-profit-first-in-13-years (accessed 10 September 2017).

Griffith, M. (2018). *The Confederacy, the Union, and the Civil War – a look at four claims about the War Between the States*. Knowsouthernhistory.net. Available at: http://www.knowsouthernhistory.net/Articles/History/WSI/four_claims.html (accessed 3 May 2018).

Guta, M. (2018). *55% of Remote Workers Now Telecommute Full Time, Survey Says*. Smallbiztrends.com. Available at: https://smallbiztrends.com/2018/08/2018-remote-working-statistics.html (accessed 5 October 2018).

Halliday, J. (2017). *Times loses almost 90% of online readership*. Theguardian.com. Available at: https://www.theguardian.com/media/2010/jul/20/times-paywall-readership (accessed 10 September 2017).

Halstead, M. (1860). *Caucuses of 1860: A history of the national political conventions of the current presidential campaign: being a complete record of the business of all the conventions; with sketches of distinguished men in attendance upon them, and descriptions of the most characteristic scenes and memorable events*. Follett, Foster and Company, p.135. Available at: https://books.google.co.uk/books?id=Tw4TAAAAYAAJ&pg=PA135&dq=her+whole+delegation+ris+ing+and+swinging+hats+and+canes&hl=en&sa=X&ved=0ahUKEwij44_z1YbjAhXoSBUIHeLvCWUQ6

AEILDAA#v=onepage&q=her%20whole%20delegation%20ris-%20
ing%20and%20swinging%20hats%20and%20canes&f=false.

Hammond, B. and Hammond, J. (1911). *The Village Labourer*. London:
Longmans.

Hannaford, A. (2017). *The Internet of Things: Could it really change the way
we live?* Telegraph.co.uk. Available at: http://www.telegraph.co.uk/
technology/2017/05/06/internet-things-could-really-change-way-live/
(accessed 11 June 2017).

Harding, M., Bradbury, D. and Lahittete, M. (2018). *OECD Revenue Statistics
2017 – Germany* (ebook). Centre for Tax Policy and Administration, p.2.
Available at: https://www.oecd.org/tax/revenue-statistics-germany.pdf
(accessed 28 March 2018).

Haskel, J. and Westlake, S. (2018). *Capitalism without Capital*. Princeton,
NJ: Princeton University Press.

Hawkins, J. (2019). *An Interview with Milton Friedman*. Rightwingnews.
com. Available at: https://rightwingnews.com/interviews/an-interview-
with-milton-friedman-2/ (accessed 1 April 2019).

Hazlitt, H. (1952). *Economics in One Lesson*. New York: Foundation for
Economic Education, p.20.

Heritage.org (2018). *2018 Index of Economic Freedom*. Available at: https://
www.heritage.org/index/about (accessed 23 December 2018).

Historylearningsite.co.uk (2018). *Henry VII*. Available at: https://www.
historylearningsite.co.uk/tudor-england/henry-vii/ (accessed 21
September 2018).

Holst, A. (2019). *Fixed telephone lines worldwide 2000–2018 | Statistic*. [online]
Statista. Available at: https://www.statista.com/statistics/273014/
number-of-fixed-telephone-lines-worldwide-since-2000/ (accessed 26
June 2019).

Hookway, A. (2019). *Searching for the owner of unregistered land*.
Hmlandregistry.blog.gov.uk. Available at: https://hmlandregistry.
blog.gov.uk/2018/02/05/search-owner-unregistered-land/ (accessed 31
March 2019).

Houlder, V. (2017). *Ten ways HMRC can tell if you're a tax cheat*. Ft.com.
Available at: https://www.ft.com/content/0640f6ac-5ce9-11e7-9bc8-
8055f264aa8b (accessed 26 October 2018).

Hudson, C. (2018). *War on the Home Front: living in a wartime economy 1792–1815*. Historicinterpreter.wordpress.com. Available at: https://historicinterpreter.wordpress.com/2015/06/17/war-on-the-home-front-living-in-a-wartime-economy-1792–1815/ (accessed 5 April 2018).

Hughes, E. (1992). *The Hampshire Hearth Tax Assessment, 1665*. Winchester: Hampshire Country Council Planning Department.

Hunt, L. (2007). *The Making of the West: Peoples and Cultures: A Concise History: Volume II: Since 1340*, 2nd edn, Boston: Bedford/St Martin's.

Imf.org (2018). *General Government Gross Debt*. Available at: https://www.imf.org/external/datamapper/GGXWDG_NGDP@WEO/OEMDC/ADVEC/WEOWORLD/JPN (accessed 24 September 2018).

Income-tax.co.uk (2018). *Tax Calculator for £27,500 salary*. Available at: https://www.income-tax.co.uk/calculator/27500/ (accessed 8 October 2018).

Indexmundi.com (2018). *Jet Fuel Daily Price*. Available at: https://www.indexmundi.com/commodities/?commodity=jet-fuel&months=240 (accessed 5 October 2018).

Info.gov.hk (2018). *Hong Kong ranked world's freest economy for 24 consecutive years*. Available at: https://www.info.gov.hk/gia/general/201802/02/P2018020200484.htm (accessed 22 December 2018).

Infoplease.com (2018). *State of the Union Address: James Buchanan (December 3, 1860)*. Available at: https://www.infoplease.com/homework-help/us-documents/state-union-address-james-buchanan-december-3–1860 (accessed 10 May 2018).

Inman, P. (2017). *This man was right all along*. Theguardian.com. Available at: https://www.theguardian.com/money/2003/may/10/tax.scamsandfraud?CMP=share_btn_tw (accessed 9 June 2017).

Internationaltaxreview.com (2017). *Global Tax 50 2017*. Available at: http://www.internationaltaxreview.com/Article/3773447/Global-Tax-50–2017.html?&es_p=6011346 (accessed 30 September 2018).

Isaac, A. (2018). *Budget splurge on NHS shows tax rises must come soon, IFS says*. Telegraph.co.uk. Available at: https://www.telegraph.co.uk/business/2018/10/30/budget-splurge-nhs-shows-tax-rises-must-come-soon-ifs-says/ (accessed 4 November 2018).

*Islam: From the Prophet Muhammad to the Capture of Constantinople: Politics and War*. Trans. Bernard Lewis, 1974. London: Macmillian.

James, S. R. (2002). *Taxation: Critical Perspectives on the World Economy.* Vol. 1. London: Routledge.

Jefferson, T. (1805). *Second Inaugural Address.* Pagebypagebooks.com. Available at: https://www.pagebypagebooks.com/Thomas_Jefferson/Second_Inaugural_Speech/Second_Inaugural_Address_p1.html (accessed 6 January 2019).

Jeffersondavis.rice.edu (2018). *Jefferson Davis' First Inaugural Address.* Available at: https://jeffersondavis.rice.edu/archives/documents/jefferson-davis-first-inaugural-address (accessed 3 May 2018).

Jenkins, P. (1989). *Mrs Thatcher's Revolution.* London: Pan Books.

Joint Association of Classical Teachers (1984). *The World of Athens.* Cambridge: CUP.

Josephus, Titus Flavius. *The Antiquities of the Jews,* AD 93–4. Trans. William Whiston, 1737.

Katz, L. F. and Krueger, A. B. (2019) 'The Rise and Nature of Alternative Work Arrangements in the United States, 1995–2015'. *ILR Review,* 72(2), pp.382–416.

Kendall, J. (1957). *Michael Faraday, Man of Simplicity.* London: Faber and Faber, p.14.

Kesselring, K. (2016). *The Trial of Charles I: A History in Documents.* London: Broadview Press.

Keynes, J. (1920). *Economic Consequences of the Peace.* London: Macmillan.

Keynes, J. M. (1963) *Essays in Persuasion.* New York: W. W. Norton & Co.

Kharas, H. and Hamel, K. (2018). *A global tipping point: Half the world is now middle class or wealthier.* Brookings.edu. Available at: https://www.brookings.edu/blog/future-development/2018/09/27/a-global-tipping-point-half-the-world-is-now-middle-class-or-wealthier/?utm_campaign=Brookings%20Brief&utm_source=hs_email&utm_medium=email&utm_content=66298094 (accessed 5 October 2018).

Kingsnorth, P. (2017). *High house prices? Inequality? I blame the Normans.* Theguardian.com. Available at: https://www.theguardian.com/commentisfree/2012/dec/17/high-house-prices-inequality-normans (accessed 12 June 2017).

Kinnock, N. (1985). *Classic Podium: End this grotesque chaos.* Independent.co.uk. Available at: https://www.independent.co.uk/arts-entertainment/

classic-podium-end-this-grotesque-chaos-1200539.html (accessed 15 September 2018).

Klingaman, W. F. (2001). *Abraham Lincoln and the Road to Emancipation*. New York: Penguin.

Knighton, H. and Lumby, J. (1964). *Chronicon Henrici Knighton vel Cnitthon, monachi Leycestrensis*. New York: Kraus Reprint.

Knupfer, S., Pokatilo, V. and Woetzel, J. (2018). *Urban Transportation Systems of 24 Cities*. Mckinsey.com. Available at: https://www.mckinsey.com/~/media/mckinsey/business%20functions/sustainability%20and%20resource%20productivity/our%20insights/elements%20of%20success%20urban%20transportation%20systems%20of%2024%20global%20cities/urban%20transportation%20systems.ashx) (accessed 21 December 2018).

Kocieniewski, D. (2018). *Airbnb, Others Pay Out Billions Beneath IRS's Radar, Study Finds*. Bloomberg.com. Available at: https://www.bloomberg.com/news/articles/2016–05-23/airbnb-others-pay-out-billions-beneath-irs-s-radar-study-finds (accessed 27 September 2018).

Laffer, A. (2004). *The Laffer Curve: Past, Present, and Future*. Heritage.org. Available at: https://www.heritage.org/taxes/report/the-laffer-curve-past-present-and-future (accessed 27 September 2018).

Laffer, A. (2011). *Cain's Stimulating '9–9–9' Tax Reform*. Wsj.com. Available at: https://www.wsj.com/articles/SB100014240529702043461045766373103153678o4 (accessed 31 March 2019).

*The Lancet* (1845). 45(1121), pp.214–16.

Lawson, N. (1992). *The View from No. 11: Memoirs of a Tory Radical*. London: Bantam.

Levels, P. (2015). *There Will Be 1 Billion Digital Nomads by 2035*. Talk for DNX Global, Berlin. Available at: https://www.youtube.com/watch?v=4IYOZ6H0UNk.

Lincoln, A. (1832). *Abraham Lincoln's First Political Announcement*. Abrahamlincolnonline.org. Available at: http://www.abrahamlincolnonline.org/lincoln/speeches/1832.htm (accessed 13 January 2019).

Lindholm, R. (1947). *German Finance in World War II* (ebook). American Economic Association, pp.121–34. Available at: http://piketty.pse.ens.

fr/files/capitalisback/CountryData/Germany/Other/Pre1950Series/
RefsHistoricalGermanAccounts/Lindholm47.pdf (accessed 1 July 2018).

Little, P. (2009). *Oliver Cromwell*. Basingstoke (England): Palgrave Macmillan.

Lordsandladies.org (2018). *Decline of Feudalism*. Available at: http://www.
lordsandladies.org/decline-of-feudalism.htm (accessed 21 September
2018).

Lordsandladies.org (2018). *Serfs*. Available at: http://www.lordsandladies.
org/serfs.htm (accessed 23 September 2018).

MacKay, A. L. (1977). *A Dictionary of Scientific Quotations*. Bristol: Institute
of Physics Publishing.

Mckinsey.com (2018). *Jobs lost, jobs gained: What the future of work will mean
for jobs, skills, and wages*. Available at: https://www.mckinsey.com/
featured-insights/future-of-work/jobs-lost-jobs-gained-what-the-future-
of-work-will-mean-for-jobs-skills-and-wages (accessed 9 October 2018).

Maldonado, C. (2018). *Price of College Increasing Almost 8 Times Faster
Than Wages*. Forbes.com. Available at: https://www.forbes.com/sites/
camilomaldonado/2018/07/24/price-of-college-increasing-almost-8-
times-faster-than-wages/#2dea3b1266c1 (accessed 22 October 2018).

Margaretthatcher.org (1997). *Speech to the First International Conservative
Congress*. Available at: https://www.margaretthatcher.org/document/
108374 (accessed 1 April 2019).

Marx, K. (2018). *The North American Civil War (1861)*. Tenc.net. Available at:
http://www.tenc.net/a/18611025.htm (accessed 10 May 2018).

Master-and-more.eu (2018). *Top 40 education systems in the world*. Available
at: https://www.master-and-more.eu/en/top-40-education-systems-in-
the-world/ (accessed 21 December 2018).

May, T. (1988). *The Crypto Anarchist Manifesto*. Activism.net. Available at:
https://www.activism.net/cypherpunk/crypto-anarchy.html (accessed
19 October 2018).

Mellon, A. (1924). *Taxation*. New York: The MacMillan Company.

Melville, L. (1913). *The Life and Letters of William Cobbett in England &
America*. London: John Lane, The Bodley Head.

Miketgriffith.com (2018). *The Tariff and Secession*. Available at: http://
miketgriffith.com/files/tariffandsecession.htm (accessed 3 May 2018).

Mill, J. (1848). *Principles of political economy with some of their Applications to Social Philosophy.* Book V, Chapter II: On the General Principles of Taxation.

Millercenter.org (2018). *Abraham Lincoln: Campaigns and Elections.* Available at: http://millercenter.org/president/lincoln/campaigns-and-elections (accessed 16 April 2018).

Mises.org (2018). Thomas J. DiLorenzo, *Lincoln's Tariff War.* Available at: https://mises.org/library/lincolns-tariff-war (accessed 6 May 2018).

Monnery, N. (2017). *Architect of Prosperity.* 1st edn. London: London Publishing Partnership.

Morrill, J. (1993). *The Nature of the English Revolution.* London: Longman.

Nase.org (2018). *Small Biz Survey – 69% of Sharing Economy Entrepreneurs Received Zero Tax Guidance.* Available at: https://www.nase.org/about-us/Nase_News/2016/05/11/small-biz-survey–69-of-sharing-economy-entrepreneurs-received-zero-tax-guidance (accessed 27 September 2018).

National Taxpayers Union (1999). *Interview with Milton Friedman* (video). Available at: https://www.youtube.com/watch?v=mlwxdyLnMXM (accessed 7 January 2019).

Nationmaster.com (2018). *Countries Compared by Economy > GDP per capita in 1950. International Statistics at NationMaster.com.* Available at: http://www.nationmaster.com/country-info/stats/Economy/GDP-per-capita-in-1950 (accessed 5 November 2018).

Newint.org (2018). *A short history of taxation.* Available at: https://newint.org/features/2008/10/01/tax-history (accessed 3 July 2018).

Newman, M. (2017). *The Next Leg of the Electric Revolution.* Presentation. Bernstein Long View Series.

News.bbc.co.uk (2018). *One in five yet to pay poll tax.* Available at: http://news.bbc.co.uk/onthisday/hi/dates/stories/august/14/newsid_2495000/2495911.stm (accessed 15 September 2018).

News.bbc.co.uk (2018). *UK settles WWII debts to allies.* Available at: http://news.bbc.co.uk/1/hi/uk/6215847.stm (accessed 7 December 2018).

Newstatesman.com (2017). *The great property swindle: why do so few people in Britain own so much of our land?* Available at: http://www.newstatesman.com/life-and-society/2011/03/million-acres-land-ownership (accessed 11 June 2017).

Norporth, H. (2018). *The American Voter in 1932: Evidence from a Confidential Survey* (ebook). American Political Science Association. Available at: https://www.gwern.net/docs/history/2018-norpoth.pdf (accessed 25 September 2018).

Novak, M. (2016). *9 Quotes From Winston Churchill That Are Totally Fake.* Paleofuture.gizmodo.com. Available at: https://paleofuture.gizmodo.com/9-quotes-from-winston-churchill-that-are-totally-fake-1790585636 (accessed 1 April 2019).

Noyes, C. (1940). *Economic Controls in Nazi Germany.* Cqpress.com. Available at: http://library.cqpress.com/cqresearcher/document.php?id=cqresrre1940110100#H2_4 (accessed 1 July 2018).

Nps.gov (2018). *Industry and Economy during the Civil War.* Available at: https://www.nps.gov/resources/story.htm%3Fid%3D251 (accessed 11 April 2018).

Nytimes.com (1861). *Sumter and the Administration.* Available at: https://www.nytimes.com/1861/04/17/archives/sumter-and-the-administration.html (accessed 12 January 2019).

Nytimes.com (2018). *A Letter from President Lincoln. Reply to Horace Greeley. Slavery and the Union. The Restoration of the Union the Paramount Object.* Available at: https://www.nytimes.com/1862/08/24/archives/a-letter-from-president-lincoln-reply-to-horace-greeley-slavery-and.html (accessed 7 May 2018).

Nytimes.com (2018). *The Emancipation Proclamation; Interesting Sketch of its History by the Artist, Carpenter.* Available at: https://www.nytimes.com/1865/06/16/archives/the-emancipation-proclamation-interesting-sketch-of-its-history-by.html (accessed 9 May 2018).

Oates, W. and Schwab, R. (2015). 'The Window Tax: A Case Study in Excess Burden'. *Journal of Economic Perspectives*, 29(1), pp.163–80.

Observationsandnotes.blogspot.com (2018). *The Decrease in Purchasing Power of the US Dollar Since 1900.* Available at: http://observationsandnotes.blogspot.com/2011/04/100-year-declining-value-of-us-dollar.html (accessed 26 September 2018).

Occhino, F., Oosterlinck, K. and White, E. (2007). *How Occupied France Financed its own Exploitation in World War II* (ebook, 2nd edn). *American Economic Review*, 97 (2), pp.295–9. Available at: https://eml.

berkeley.edu/~webfac/eichengreen/e211_fa05/white.pdf (accessed 1 July 2018).

Oecd.org (2018). *General government spending*. Available at: https://data. oecd.org/gga/general-government-spending.htm (accessed 13, 22 September 2018).

Oecd.org (2018). *OECD Revenue Statistics 2017 United States*. Available at: https://www.oecd.org/tax/revenue-statistics-united-states.pdf (accessed 15 July 2018).

Oecd.org (2018). *Tax on personal income*. Available at: https://data.oecd. org/tax/tax-on-personal-income.htm (accessed 22 September 2018).

Oecd.org (2019). *Economic Outlook Annex Tables*. Available at: http://www. oecd.org/economy/outlook/economicoutlookannextables.htm (accessed 20 March 2019).

Official Report of Proceedings of the Hong Kong Legislative Council (1961). Legco.gov.hk. Available at: https://www.legco.gov.hk/yr97-98/ english/former/lc_sitg.htm (accessed 19 December 2018).

Officialdata.org (2018). *£100 in 1938 → 1951*. Available at: https://www. officialdata.org/1938-GBP-in-1951?amount=100 (accessed 29 June 2018).

Okrent, D. (2010). *Wayne B. Wheeler: The Man Who Turned Off the Taps*. Smithsonianmag.com. Available at: https://www.smithsonianmag. com/history/wayne-b-wheeler-the-man-who-turned-off-the-taps-14783512/ (accessed 14 June 2018).

Ormrod, W. (1990). 'The Peasants' Revolt and the Government of England'. *Journal of British Studies*, Vol. 29 (No.1), pp.1–30. Available at: https://www.jstor.org/stable/175483 (accessed 17 September 2018).

Ortiz-Ospina, E. and Roser, M. (2018). *Public Spending*. Ourworldindata. org. Available at: https://ourworldindata.org/public-spending (accessed 10 July 2018).

Ortiz-Ospina, E. and Roser, M. (2018). *Taxation*. Ourworldindata.org. Available at: https://ourworldindata.org/taxation (accessed 5 July 2018).

Ourworldindata.org (2018). *Number of countries having implemented Value Added Taxes*. Available at: https://ourworldindata.org/grapher/number-of-countries-having-implemented-a-vat (accessed 11 July 2018).

Oxfam.org (2018). *Richest 1 percent bagged 82 percent of wealth created last year – poorest half of humanity got nothing*. Available at: https://www.oxfam.

org/en/pressroom/pressreleases/2018–01-22/richest-1-percent-bagged-82-percent-wealth-created-last-year (accessed 24 November 2018).

Oxforddictionaries.com (2018). *Definition of task in English by Oxford Dictionaries*. Available at: https://en.oxforddictionaries.com/definition/task (accessed 11 November 2018).

Packman, A. (2016). *Tax transparency and country by country reporting*. Pwc.com. Available at: https://www.pwc.com/gx/en/tax/publications/assets/tax-transparency-and-country-by-country-reporting.pdf (accessed 30 September 2018).

Paine, T. (1797). *Agrarian Justice*. Geolib.pair.com. Available at: http://geolib.pair.com/essays/paine.tom/agjst.html (accessed 23 December 2018).

Painter, S. (1933). *William Marshal, Knight-Errant, Baron, and Regent of England*. Baltimore: Johns Hopkins Press.

*The Parliamentary Debates (Authorized Edition)* (1833). Wyman, Vol. 20.

Parliament.uk (2018). *The 1816 repeal of the income tax*. Available at: https://www.parliament.uk/business/committees/committees-a-z/commons-select/petitions-committee/petition-of-the-month/war-petitions-and-the-income-tax/ (accessed 8 April 2018).

Parliament.uk (2018). *The cost of war*. Available at: https://www.parliament.uk/about/living-heritage/transformingsociety/private-lives/taxation/overview/costofwar/ (accessed 13 June 2018).

Parliament.uk (2019). *Taxation during the First World War*. Available at: https://www.parliament.uk/about/living-heritage/transformingsociety/private-lives/taxation/overview/firstworldwar/ (accessed 11 March 2019).

Pettinger, T. (2018). *David Lloyd George Biography*. Biographyonline.net. Available at: https://www.biographyonline.net/politicians/uk/lloyd-george.html (accessed 15 December 2018).

Phillips, M. (2018). *The Long Story of US Debt, from 1790 to 2011, in 1 Little Chart*. Theatlantic.com. Available at: https://www.theatlantic.com/business/archive/2012/11/the-long-story-of-us-debt-from-1790-to-2011-in-1-little-chart/265185/ (accessed 29 June 2018).

Plato (2007). *Republic*. Oxford: Aris & Phillips.

Pope, T. and Waters, T. (2016). *A Survey of the UK Tax System*. Ifs.org.uk. Available at: https://www.ifs.org.uk/bns/bn09.pdf (accessed 15 July 2018).

Positivemoney.org (2017). *House prices: why are they so high?* Available at: http://positivemoney.org/issues/house-prices/ (accessed 11 June 2017).

Positivemoney.org (2018). *Infographic: Why are House Prices So High?* Available at: http://positivemoney.org/2012/09/infographics-why-are-house-prices-so-high/ (accessed 11 September 2018).

Presidency.ucsb.edu (2018). *John F. Kennedy: Address and Question and Answer Period at the Economic Club of New York.* Available at: http://www.presidency.ucsb.edu/ws/?pid=9057 (accessed 4 June 2018).

Preyer, N. W. (1959). 'Southern Support of the Tariff of 1816: A Reappraisal', *Journal of Southern History*, XXV, pp.306–22, in *Essays on Jacksonian America*, ed. Frank Otto Gatell, New York: Holt, Rinehart and Winston, Inc., 1970.

Price, M. (1980). *The Peasants' Revolt.* London: Longman.

Pwc.co.uk (2018). *UK Economic Outlook.* Available at: https://www.pwc.co.uk/services/economics-policy/insights/uk-economic-outlook.html#dataexplorer (accessed 9 October 2018).

Quod.lib.umich.edu (2018). *Collected Works of Abraham Lincoln. Volume 3.* Available at: https://quod.lib.umich.edu/l/lincoln/lincoln3/1:122.1?rgn=div2;view=fulltext (accessed 27 April 2018).

Quoteinvestigator.com (2019). *The Hardest Thing in the World to Understand is Income Taxes.* Available at: https://quoteinvestigator.com/2011/03/07/einstein-income-taxes/ (accessed 9 January 2019).

Reaction.life (2017). *How to switch taxation to a subscriber model.* Available at: https://reaction.life/switch-taxation-subscriber-model/ (accessed 10 September 2017).

Recode.net (2018). *The US government doesn't know how big the gig economy is.* Available at: https://www.recode.net/2018/7/24/17603482/the-u-s-government-doesnt-know-how-big-the-gig-economy-is (accessed 1 October 2018).

Reichsfinanzministerium-geschichte.de (2018). *Historikerkommission – Reichsfinanzministerium von 1933–1945.* Available at: http://www.reichsfinanzministerium-geschichte.de/ (accessed 30 June 2018).

Reid, J., Nicol, C., Burns, N. and Chanda, S. (2018). *Long Term Asset Return Study – the Next Financial Crisis* (ebook). London: Deutsche Bank Global Research. Available at: https://www.dbresearch.com/PROD/

RPS_EN-PROD/Publications_reportsanalysis_and_studies_by_Jim_Reid_for_download/JIM_REID.alias (accessed 25 September 2018).

Reid, J., Nicol, C., Burns, N. and Mahtani, S. (2018). *The History (and Future) of Inflation*. London: Deutsche Bank Research.

Reinhart, C. and Rogoff, K. (2013). *Reflections on the 100th Anniversary of the Federal Reserve* (ebook). San Diego. Available at: http://www.aeaweb.org/aea/2013conference/program/retrieve.php?pdfid=485 (accessed 25 September 2018).

Rivlin, A. M. and McClellan, M. B. (2017) *How to Take on Health Inequality in America*. brookings.edu.

Roantree, B. and Miller, H. (2018). *Tax revenues: where does the money come from and what are the next government's challenges?* Ifs.org.uk. Available at: https://www.ifs.org.uk/publications/9178 (accessed 28 March 2018).

Roberts, J. and Westad, O. (2014). *The Penguin History of the World*. London: Penguin Books.

Roberts, R. (2018). *Neil Monnery on Hong Kong and the Architect of Prosperity* (podcast). Econtalk.org. Available at: http://www.econtalk.org/neil-monnery-on-hong-kong-and-the-architect-of-prosperity/#audio-highlights (accessed 17 December 2018).

Roosevelt, F. (1942). *State of the Union 1942*. Let.rug.nl. Available at: http://www.let.rug.nl/usa/presidents/franklin-delano-roosevelt/state-of-the-union-1942.php (accessed 1 April 2019).

Rothwell, H. and Douglas, D. (1996). *English Historical Documents*. London: Routledge.

Sakoulas, T. (2017). *Parthenon*. Ancient-greece.org. Available at: http://ancient-greece.org/architecture/parthenon.html (accessed 17 February 2017).

as-Sallaabee, A. M. (2007). *The Biography of Abu Bakr as Siddeeq*. Riyadh: Darussalam Publisher.

Scencyclopedia.org (2018). *Secession crisis of 1850–1851*. Available at: http://www.scencyclopedia.org/sce/entries/secession-crisis-of-1850%C2%961851/ (accessed 27 April 2018).

Schwab, K. (2016). *The Fourth Industrial Revolution*. Geneva, Switzerland: World Economic Forum.

Scmp.com (2018). *Hong Kong's budget surplus underestimated for eighth year in a row*. Available at: https://www.scmp.com/news/hong-kong/article/1723421/hong-kongs-budget-surplus-underestimated-eighth-year-row (accessed 21 December 2018).

Shaw, G. (1944). *Everybody's Political What's What?* New edn. London: Constable.

Shaxson, N. (2014). *Treasure Islands*. New York: St Martin's Press.

Shoard, C. (2019). *BAFTA nominations 2019: The Favourite is queen but Steve McQueen snubbed*. Theguardian.com. Available at: https://www.theguardian.com/film/2019/jan/09/baftas-2019-the-favourite-nominations-steve-mcqueen (accessed 9 January 2019).

Sinclair, J. (1785). *The History of the Public Revenue of the British Empire*. W. and A. Strahan for T. Cadell.

Singleton, A. (2006). *Obituary: Sir John Cowperthwaite*. Theguardian.com. Available at: https://www.theguardian.com/news/2006/feb/08/guardianobituaries.mainsection (accessed 21 December 2018).

Sloan, B. (2018). *Taxation Trends in Mainland Europe*. Ec.europa.eu. Available at: https://ec.europa.eu/taxation_customs/sites/taxation/files/taxation_trends_report_2017.pdf (accessed 15 July 2018).

Smith, A. (1793). *An Inquiry into the Nature and Causes of the Wealth of Nations*. London: printed for A. Strahan and T. Cadell.

Smith, D. (2006). *Living with Leviathan*. London: Institute of Economic Affairs.

Smith, N. (2017). *Who Has the World's No. 1 Economy? Not the US*. Bloomberg.com. Available at: https://www.bloomberg.com/opinion/articles/2017–10-18/who-has-the-world-s-no-1-economy-not-the-u-s (accessed 22 December 2018).

Sourcebooks.fordham.edu (2018). *Medieval Sourcebook: Anonimalle Chronicle: English Peasants' Revolt 1381*. Available at: https://sourcebooks.fordham.edu/source/anon1381.asp (accessed 19 September 2018).

Spartacus-educational.com (2016). *John Wycliffe*. Available at: http://spartacus-educational.com/NORwycliffe.htm (accessed 17 September 2018).

Spartacus-educational.com (2016). *John Ball*. Available at: http://spartacus-educational.com/YALDballJ.htm#section6 (accessed 19 September 2018).

Spartacus-educational.com (2018). *The Peasants' Revolt of 1381.* Available at: http://spartacus-educational.com/Peasants_Revolt.htm (accessed 21 September 2018).

Spence, P. (2015). *Half of all British jobs could be replaced by robots, warns Bank of England's chief economist.* Telegraph.co.uk. Available at: https://www.telegraph.co.uk/finance/bank-of-england/11991704/Half-of-all-British-jobs-could-be-replaced-by-robots-warns-Bank-of-Englands-chief-economist.html (accessed 9 October 2018).

Stampp, K. A., ed. (1965). *The Causes of the Civil War.* Englewood Cliffs, NJ: Prentice-Hall Inc.

Statcounter.com (2018). *Social Media Stats Worldwide.* Available at: http://gs.statcounter.com/social-media-stats (accessed 31 October 2018).

Statista.com (2018). *Apple: number of employees 2017.* Available at: https://www.statista.com/statistics/273439/number-of-employees-of-apple-since-2005/ (accessed 29 October 2018).

Statista.com (2018). *Facebook: number of employees 2017.* Available at: https://www.statista.com/statistics/273563/number-of-facebook-employees/ (accessed 27 September 2018).

Statista.com (2018). *IoT: number of connected devices worldwide 2012–2025.* Available at: https://www.statista.com/statistics/471264/iot-number-of-connected-devices-worldwide/ (accessed 3 November 2018).

Statista.com (2018). *Number of Google employees 2017.* Available at: https://www.statista.com/statistics/273744/number-of-full-time-google-employees/ (accessed 27 September 2018).

Statista.com (2018). *Search engine market share worldwide.* Available at: https://www.statista.com/statistics/216573/worldwide-market-share-of-search-engines/ (accessed 31 October 2018).

Stolper, G., Hauser, K. and Borchardt, K. (1967). *The German Economy, 1870–1940.* London: Weidenfeld and Nicolson.

Storey, D., Steadman, T. and Davis, C. (2016). *Is the gig economy a fleeting fad, or an enduring legacy?* Gigeconomy.ey.com. Available at: https://gigeconomy.ey.com/Documents/Gig%20Economy%20Report.pdf (accessed 2 October 2018).

Susskind, J. (2018). *Future Politics.* 1st edn. Oxford: Oxford University Press.

Tanzi, V. and Schuknecht, L. (2000). *Public Spending in the 20th Century*. Cambridge: CUP.

Taplin, J. (2017). *Move Fast and Break Things*. New York: Little, Brown and Company.

Taplin, J. (2017). *Why is Google spending record sums on lobbying Washington?* Theguardian.com. Available at: https://www.theguardian.com/technology/2017/jul/30/google-silicon-valley-corporate-lobbying-washington-dc-politics (accessed 3 November 2018).

Taussig, F. (1910). *The Tariff History of the United States*. New York: G. P. Putnam's Sons.

Taxation.co.uk (2018). *Taxing horses, dogs, guinea-pigs and seals*. Available at: https://www.taxation.co.uk/Articles/2007/01/25/220271/taxing-horses-dogs-guinea-pigs-and-seals (accessed 1 April 2018).

Taxfoundation.org (2016). *The Compliance Costs of IRS Regulations*. Available at: https://taxfoundation.org/compliance-costs-irs-regulations/ (accessed 26 November 2018).

Taxfoundation.org (2018). *What Are Payroll Taxes and Who Pays Them?* Available at: https://taxfoundation.org/what-are-payroll-taxes-and-who-pays-them/ (accessed 28 March 2018).

Taxhistory.org (2018). *Tax History Project – The Seven Years War to the American Revolution*. Available at: http://www.taxhistory.org/www/website.nsf/Web/THM1756?OpenDocument (accessed 26 May 2018).

Taxinsights.ey.com (2018). *Tax function of future to prioritize cost, value and risk*. Available at: https://taxinsights.ey.com/archive/archive-articles/future-of-tax-tax-function-will-be-very-different.aspx (accessed 30 September, 1 October 2018).

Taylor, A. (1982). *Politicians, Socialism, and Historians*. New York: Stein and Day.

Taylor, B. (2018). *The Century of Inflation*. Globalfinancialdata.com. Available at: https://www.globalfinancialdata.com/GFD/Article/the-century-of-inflation (accessed 25 September 2018).

Taylor, C. (2017). *Ireland named best country for high-value FDI for sixth year in a row*. Irishtimes.com. Available at: https://www.irishtimes.com/business/economy/ireland-named-best-country-for-high-value-fdi-for-sixth-year-in-a-row-1.3204594 (accessed 18 October 2018).

Telegraph.co.uk (2006). *Sir John Cowperthwaite*. Available at: https://www.telegraph.co.uk/news/obituaries/1508696/Sir-John-Cowperthwaite.html (accessed 19 December 2018).

Theglobaleconomy.com (2018). *Capital investment, percent of GDP by country, around the world*. Available at: https://www.theglobaleconomy.com/rankings/Capital_investment/ (accessed 10 July 2018).

Thornton, M. and Ekelund, R. (2004). *Tariffs, Blockades and Inflation*. Wilmington, Del.: SR Books.

Time.com (2018). *The TIME Vault: October 19, 1942*. Available at: http://time.com/vault/issue/1942–10-19/page/23/ (accessed 28 June 2018).

Tinniswood, A. (2004). *By Permission of Heaven*. London: Pimlico.

Tolkien, J. (2015). *Fellowship of the Ring*. London: HarperCollins Publishers Limited, 'The Song of Aragorn'.

Toynbee, P. (2018). *The NHS is our religion: it's the only thing that saves it from the Tories*. Theguardian.com. Available at: https://www.theguardian.com/commentisfree/2018/jul/03/nhs-religion-tories-health-service (accessed 5 September 2018).

Tradingeconomics.com (2018). *United Kingdom Money Supply M3*. Available at: https://tradingeconomics.com/united-kingdom/money-supply-m3 (accessed 26 September 2018).

Uber.com (2018). *Company Information*. Available at: https://www.uber.com/en-GB/newsroom/company-info/ (accessed 27 September 2018).

Ukpublicspending.co.uk (2017). *Charts of Past Spending*. Available at: http://www.ukpublicspending.co.uk/past_spending (accessed 11 June 2017).

Us1.campaign-archive.com (2012). *TaxPayers' Alliance reveals cost of collecting tax has barely fallen in over 50 years*. Available at: https://us1.campaign-archive.com/?u=cc07cd0ccd07d854d8da5964f8&id=ad07b30f56 (accessed 26 November 2018).

Usgovernmentspending.com (2018). *US Government Defense Spending History with Charts*. Available at: https://www.usgovernmentspending.com/defense_spending (accessed 10 July 2018).

Utzke, D. (2017). *IRS Affidavit for Coinbase*. Scribd.com. Available at: https://www.scribd.com/document/342374347/IRS-Affidavit-for-Coinbase?campaign=SkimbitLtd&ad_group=58287X1517249X4494521

015d9a87485a7bdaeeaeec496&keyword=660149026&source=hp_affiliate&medium=affiliate (accessed 21 October 2018).

Vaclavik, B. (2018). *7 2018 Remote Work Statistics*. Dontpanicmgmt.com. Available at: https://www.dontpanicmgmt.com/2018-remote-work-statistics/ (accessed 5 October 2018).

Vermilya, D. (2019). *Walker Tariff of 1846: Definition & Summary | Study. com*. [online] Study.com. Available at: https://study.com/academy/lesson/walker-tariff-of-1846-definition-summary-quiz.html (accessed 28 June 2019).

Visionofbritain.org.uk (2019). *History of the Census of Population*. Available at: http://www.visionofbritain.org.uk/census/ (accessed 4 January 2019).

Vitalone, P. (2011). *The Not-So-Dark-Age: Light in 14th Century Britain*. Masshumanities.org. Available at: http://masshumanities.org/ph_the-notsodarkage-light-in-14th-century-britain/ (accessed 24 February 2019).

Wallis, J. (2000). 'American Government Finance in the Long Run: 1790 to 1990'. *Journal of Economic Perspectives*, 14(1), pp.61–82.

Walsingham, T. and Riley, H. (1863). *Historia Anglicana*. London: HMSO.

Web.archive.org (2009). *Exchange Rate – New Liberty Standard*. Available at: https://web.archive.org/web/20091229132610/http://newlibertystandard.wetpaint.com/page/Exchange+Rate (accessed 21 October 2018).

Web.archive.org (2018). *Magna Carta – Statute Law Database*. Available at: https://web.archive.org/web/20070905014018/http://www.statutelaw.gov.uk/content.aspx?activeTextDocId=1517519 (accessed 1 April 2018).

Web.archive.org (2018). *US Treasury – Fact Sheet on the History of the US Tax System*. Available at: https://web.archive.org/web/20101204034946/http://www.treasury.gov/education/fact-sheets/taxes/ustax.shtml (accessed 3 October 2018).

Web.archive.org (2019). *US Treasury – Fact Sheet on the History of the US Tax System*. Available at: https://web.archive.org/web/20101204034946/http://www.treasury.gov/education/fact-sheets/taxes/ustax.shtml (accessed 11 January 2019).

Webarchive.nationalarchives.gov.uk (2018). *HM Revenue & Customs: Taxation: A tax to beat Napoleon*. Available at: http://webarchive.

nationalarchives.gov.uk/20130127153155/http://www.hmrc.gov.uk/history/taxhis1.htm (accessed 7 April 2018).

Williams, D. R. McClellan, M. B. and Rivlin, A. M. (2010). 'Beyond the Affordable Care Act: Achieving Real Improvements in Americans' Health', *Health Affairs*, 29, No.8, pp.1481–8.

Willshire, A. (2017). *How to switch taxation to a subscriber model*. Reaction. life. Available at: https://reaction.life/switch-taxation-subscriber-model/ (accessed 24 March 2019).

World Bank (2017). *The Global Findex Database 2017*. Washington DC: The World Bank.

Xiaoping, D. (1984). *Build Socialism with Chinese Characteristics*. Academics. wellesley.edu. Available at: http://academics.wellesley.edu/Polisci/wj/China/Deng/Building.htm (accessed 21 December 2018).

Yablon, J. (2015). *As Certain as Death*. 9th edn. Arlington, Va.: Tax Analysts.

Youyou, W., Kosinski, M. and Stillwell, D. (2015). *Computer-based personality judgments are more accurate than those made by humans*. Pnas.org. Available at: http://www.pnas.org/content/112/4/1036 (accessed 29 October 2018).

Zimmerman, C. (2014). *Who holds federal debt?* Fredblog.stlouisfed.org. Available at: https://fredblog.stlouisfed.org/2014/05/who-holds-federal-debt/ (accessed 13 September 2018).

Zucman, G. (2015). *The Hidden Wealth of Nations*. Chicago: University of Chicago Press.

# Notes and Sources

## Chapter 1: Daylight Robbery

1  This famous saying is thought to have been uttered around 1665 (see James), but it cannot be found in print and so, ultimately, can only be attributed.

2  Based on figures from website Measuring Worth, which calculates relative worth over time. Measuringworth.com:
The historic standard of living value of 20 shillings is £120.51.
The labour earnings is £2,010.00.
The economic status value is £3,431.00.
The economic power value is £24,040.00.
I use a pound–dollar exchange rate of 1.4, and round numbers where appropriate.
The likelihood is that the relative number was higher.

3  Dowell, pp.167–8.

4  1 Will. & Mar. s. 1, c. 10.

5  *The Lancet.*

6  Mill, Ch. 3, Section 27.

7  Oates and Schwab.

8  Visionofbritain.org.uk.

9  Demographia.com.

10  'QI: Quite Interesting'. Qi.com (2017). Available at: http://qi.com/infocloud/taxes (accessed 10 February 2017).

11  Austen, p.150.

12  Smith, *Wealth of Nations.*

13  *The Lancet.*

14  *First [and second] Report[s] of the Commissioners.*

15  Dickens, *Household Words*, Vol. 1, p.461.

16 The first use of the expression 'daylight robbery' in print appears in the 1916 play *Hobson's Choice*, by Harold Brighouse. Brighouse has his character Ada Figgins cry, 'It's daylight robbery', meaning a charge so outrageous it is tantamount to brazen theft. Another theory has it that the expression derives from bold highwaymen acting in broad daylight.

17 Novak.

## Chapter 2: How an Extraordinary Situation Could Offer an Extraordinary Solution

1 Monnery, p.18.

2 Roberts.

3 Ibid.

4 Official Report of Proceedings of the Hong Kong Legislative Council, 27 March 1968, p.212.

5 Ibid., 27 February 1963, p.47.

6 Ibid., 30 March 1962, p.133.

7 Ibid.

8 Ibid.

9 Ibid., 24 March 1971, p.531.

10 Ibid., 29 March 1967, p.248.

11 Ibid., 27 February 1963, p.50.

12 Ibid., 24–25 March 1966, p.213.

13 Ibid., 29 March 1963, p.134.

14 Ibid., 9 October 1970, p.116.

15 Ibid., 27 March 1968, p.212.

16 Telegraph.co.uk.

17 Official Report of Proceedings of the Hong Kong Legislative Council, 29 March 1967, p.253.

18 Ibid., 27 March 1968, p.215.

19 Singleton.

20 Friedman, *The Hong Kong Experiment*.

21 Official Report of Proceedings of the Hong Kong Legislative Council, 25 March 1970, p.495.

22  Singleton.

23  Roberts.

24  Ching.

25  Friedman, *The Hong Kong Experiment*.

26  Data.worldbank.org (2018), *GDP per capita, PPP (current international $)* (accessed 5 November 2018).

27  Data.worldbank.org (2018), *GDP per capita, PPP (current international $)* (accessed 21 December 2018).

28  Monnery, p.4.

29  Official Report of Proceedings of the Hong Kong Legislative Council, 29 March 1967, p.248.

30  Scmp.com.

31  Heritage.org.

32  Info.gov.hk.

33  Master-and-more.eu.

34  Bloomberg.com.

35  Ibid.

36  Knupfer, Pokatilo and Woetzel.

37  Official Report of Proceedings of the Hong Kong Legislative Council, 26 February 1969, p.104.

38  Ibid.

39  Ibid.

40  Ibid., 28 February 1962, p.51.

41  Monnery, p.90.

42  Gibson.

43  Ibid.

44  Xiaoping.

45  Smith, *Who Has the World's No. 1 Economy?*

46  Telegraph.co.uk.

# Chapter 3: Why Tax?

1  Benjamin Franklin will always be credited with this phrase, which he wrote, in French, in a letter to scientist Jean-Baptiste Leroy in 1789, at

the age of 83. But the first example in print actually pre-dated him by some 73 years in the little-known farce of 1716, *The Cobbler of Preston*.

2 One Alulim, reputedly a contemporary of Adam and Eve, who ruled in antediluvian times for an impressive 28,800 years.

3 Danesi, p.48.

4 Booth and Bourne, p.9.

5 The precise figure is almost impossible to calculate. Booth and Bourne have it at 44%. Former MP Douglas Carswell has it at 46% in the UK (Carswell, p.13). Website Simple Financial Solutions argues the figure is closer to 65% (*How Much Tax Will I Pay On £100 Earned?* 3 June 2018. Available at http://www.simplefs.co.uk/press-release/how-much-tax-on-100-pounds.asp).

6 Booth and Bourne, p.9.

7 Ibid.

8 Smith, *Living with Leviathan*, p.27.

9 Urine was used for tanning, laundering, even brushing teeth. Collecting it became such a lucrative activity that Nero levied a tax.

10 James Connington, 'Middle-Class Professional? Your Lifetime Tax Bill Could Be £3.6M', http://www.telegraph.co.uk/tax/income-tax/middle-class-professional-your-lifetime-tax-bill-could-be-36m/ (accessed 10 February. 2017).

11 The Adam Smith Institute's Cost of Government Day in the UK falls on 24 June – roughly the mid-point of the year – with Tax Freedom Day falling three weeks earlier. Assuming a working life of 45 years, comfortably more than 20 is spent in service to the taxman. The specific number is imprecise.

12 The famous line is usually credited to Supreme Court Justice Oliver Wendell Holmes Jr.

## Chapter 4: The Cradle of Taxation

1 Cottrell and Davidson, p.2.

2 *The Assyrian Dictionary of the Oriental Institute of the University Of Chicago*, Volume 4, pp.369–70.

3  Samuel Noah Kramer, professor emeritus of Assyriology at the University of Pennsylvania, 'Gov. Urukagina's Message for Mr Reagan', letter to the *New York Times*, 30 January 1981. Available at: http://www.nytimes.com/1981/01/30/opinion/l-gov-urukagina-s-message-for-mr-reagan-245065.html (accessed 12 February 2017).

4  Cooper, J. S., 'Clay Cones La 9.1 Presargonic Inscriptions'.

5  Ibid.

6  Genesis 14:20, English Standard Version (ESV).

7  Genesis 28:22, King James Version (KJV).

8  Numbers 18:21–23, KJV.

9  1836 Tithe Commutation Act.

10  Toynbee.

11  Lawson, p.613.

12  Bevan.

13  *The Rosetta Stone: Translation of the Greek Section*. Available at: https://sourcebooks.fordham.edu/ancient/rosetta-stone-translation.asp (accessed 15 February 2017).

14  Ibid.

15  Ibid.

16  Aristotle, *Magna Moralia*, 1194a.

17  Aristotle, *Art of Rhetoric*, 1361a 28–43.

18  Hippocrates, *Precepts*, Part VI.

19  Joint Association of Classical Teachers, p.228.

20  Some historians have argued that antidosis didn't actually exist, though both Demosthenes and Xenophon mention it.

## Chapter 5: Judaism, Christianity, Islam – and Tax

1  Adams, p.25.

2  Titus Flavius Josephus, 2.201.

3  Exodus 1: 9–10, KJV.

4  Graetz.

5  Exodus 1:11–14, KJV.

6  Ibid.

7  Luke 2:1–5, KJV.

8  Matthew 17:27, KJV.

9  Luke 19:45, KJV.

10  Matthew 22:21, New International Version (NIV).

11  Luke 20:20, NIV.

12  Matthew 18:18–21, KJV.

13  Luke 23:2, KJV.

14  Ali.

15  Dennett.

16  Boyce.

17  Adams, p.131.

18  Dennett, pp.189–90, 231–2.

19  Adams, p.128.

20  Ibid.

21  Ali.

22  Ibid.

23  *Islam: From the Prophet Muhammad*, Vol. 1, p.230.

24  At-Turtushi, 'On Taxation and its Effects, 9th to 12th Centuries', in *Islam*, op. cit., Vol. 1, pp.134–5, cited in Adams, p.133.

25  Adams, p.135.

26  Ibid., p.134.

27  At-Turtushi, op. cit., cited in Adams, p.133.

28  as-Sallaabee.

29  Mellon, p.16.

30  Laffer, *The Laffer Curve*.

31  Presidency.ucsb.edu.


# Chapter 6: The Greatest Constitutional Document
## of All Time

1  *Robin Hood* (1973), directed by W. Reitherman.

2  Cazel.

3  This land tax was based on carucates – the amount of land that can be ploughed by eight oxen in a year.

4  Painter, p.289.

5  Denning, p.922.

6  Danziger and Gillingham, p.268.

7  A. E. Dick Howard, 'Magna Carta Comes to America', Fourscore, 2008, p.28.

8  'The Magna Carta', National Archives, 2018. Web, 1 April 2018.

9  Ibid.


## Chapter 7: How the Black Death Changed the Tax Structure of Europe

1  Benedictow.

2  Knighton and Lumby.

3  Dyer, p.279.

4  Ibid., p.285.

5  Spartacus-educational.com, *John Ball*.

6  John Ball, Sermon at Blackheath, 12 June 1381, quoted by Jean Froissart, *Chronicles*, *c*.1395.

7  Walsingham and Riley.

8  Henry Knighton, quoted in Spartacus-educational.com, *John Ball*.

9  Thomas Walsingham, quoted in ibid.

10  John Ball, Sermon at Blackheath, 12 June 1381, quoted by Froissart, op. cit.

11  Ibid.

12  *Anonimalle Chronicle*, cited in Dobson, p.160, and also in Ormrod, p.3.

13  Dunn, pp.85–7.

14  Sourcebooks.fordham.edu.

15  Ibid.

16  Ibid.

17  Ibid.

18  Ibid.

19  *Anonimalle Chronicle*, quoted in Spartacus-educational.com, *The Peasants' Revolt of 1381*.

20  Burns, p.10.

## Chapter 8: How Taxes Gave Us the Modern Nation States
## We Know Today

1  Cobbett, p.519.

2  Kesselring, p.32.

3  Little, p.198.

4  Adams, p.297.

5  Taxhistory.org.

6  Adams, p.297.

7  Founders.archives.gov.

8  *The Parliamentary Debates*, p.523.

9  Ibid.

10  Bluche, p.50.

11  Chanel, p.76.

12  Davidson, pp.427–31.

13  Hunt.

14  Chanel, p.76.

15  Adams, p.354.

16  Ibid., p.355.

17  Booth and Bourne. Sources: Tanzi and Schuknecht; OECD Economic Outlook (June 2016, Annex Table 29), and OECD data bank. 2018 figures from Oecd.org (2019).

## Chapter 9: War, Debt, Inflation, Famine – and Income Tax

1  Archive.spectator.co.uk.

2  Harding, Bradbury and Lahittete. These calculations include income taxes and social security contributions – for example, payroll taxes in the US and National Insurance in the UK – which are based on earnings. Although employers pay some payroll taxes, the actual tax burden effectively falls on employees. See Taxfoundation.org, *What Are Payroll Taxes And Who Pays Them?* and Entin.

3  Harding, Bradbury and Lahittete. Social security contributions in Germany run especially high at 39%.

4  Ibid. See also Roantree and Miller.

5  Fritschy.

6  Sinclair.

7  Walsingham and Riley, pp.369, 370.

8  *National Geographic*, Vol. 208, Issues 4–6, p.60.

9  Coffield, pp.90–94.

10  Hudson.

11  Coffield, pp.90–94.

12  Ibid.

13  Hudson.

14  Ibid.

15  Webarchive.nationalarchives.gov.uk.

16  *James Gillray on War and Taxes during the War against Napoleon*. Retrieved from Online Library of Liberty (5 June 2015): http://oll.libertyfund.org/pages/james-gillray-on-war-and-taxes-during-the-war-against-napoleon.

17  Taxation.co.uk.

18  A: income from land and buildings. B: farming profits. C: public annuities. D: self-employment and other items not covered by A, B, C or E. E: salaries, annuities and pensions.

19  Webarchive.nationalarchives.gov.uk.

20  Parliament.uk, *The 1816 repeal of the income tax*.

21  Webarchive.nationalarchives.gov.uk.

22  Parliament.uk, *The 1816 repeal of the income tax*.

23  From a letter of 1804. See Melville, p.203.

24  Coffield, pp.90–94.

25  Ibid., p.101.

26  Ibid., p.121.

27  Coffield, p.120.

28  Api.parliament.uk.

29  Ibid.

30  Hammond and Hammond.

31  Ibid., p.125.

32  Bloy.

33  *The Lancet*.

34  1847 [799] Distress (Ireland). Treasury minute, dated 10 March 1847.

## Chapter 10: *The Real Reason for the US Civil War*

1 Archive.org, *The address of the people of South Carolina.*
2 Burgan, p.36.
3 Jefferson.
4 Web.archive.org (2019), *US Treasury – Fact Sheet on the History of the US Tax System.*
5 Benson, p.26.
6 Preyer.
7 Thornton and Ekelund, p.10, citing Taussig.
8 Adams, p.327.
9 Freehling, pp.253–70.
10 Benson, pp.84–86.
11 Ibid., pp.107–12.
12 Vermilya.
13 Scencyclopedia.org.
14 Benson, p.142.
15 Ibid.
16 Taussig, p.159.
17 Lincoln.
18 Basler, ed., p.49 (Letter from Abraham Lincoln to Edward Wallace, 12 May 1860).
19 Ibid., p.211 (Speech in Pittsburgh, 11 February 1861).
20 Millercenter.org.
21 Abrahamlincolnonline.org, *Abraham Lincoln's 1855 Letter to Joshua Speed.*
22 Halstead.
23 Archive.org, *The address of the people of South Carolina.*
24 Ibid.
25 Henry Carey, letter to Lincoln, 2 January 1861, Abraham Lincoln Papers at the Library of Congress, transcribed and annotated by the Lincoln Studies Center, Knox College, Galesburg, Ill.
26 Avalon.law.yale.edu, *The Avalon Project: First Inaugural Address of Abraham Lincoln.*

27 Ibid.

28 Avalon.law.yale.edu, *Avalon Project: Constitution of the Confederate States; March 11, 1861.*

29 Ibid.

30 Jefferson Davis, letter to Lincoln, 27 February 1861.

31 Mises.org.

32 Archive.org, *Full text of 'Interview between President Lincoln and Col. John B. Baldwin'.*

33 Ibid.

34 Mises.org.

35 Archive.org, *Full text of 'Interview between President Lincoln and Col. John B. Baldwin'.*

36 Ibid.

37 Miketgriffith.com.

38 Infoplease.com.

39 Archive.org, *Full text of 'Interview between President Lincoln and Col. John B. Baldwin'.*

40 Nytimes.com, *Sumter and the Administration.*

41 Klingaman, p.45.

42 Avalon.law.yale.edu, *The Avalon Project: First Inaugural Address of Abraham Lincoln.*

43 Nytimes.com, *Sumter and the Administration.*

44 Civil War Trust, *Civil War Facts.*

45 Francis Simkinds, quoted in Miketgriffith.com.

46 *New Orleans Daily Crescent*, 21 January 1861, in Stampp, ed., p.75.

47 Stampp, ed., p.91.

48 John Ford Rhodes, *Lectures on the American Civil War*, New York, 1913, pp.2–16, cited in Adams, p.332.

49 Nytimes.com, *A Letter from President Lincoln.*

50 Nytimes.com, *The Emancipation Proclamation.*

51 William J. Cooper, *Jefferson Davis, American*, pp.552–3.

52 Klingaman, p.113.

53 Dickens, 'The Morrill Tariff'. Dickens, though he published the article, was likely not the author.

## Chapter 11: The Birth of Big Government

1  R. Ver, *My Story of Being Tortured in Prison*, 2019. Available at: https://www.youtube.com/watch?v=hJo7sM5w_Dk&t=296s (accessed 7 April 2019).

2  Belloc.

3  T. Pettinger, David Lloyd George biography.

4  Coffield, p.153.

5  Ibid., p.164.

6  Parliament.uk, *The cost of war*.

7  Newint.org.

8  Coffield has the figure at 25%. Balderston has it at 19%.

9  Bbc.co.uk, *Government to pay off WW1 debt*.

10  Coffield, p.165.

11  Balderston; Feldman, pp.41ff.; Fairchild.

12  Okrent (main source for this chapter).

13  Ibid.

14  Ibid.

15  Occhino, Oosterlinck and White.

16  Okrent.

17  David Hanson, *Wheeler, Wayne Bidwell*, American National Biography Online, February 2000.

18  Wallis, pp.61–82.

19  Norporth.

## Chapter 12: The Second World War, the US and the Nazis

1  Time.com.

2  Roosevelt.

3  Occhino, Oosterlinck and White.

4  Time.com.

5  Cbsnews.com.

6 Bank, Stark and Thorndike, p.6 citing American Enterprise Institute, 'Public Opinion on Taxes', AEI Studies in Public Opinion.

7 *United States – World War II*, Encyclopedia Britannica Online, 2018.

8 Occhino, Oosterlinck and White.

9 Phillips.

10 Occhino, Oosterlinck and White.

11 Galofré-Vilà et al.

12 Aeon.co.

13 Noyes.

14 Stolper, Hauser and Borchardt, p.264.

15 Cesarani.

16 Aly, p.52.

17 Ibid.

18 Ibid, pp.288–91.

19 Lindholm, p.128.

20 Ibid.

21 Stolper, Hauser and Borchardt, p.264.

22 Lindholm.

23 Reichsfinanzministerium-geschichte.de.

24 Ibid.

25 Ibid.

26 Bibula.com.

27 Allen, *The Business of Genocide*, p.1.

28 Clark and Dilnot.

29 Coffield, p.178.

30 Officialdata.org.

31 Coffield, p.187.

32 News.bbc.co.uk, UK settles WWII debt to allies.

## Chapter 13: The Evolution of Social Democracy

1 Shaw.

2 Clark and Dilnot.

3  Ibid.

4  Oecd.org, *General government spending*.

5  Ibid.

6  Booth and Bourne. Sources: Tanzi and Schuknecht; OECD Economic Outlook (June 2016, Annex Table 29), and OECD data bank. 2018 figures from Oecd.org (2019).

7  Ortiz-Ospina and Roser.

8  Clark and Dilnot.

9  Ibid.

10  Wallis, pp.61–82.

11  Ibid.

12  Ibid.

13  Web.archive.org (2018), *US Treasury – Fact Sheet on the History of the US Tax System*.

14  Ourworldindata.org.

15  Harding, Bradbury and Lahittete.

16  Pope and Waters.

17  Sloan.

18  Oecd.org, *OECD Revenue Statistics 2017 United States*.

19  Ortiz-Ospina and Roser.

20  Ibid.

21  Ibid.

22  Laffer, *Cain's Stimulating '9–9–9' Tax Reform*.

23  Figure includes total military spending, veterans and foreign aid. Usgovernmentspending.com.

24  Data.worldbank.org, *Military expenditure (% of GDP)*.

25  Ibid.

26  Clark and Dilnot.

27  Ibid.

28  Theglobaleconomy.com.

29  Ibid.

30  Ortiz-Ospina and Roser.

31  Isaac.

32  Clark and Dilnot.

33  Deloitte Czech Republic.

## Chapter 14: The Unofficial Taxes: Debt and Inflation

1 Herbert Hoover, Address to the Nebraska Republican Conference, Lincoln, Nebraska, 16 January 1936.

2 Cosgrave.

3 Reid et al., *Long Term Asset Return Study*.

4 Imf.org.

5 Graeber.

6 Reid et al., *Long Term Asset Return Study*.

7 Copernicus.

8 Ibid.

9 Keynes, *Economic Consequences*, Chapter VI, pp.235–6.

10 Hazlitt, p.20.

11 Friedman, *Monetary Correction*, p.4.

12 Taylor, *The Century of Inflation*.

13 Faber.

14 Friedman, *Monetary Correction*, p.4.

15 Reinhart and Rogoff.

16 Allen, *Inflation: the Value of the Pound*.

17 Ibid.

18 Reinhart and Rogoff.

19 Allen, *Inflation: the Value of the Pound*.

20 I am using MZM here. Whether you choose to use M2, M3 or MZM, the growth is astounding. Fred.stlouisfed.org.

21 Tradingeconomics.com.

22 Reid et al., *The History (and Future) of Inflation*, p.2.

23 Positivemoney.org, *Infographic*.

24 Economicshelp.org (2018). Available at: https://www.economicshelp.org/blog/5709/housing/market/ (accessed 11 September 2018), using data from Nationwide.co.uk (2018), House Prices Data Download. Available at: https://www.nationwide.co.uk/about/house-price-index/download-data#tab:Downloaddata (accessed 11 September 2018).

25 Positivemoney.org, *Infographic*.

26 Davies.

27  This famous quote first appeared in print in John Maynard Keynes'
    *Economic Consequences of the Peace*. Keynes claimed Lenin was 'said to
    have said' it. Lenin later read the book, and on occasion even cited it
    (for example in a July 1920 speech to the Comintern), and never made
    any denial of the attribution. Keynes used it as a starting point for his
    own arguments about currency debasement.
28  Ibid.

## Chapter 15: The Future of Work

 1  Delaney.
 2  Bls.gov.
 3  Gigeconomydata.org.
 4  Recode.net.
 5  *How the Freelance Generation is Redefining Professional Norms*, blog.
    linkedin.com, 2017.
 6  Storey, Steadman and Davis.
 7  Katz and Krueger.
 8  *Tax System Struggles to Cope with Rise of Gig Economy*, ft.com, 2017.
 9  Storey, Steadman and Davis.
10  Hilary Osborne, *London's 'Gig Economy' Has Grown By More than 70%
    Since 2010*, theguardian.com, 2017.
11  *LFS: Self-Employed: UK: All: 000S: SA: Annual = 4 Quarter Average-Office
    For National Statistics*, ons.gov.uk, 2017.
12  *How the Freelance Generation Is Redefining Professional Norms*, blog.
    linkedin.com, 2017.
13  Storey, Steadman and Davis.
14  Taxinsights.ey.com.
15  Statista.com, *Facebook: number of employees 2017*.
16  Statista.com, *Number of Google employees 2017*.
17  Statista.com, *Apple: number of employees 2017*.
18  Uber.com.
19  Chesky et al.
20  Kocieniewski.

21  Nase.org.

22  Katie Allen, *Booming Gig Economy Costs £4Bn in Lost Tax and Benefit Payouts, Says TUC*, theguardian.com, 2017.

23  Ibid.

24  Income-tax.co.uk.

25  Cervantes.

26  Bloom, *The digital nomads wandering the world.*

27  Levels.

28  Ibid.

29  Elliott.

30  Indexmundi.com.

31  Elliott.

32  Browne.

33  Guta.

34  Ibid.

35  Vaclavik.

36  Guta.

37  Levels.

38  Kharas and Hamel.

39  Hardcover business best-sellers, *New York Times*, 1 May 2011.

40  Levels.

41  https://twitter.com/paulypilot/status/869684418562097152.

42  Schwab.

43  Edwards and Edwards.

44  Spence.

45  Edwards and Edwards.

46  Mckinsey.com.

47  Pwc.co.uk.

## Chapter 16: Crypto Money: the Taxman's Nightmare

1  Web.archive.org, *Exchange Rate – New Liberty Standard.*

2  May.

3  Bartlett, *The People vs Tech*, p.167.

4  Cato Unbound (2017).
5  Satoshi Nakamoto, *Bitcoin 0.3 released!*, Sourceforge, 6 July 2010. Available at: http://bit.ly/1tru7NE (accessed 22 May 2014).
6  Utzke.
7  Dailymail.co.uk.
8  Ericsson.com.
9  Ibid.
10  Holst.
11  World Bank.

## Chapter 17: Digital Breaks Free

1  MacKay, p.140. Probably attributed.
2  Allen, *Technology and Inequality*, p.16; Europa.eu, *State aid*.
3  Ibid.
4  Brown.
5  Bartash.
6  Taylor, *Ireland named best country for high-value FDI*.
7  Europa.eu, *State of the Union 2018*.
8  Barlow.
9  Kendall.
10  Ebenstein, p.251.

## Chapter 18: Data: the Taxman's New Friend

1  Youyou, Kosinski and Stillwell.
2  Bartlett, *The People vs Tech*, p.75.
3  Houlder.
4  Susskind, p.139.
5  Ibid., p.173.
6  Ibid.
7  Shaxson, p.8.

8  Zucman, p.39.

9  Barlow.

## Chapter 19: The System is Broken

1  Plato, *Republic*, 1, 343e.

2  Oxfam.org.

3  Ibid.

4  Oxfam calculations using wealth of the richest individuals from Forbes Billionaires listing and wealth of the bottom 50% from Credit Suisse Global Wealth Databook 2016. See Deborah Hardoon, 'An Economy for the 99%', Oxfam, January 2017. Available at: https://www.oxfam.org/en/research/economy-99.

5  *UK Health Gap Between Rich and Poor Widest Ever*, theguardian.com, 2017.

6  *Health Gap Between Rich and Poor Has Increased Under Labour*, telegraph.co.uk, 2017. This study was from 2010, but current numbers are no better.

7  Williams, McClellan and Rivlin.

8  Rivlin and McClellan.

9  Sally Weale, *The large majority of top jobs in the UK still go to the 7% of students who are educated privately*, theguardian.com, 2017.

10  Frisby, p.133.

11  *A New, Simple, Revenue Neutral Tax Code*, cps.org.uk, 2017.

12  Taxfoundation.org, *The Compliance Costs of IRS Regulations*.

13  Quoteinvestigator.com.

14  Taxfoundation.org, *The Compliance Costs of IRS Regulations*.

15  Ibid.

16  Us1.campaign-archive.com.

17  Keynes, *Essays in Persuasion*, pp.358–73.

18  Carswell, p.14.

19  Bartlett, *The end of a world of nation-states may be upon us*.

20  Isaac.

21  Haskel and Westlake, pp.23–6.

22  Ibid.

23  Data.worldbank.org, *GDP per capita, PPP (current international $)* (accessed 5 November 2018).

24  Nationmaster.com.

# Chapter 20: Designing Utopia

1   Milton Friedman (on the Bush tax cuts), interview by John Hawkins, 16 September 2003.

2   Today, however, the leasing system is not so ideal. If the government wants to expand an area, it auctions a lease. But the upfront payment is so high that only the richest developers are able to afford it and the building industry has become something of a cartel.

3   Churchill.

4   Mill, p.363.

5   Currently about 15% of UK real estate remains unregistered. See Hookway. One consequence of the tax will be to get land closer to 100% registration.

6   Interview with *The Times Herald*, Norristown, Pennsylvania (1 December 1978).

7   Cahill.

8   Willshire.

# Index